Order this book online at www.trafford.com
or email orders@trafford.com

Most Trafford titles are also available at major online book retailers.

Printed in the United States of America.

ISBN: 978-1-4269-5763-5 (sc)
ISBN: 978-1-4269-5764-2 (e)

Library of Congress Control Number: 2011902479

Trafford rev. 05/02/2011

 www.trafford.com

North America & international
toll-free: 1 888 232 4444 (USA & Canada)
phone: 250 383 6864 ♦ fax: 812 355 4082

TABLE OF CONTENTS

PREFACE

THE REASONS WHY I WROTE THIS BOOK:

I To feature the City of Toledo, as it appeared and existed more than a half century ago; especially the downtown area. It was dominated by several huge department stores: Tiedtkes, LaSalle's, Lion, Sears and Lamsons.

There were many cinemas, including the Paramount, Rivoli, Valentine, Esquire, Princess, Pantheon and the Palace. (The Valentine is the only survivor and is now a Dinner Theatre)

The Commodore Perry, Secor, Willard, Waldorf and the Hillcrest were bustling hotels. (The Commodore was remodeled into apartments and the Hillcrest has recently been Renovated).

The Maumee River still flows through the city, separating the East and West sides. Several impressive bridges span her width, but the Anthony Wayne Bridge (known as the High Level) will always be especially memorable to me.

The thought of all these places and things will always bring vivid memories of yester-years to my mind. In my opinion the photographs of "ol' Toledo" are worth the price of the book.

II To illustrate to the public today the hardships of being a police officer during the 50's and 60's. To begin with, the annual pay ($4200) for a 48 hour week was grossly inadequate, considering the perils a police officer was exposed to.

There was no pay for court time and overtime was frowned upon and seldom authorized.

Uniformed police officers were assigned to one of three shifts and were mandated to change shifts the first day of each month. This compelled officers of two shifts to "double- back", requiring them to return to work in less than an eight hour period.

Also, to maintain a four-day-on and one-day-off work schedule officers had to give up one-day-off a month which caused them to work a nine day stretch each month. This was bad enough on the 7 AM and 3 PM shifts, but it was definitely more taxing to the officers on the 11 PM shift.

(Today, officers may work a permenant shift, based on seniority.)

There was no provisions to take time off for a sick family member. Eventually, this was remedied through police unions bargaining with the city.

A newly appointed officer's cost for a first-issue of uniforms and equipment was two hundred and ninety dollars ($290); nearly a month's pay. And this did not cover rain gear, handcuffs, flashlights and traffic whistles. If officers desired those items they had to purchase them "out of pocket."

Compare to today's technology, equipment was either anticated or didn't even exist: Modern bullet-proof vests were not available until 1965; the cost of a Second Chance vest was $245.00; much too expensive for the individual officer, at that time.

There were no walkie-talkie radios. When officers left their vehicles for any reason, they were out of contact with the police dispatcher and on their own.

Beat officers had to rely on call-boxes which were located at almost every major intersection, but in some areas of the city there were several blocks between them. If a beat officer was in trouble any distance from a call-box, he also had to fend for himself. (Portable radios were not perfected and made available until 1966. They were large and cumbersome, but very welcome.)

There were no air conditioners in police vehicles; motors had to be left running at all times during all four seasons to prevent the police radios from depleting the car batteries . (Toledo police officers did not have air conditioned vehicles until 1974.)

Colt, six-shot, .38 caliber revolvers with five inch barrels were the issued sidearm for patrol officers; they carried an additional 12 rounds on their gun belt.

In 1958 they were replaced with stainless steel Smith & Wesson, .38 caliber revolvers with four-inch barrels.

Today, most police departments equip their officers with Glocks or similar 9 mm. semi-automatic pistols capable of holding a minimum of 17 rounds in a clip. With two additional clips, their firepower is drastically greater than that of the officers who were armed with revolvers.

Prior to computer technology any information a patrol officer needed had to be obtained via phone or radio through a police operator. To check out a suspect an officer had to wait until the operator contacted the Record Bureau, then wait until a clerk obtained the data and relayed it back to the operator, who in turn informed the officer seeking the information. Depending on how busy the Record Bureau clerks were such transactions could take as long as 15 minutes or more.

During that time a suspect could become unruly, or a crowd could gather and attempt to aid the suspect or interfere with the officer's duty. Therefore, during this time an officer's safety could be jeopardized.

Now, officers have computers in their vehicles and can obtain data directly and rapidly without going through any other agent.

Presently, many police departments have eliminated foot patrols; although, some do have bicycle patrols with officers patrolling in pairs.

III Several years after my retirement I realized that many of my police experiences paralleled fiction; defying belief. I decided to use this data for the contents of this book.

Names, with an asterisk, are real. All others have been changed. Some locations have been changed, also to protect the innocent. However, all the events actually occurred and have been related to the best of my recollection.

My only regret is that so many police veterans, answered their last call before this book was published. May they rest in peace.

ACKNOWLEDGEMENTS

My sincere gratitude is extended to the following persons for their tireless efforts to help me make the publication of this book possible:

Mr. Norman Joseph Vahey, for his knowledge and skills in scanning and reproducing a number of the photographs herein.

The Toledo Blade Newspaper's Library Staff for allowing me access to their library and for the privilege and their assistance in obtaining the many photographs of ol' Toledo. I consider the photos a major asset to this book. Also, may I extend my deep gratitude to Assistant Managing Editor Luann Sharp for obtaining permission for me to use the photographs.

My daughter, Therese, for helping me to conquer the intracacies of my computer and for assisting me with computer techniques. And especially for her countless hours she spent working with the publisher in formatting the materials and photos for this book. This book would never have been published without her superb efforts.

My sons Steve and Tim for their generous gift of a digital camera; Steve for taking some great photographs for this book as well.

DEDICATION

This book is dedicated to my beloved wife, Mary Ann, for her never ending love and loyal support.

And to our son, Michael, who suffered severely with asthma, which finally claimed his life while he was in his prime. May God Bless his soul.

AERIAL PHOTO OF TOLEDO, OHIO WITH VIEW OF THE MAUMEE RIVER AND THE ANTHONY WAYNE BRIDGE, ALSO CALLED THE "HIGH LEVEL".

The Maumee River separates the West and East sides of Toledo. The city covered 86 square miles with a population of about 400,000 Citizens at the time of this photo. Circa 50's.

PATROLMAN ORVILLE SWANTEK DIRECTING TRAFFIC AT THE INTERSECTION OF
ADAMS AND SUMMIT, IN DOWNTOWN TOLEDO. AT THE TIME, TOLEDO POLICE
OFFICERS CARRIED COLT .38 CALIBER REVOLVERS, LOADED WITH SIX ROUNDS,
WITH AN ADDITIONAL TWELVE CARTRIDGES ON THEIR GUNBELTS. CIRCA 1950'S

Author James B. Moore as a Patrolman in 1964.

CHAPTER I

PERSONAL EXPERIENCES WITH TOLEDO POLICE

EPISODES

1. POLICE BRUTALITY

2. THE DRIVER TEST

3. AN OFFICER AND A GENTLEMAN

4. FOR A GOOD CAUSE

5. THE HEARING TEST

6. THE TRAFFIC VIOLATION

7. THE INTERVIEW

POLICE BRUTALITY

At 10 A.M. on a Saturday morning in June of 1945, I was waiting for a bus on the corner of St. Clair and Orange Street in downtown Toledo. Across the street, two elderly, intoxicated men were arguing loudly. Suddenly they began to swing at each other. They were so inebriated that their blows whiffed the air without impact. It was like a Keystone comedy and ironically, it was taking place under the marquee of the old abandoned Town Hall Burlesque Theatre.

Apparently someone took a different view of it and called the police. A paddy-wagon pulled up and two seasoned, middle-aged police officers jumped out with billy clubs in hand. Without provocation they each grabbed one of the harmless combatants and clubbed him over the head. Blood poured over the faces of the unfortunate drunks, as the policemen manhandled them into the rear of the wagon and sped away.

At the age of 14, I never forgot that incident. It was the worst case of police brutality that I have ever witnessed, including during the years I served as a Toledo Police Officer.

As a cadet in the Toledo Police Academy, I was trained in the proper use of a club and instructed that human skulls are of various thicknesses and a blow to the head may result in a skull fracture. Police are trained to strike other areas of the body instead.

THE DRIVER TEST

When I was sixteen I appeared at the East Side Toledo Police Station at 722 Second St. to take my driver test in my 1935 Dodge sedan. My Uncle Tony accompanied me.

My examiner was a middle-aged, obese detective in plain clothes. He settled in the right front seat of my car with an official form attached to a clip-board. From where I was parked on Second Street, in front of the police station, he directed me to drive to the intersection at Oswald and to turn right; then to turn right again onto Sixth Street and a third right turn at Pratt Street and a final right turn back onto Second Street. Thus we ended up where we had started from by the police station.

My road test consisted of a total of four right turns over a distance of six square blocks. The detective told me that I had passed and to get a cracked window fixed. He then alighted from my car and returned to his office inside the police station. There was no written test.

AN OFFICER AND A GENTLEMAN

On a June evening of 1953, three months after being honorably discharged from the U.S. Marines Corps., I was driving my new 1952 Chevrolet, West on Madison Avenue. The traffic light at 17th. Street was red, but as I approached the intersection it changed to green. As I proceeded into the intersection I sensed a car bearing down on my left. When I looked it appeared as large as a locomotive just before it rammed the left side of my car.

The force of the collision threw me to the passenger side of my sedan (there was no seat belts then) and my auto veered into a steel light pole on the Northwest corner. The second impact propelled my head partially through the windshield rendering me unconscious for a brief time. When I regained my senses I was aware of a crowd of spectators around my car and as I emerged from the wreckage a police crew arrived.

Stunned, I observed several strands of my hair dangling from the broken windshield and felt pain in my left knee, right shoulder and back. When I looked at my watch to see what time it was my wrist was exposed where the face of my watch should have been; the works was missing from the case. It was an expensive watch which I had purchased from the P.X. (Post Exchange) prior to leaving the Marines.

A police officer interviewed me and informed me that witnesses verified that the other driver was at fault. When I mentioned my damaged watch he took time to locate the missing works and placed it in a plastic bag for me. He informed me that a female passenger in the other car had suffered a fractured skull and that an ambulance was on the way. He also suggested that I get an attorney.

The girl and I were both transported to Mercy Hospital. The other driver rode along to be with his girlfriend. I recognized him from high school but we did not communicate. Over the years his name had escaped my memory.

Officer James Wagner* had conducted himself in a true professional manner at the scene of that accident and I'll always be indebted to him for his kind consideration and courtesy.

Several years later while Officer Wagner was assigned to the motorcycle squad an errant motorist ran a stop sign and drove directly into his path. Officer Wagner struck the car broadside and was flipped from his cycle, over the vehicle, and onto the pavement; suffering serious injuries.

Just before I was appointed to the force Officer Wagner had left the ranks of the Toledo Police Department, but I'll always remember him.

The girl? She recovered and married the driver of the car that struck me.

The watch? It was never the same after I had it repaired.

My car? It was a total loss and I had to buy a new one. A 1953 Chevrolet.

Myself? I had suffered a concussion, a broken front tooth and an injured knee. A fractured lower left rib went undetected . I went to work the next day driving a truck and never realized that I had a broken rib. Over time it healed naturally without medical attention.

FOR A GOOD CAUSE

In December of 1953, six months before I was appointed to the Toledo Police Department, I was single and dating a girl named Traci; an attractive blond.

On a Saturday evening we were in a bar which featured a live band when a Toledo police officer entered. He was wearing a black, leather jacket and shiny, black leather leggings. He was big, brash and brandishing a container of money. He announced that he was soliciting funds for needy families for Christmas. The patrons were in a festive mood and began to cram the container with their donations.

The band began to play a lively tune and someone shouted for the cop to dance. Without a word the cop grabbed Traci and pulled her to the tiny dance floor. He mauled her as he wiggled and jiggled; his holstered revolver flopping at his side. Traci was bouncing and swinging trying to keep in step with the music. The crowd loved it! When the song ended the cop, sweating profusely and panting for breath, towed Traci back to me. He yelled a shrill "Thank You" to everyone; whacked me on the back and with his container brimming with cash he scooted out the door.

Traci was gasping for breath as beads of perspiration rolled down her face marring her make-up. Her hair was askew and she appeared to be dazed from all the exertion.

"Are you all right, Traci?" I was concerned, slightly amused and slightly upset over the officer's impudence. Traci regained her composure, repaired her make-up and with a little chortle exclaimed, "That was some workout."

I calmed down and began to laugh with her; then I thought: "What the hell; it was for a good cause."

THE HEARING TEST

The only real concern I harbored regarding my appointment to the Toledo Police Department was passing any kind of hearing test.

At the age of five I suffered a severe case of tonsillitis. Although my tonsils were removed as soon as the condition was diagnosed, doctors feared that I was going to lose all of my hearing. As it turned out I did lose some of my sense of hearing but I was not rendered deaf.

Later in life, what also effected my condition negatively was all the training in rifle and pistol shooting that I under went in the Marine Corps. As a member of a Marine Pistol Team, I participated in pistol matches prior to my discharge. In those times no one used commercial hear-guards.

The physical examination held prior to appointment to the Toledo Police Department was conducted in the gymnasium of Macomber High School. When I discovered what the hearing test consisted of I was dumbfounded but elated.

Examinees stood at a mark while a Counselor held a Big Ben alarm clock to one of their ears then slowly moved the clock away from the subject's head. When the examinee could no longer hear the clock ticking he was to signal the Counselor. Each ear was tested in this manner.

There were two examinees ahead of me to be tested. I closely observed the distance the clock was from their ears when each man signaled that he could no longer hear the clock ticking. When it was my turn I allowed the Counselor to take the clock about the same distance from my ear before giving him the signal. Actually, I could not hear the clock some distance prior to my signal.

When this primitive exercise was over the Counselor informed me that I had passed. I wouldn't blame anyone for not believing this but it is absolutely true. I believe that if there had been any kind of a sophisticated hearing test administered my police career would have been over before it had begun.

Macomber High School

THE TRAFFIC CITATION

The Railway Express Agency was still my employer and shortly before my appointment to the Toledo Police Department I was driving a company truck North on Sumner Street in the South End of Toledo. I passed Eastern Avenue, made a delivery and returned the way I had come. However, as I approached Eastern Ave. I observed a stop sign for Sumner traffic which I knew was not there a few minutes before.

Confused, I drove past the stop sign without stopping. Immediately there was a police car behind me signaling me to pull over. A young officer asked to see my driver license and Inquired if I had seen the stop sign.

"Yes," I admitted, "But there was no sign there a little while ago. I don't understand."

"It's a folding sign in a school zone and it's only used on school days before school, at lunch and after school." he explained.

"I never knew it was there," I truthfully stated.

"According to your license you live just a short distance from here; you must have been aware of it." He then proceeded to issue me a citation.

I observed that a second officer sitting in the police car was older and I had a feeling that the younger patrolman was expected to write a citation in order to prove his merit, or to meet with the veteran officer's approval.

I knew that It was useless to say anything more to the officer but I fully intended to take the matter to traffic court. However, as the court date approached I was extremely busy trying to stay employed and was working various shifts at the R.E.A. The fine was only five dollars so I decided to pay it and forget it.

The main reason I have related this incident is because a couple of years after I was appointed to the Toledo Police Department, that same police officer who issued that ticket to me became not only a close friend, but my mentor.

The only way individual police officers could gain an increase in pay was to achieve rank and it was he whom inspired and encouraged me to strive for promotion. One of his exact statements to me was: "If you did as much studying as you do shooting, you'd be a sergeant."

(The words of CAPTAIN ROBERT E. GRAY* Retired, proved to be true indeed. After he retired I was promoted to captain. To my dismay, he passed away before this book was finished. May God bless him.)

THE INTERVIEW

The Toledo Police Academy was located at the East Side Station on Second St. at Oswald. It occupied the entire second floor. On a balmy April morning of 1954, I was on time for my interview and I felt confident.

Entering the office, I was confronted by a command officer wearing the gold oak leafs of a major. He was tall, ram-rod straight and partially bald with a lean, stern face. He gestured for me to take a seat in front of his desk. A uniformed patrolman was seated to one side.

The stern one made introductions: "I'm Inspector Karl Thor, Commandant of the Toledo Police Academy. And this is Officer John Mahoney, one of our fine Instructors."

I acknowledged the introductions and placed my military discharge document on the desk near Mahoney.

Thor continued: "You are James B. Moore, a candidate on our eligibility list and according to our research you did not complete high school. Is that correct?"

"Yes, Sir." I replied.

"Why?" Thor demanded. His voice was flat.

"Well, Sir," I tried to read Thor's face but it was like a granite mask.

"Macomber High School had an unique program whereby studies would alternate weekly; one week of shop and then a week of academic subjects. In my opinion, with the exception of Commercial Art, the subjects were boring and some of the instructors were grossly inept."

Thor's eyes narrowed. "In May of 1948 you were charged with being a suspicious person; explain, please."

"That's a mistake, Sir!"

"Damn it! We don't make mistakes!" Thor thundered and struck the desk top with his fist with such force that his coffee mug jumped up into the air. "Well, that's a mistake!" I retorted. "If Officer Mahoney will look on the back of my discharge paper it will reveal that I sailed from the United States on April 28th of 1948 aboard the USS Grant, for Guam. I wasn't even in the continental United States in May."

"That's right, inspector." Mahoney assured him.

I sat back in an air of righteousness even though I knew the charge was not entirely in error.

Agitated, Thor grabbed the desk phone. "We'll see about this," he spewed. He dialed three digits, waited a moment, then shouted into the handset: "Let me talk to Captain Bosch, now!"

After a brief wait Thor continued: "Tony, Thor here. I have a candidate by name of James B. Moore, with two O's. There seems to be a question about a suspicious person charge in May of 1948, can you verify that for me? I'll wait."

Soon he spoke again: "What year? Oh, I see." Thor's face caved into an expression of disappointment. "All right, Tony, I'll take your word for that. Thank you."

Thor slowly hung up the phone and looked directly at me as he spoke, "You were involved in a minor juvenile matter in May of 1941 at the age of ten. My associate said it didn't amount to a nickel's worth of concern so I'm going to let that go as is."

Thor's voice lost its edge, but his eyes narrowed once more as he resumed. "There is still the matter of your lack of a formal education. I don't believe you are qualified to complete the requirements of my ... err, the Toledo Police Academy. It would be a waste of our time and money and would deprive a candidate with a higher - -"

I leaped to my feet, snatched my paper from the desk, looked Thor in the eye and spoke in a firm voice: "I'll put myself up against anyone, physically, mentally, morally or any way you want to cut the cake. If that's not good enough then I don't know what is!"

I bolted out the door and left it ajar. By the time I reached my car my anger had collapsed into despair. "Well, that's the end of that." I said to myself.

However, in May I was summoned to a hearing before the chief of police, the safety director and Thor. The inspector informed me that I needed two votes out of three and his was against me. He pulled no punches but he was honest; I gave him that.

The chief and the safety director over-rode Thor and I was appointed to the Toledo Police Academy's 12th Cadet Class.

(While assigned as Captain of the Toledo Police Training Academy I had access to a number of files. While seeking information on a different matter I discovered that there was six other cadets in my class, besides me, that didn't finish high school. Yet, I don't believe that any of them were challenged about it as I was. I truly believe that Inspector Thor wanted to eliminate me as a candidate for the T.P.D. solely because I stood up to him during my original interview.)

CHAPTER 2

TOLEDO POLICE ACADEMY EXPERIENCES

EPISODES

1. CURRICULUM OUTLINE

2. MARKSMANSHIP QUALIFICATIONS

3. A CADET'S REBUKE

4. FUNERAL MANEUVERS

5. REPRIEVE AT A PUB

CURRICULUM OUTLINE

Immediately after the 12th. Cadet Class of the Toledo Police Department was sworn in, we received our uniforms, equipment, official books and training manuals and signed for a credit union loan of $290; a hefty sum in those days, almost equivalent to a month's pay.

That didn't cover black shoes and socks, raincoat and rain-cap-cover, a set of handcuffs with case and a traffic whistle. With the exception of the foot wear, if one chose not to obtain the other items, one simply went without.

At the time, Toledo Police Cadet Training Classes received a minimum of 280 hours of training as mandated by the State of Ohio. The Toledo Police Academy's training agenda exceeded that requirement by about 40 hours, which was the duration of training on the Toledo Police Pistol Range.

The said training class was not scheduled to graduate until the end of August, but a directive from the chief's office threw Thor's entire schedule into disarray. Because manpower was so low and the need for officers to fill in for summer vacations was so great, a precedent was set:

The 12th. Cadet Class would be assigned to the streets on July 19th,: a month and a half before their scheduled graduation. This meant that the cadets would be working the streets in the full capacity of police officers with only about 35 days of formal training.

Inspector Thor was aghast. He had to adjust the academy curriculum to afford the cadets marksmanship training. That was a must! "That will take away 40 hours of classroom instruction, alone," he fretted.

When this class resumed their academy training on October 1st. the Inspector avowed: "To never let it happen again."

Inspector Thor commanded the academy with an iron hand; he would not tolerate any foolishness from either cadets or members of his hand-picked staff. He tried to present himself as one with military bearing and relished being saluted, but in reality, he was never in the military.

It was no secret that he craved for the position of chief, but he knew as well as everybody else that it would never be. He was no politician and for a person of his stature he lacked any real skills in diplomacy; he was short-tempered and impatient.

His greatest quality, in my opinion, was his absolute honesty. I don't think that anyone was ever in doubt where one stood with him, at least not for very long.

A representative from each police bureau, usually a command officer, addressed the class and explained the functions of that bureau and the elements of the particular crime that they primarily dealt with: robbery, burglary, larceny, auto theft, homicide, etc. and how it's operation fit in with the department as a whole; from communications and the vice squad to the records & identification section to the jails and everything in between. There was even a presentation from the city traffic engineer. Also, the city physician, who brought in several placentas from new births, instructed us on how to deliver a baby, if it was ever necessary.

Inspector Thor's main subjects were The Laws of Arrest and Constitutional Law, while Captain Gladieux * lectured on Search and Seizure; all serious topics.

However, many afternoons were spent revising our copies of the City Ordinance Manual, it dated back to the early 1900's. Among other subjects it covered was, " How To Care For Your Horse." We were instructed to scratch those paragraphs out.

The manual was a small soft-covered booklet with small type. We had to correct each ordinance that had been changed and/or insert each new ordinance, which meant writing between the narrow-spaced sentences and on the margins of the pages. When we finished this massive, monotonous task, our manuals resembled a book of directions for a "Chinese Fire Drill".

Also, a lecture by Captain Gladieux entitled: "What To Do in Case of Atomic Attack," was truly a waste of time.

Training in self-defense and rescue tactics was scant, but I'll always remember executing a "firemen's carry" on Norbert DeClercq,* He didn't appear to be heavy, but he weighed a solid 200 pounds which afforded me a good reason to fear suffering a hernia. I weighed about 25 pounds less than him.

Chief of Police Ray E. Allen presenting Toledo Police Academy certificates to
Patrolmen John Potrezbowski & James McCormick. Circa 50's.

THE TOLEDO POLICE 12ᵀᴴ. ALUMNI CLASS

ON THE FIRST DAY OF JUNE, 1954,
SIXTEEN MEN ANSWERED THE CALL
TO WEAR A BADGE AND A GUN
AND SWORE TO UPHOLD THE LAW.

ONLY FORTY-NINE DAYS LATER
THEY WERE PLACED UPON THE STREETS;
ASSIGNED TO VEHICLES AND UPON FOOT
TO PATROL THE CITY'S BEATS.

THE TOLEDO POLICE 12ᵀᴴ. ALUMNI CLASS

CHALLENGING THEIR MINDS AND BODIES,
EACH OFFICER WAS PUT TO THE TEST,
AS THEY GAVE THEIR MAXIMUM EFFORT
AND PROVED TO BE THE VERY BEST.

AFTER THEIR FALL GRADUATION,
FOLLOWING ADDITIONAL TRAINING;
IT WAS PREDICTED THAT UPON THIS CLASS
THE STARS AND BARS WOULD BE RAINING.

THE TOLEDO POLICE 12TH. ALUMNI CLASS

LET US SALUTE OUR BRETHREN LAID TO REST,
AS WE RECALL OUR ACTIVE YEARS
FILLED WITH HAUNTING MEMORIES;
WROUGHT THROUGH SACRIFICE AND TEARS.

A TOAST TO THOSE OF US REMAINING
AND MAY WE SHARE IN THIS PRAYER I GIVE:
THAT WE MAY LIVE AS LONG AS WE WANT
AND NEVER WANT AS LONG AS WE LIVE.

THE TOLEDO POLICE 12TH. ALUMNI CLASS… GOD BLESS!

BY JAMES B. MOORE

MARKSMANSHIP QUALIFICATIONS

The last week of June our class reported to the Toledo Police Pistol Range. Our class consisted of 16 Caucasian males, all military veterans. I'm positive that all of us had prior firearms training, but pistol shooting was a special interest of mine.

Our initial training was on paper bull's eye targets at 25 yards.

Although I had never fired a .38 cal. revolver before, I lead the class right up to the qualification match on Friday morning of that week. No brag … just fact. The final match consisted of five volleys of ten shots each at a bull's eye target fired from 25 yards with the strong hand only. The maximum score for each target was 100 points.

On my first two targets I scored a pair of 92's. I was informed that Norbert DeClercq was right behind me with a pair of 89's. On my next two targets, I fired a 94 and a 96; and on my final target I shot a 98. I was determined to win.

When all the targets were scored and the range cleared, one cadet topped the class in Marksmanship. To Thor's dismay that cadet was James B. Moore, spelled with two O's. (Thirty years later, in retirement, Norbert confided to me that he had not only wanted to be the top cadet in the class, but he also had wanted to be the top shot. He admitted that he had practiced surreptitiously with expectations to surprise everyone with the winning score on qualification day. He expressed disappointment to that day that I had excelled him.)

MAJOR CHARLES ROTH, TRAINING COMMANDER, INSTRUCTING MARKSMANSHIP TO A ROOKIE CLASS, AT THE ORIGINAL TOLEDO POLIICE PISTOL RANGE.

This monument was dedicated to Toledo Police Officers killed on duty. Located at the pistol range, it was destroyed when the range was demolished to make way for a municipal golf course.

The Anatomical Man: This target was a steel silhouette with 6 apertures at vital points. The apertures had hinged up-rights covering them from the back. A Trainee stood 30 feet from it and was required to fire six shots in ten seconds, double action at the apertures. A point was scored for each aperture's cover which was hit and fell away.

A CADET'S REBUKE

Nate Taylor was a handsome man with smooth facial features, large blue eyes and sandy, wavy hair. He was tall with a good build and since being divorced, he had women swarming all over him.

Greg Norris had not only been divorced, but had re-married and his current wife was a teenager. Norris had to endure a special hearing and also prevailed. Our friendship began with that much in common and over the years we became solid friends.

It was obvious that Captain Gladieux was less than fond of Cadet Norris for reasons I'm not sure of. One morning before class Norris approached the captain on a subject that didn't gain him any points.

" I've got a problem, captain," Norris, began. "You see, I can shoot with either hand, but I'm not sure if I ordered the correct holster."

"What hand do you write with?" the captain inquired.

"My left hand, Sir."

"What holster did you order?" the captain persisted.

"A left-handed one, Sir." Norris answered.

"Well," the captain exhaled with a sigh of exasperation, "Your problem should be resolved, wouldn't you say?" The captain then walked away.

Captain Gladieux, second in command of the police academy, was delivering a lecture to the class when Inspector Thor burst through the closed classroom door like a cyclone. Thor was obviously upset. His face was crimson, his eyes were bulging and a vein near his right temple was protruding, as he spoke rapidly.

"Sorry to interrupt, captain, I just received an upsetting phone call and must bring something to the attention of the cadets immediately."

"Gentlemen! This academy is a place of business and your instruction here is serious business. I will not stand for our classes or my office to be interrupted for personal phone calls; especially from women whom have nothing better to do."

"Each of you should be well aware that with the exception of emergencies no outsiders are to call here to engage any of you about personal matters. How dare a female caller direct me to summon one of you from class! I do not wish to mention any names, but it better not happen again."

"Carry on, captain and again, my apologies for the intrusion."

As Thor strode towards the door he shouted: "Cadet Taylor! Come to my office!"

Poor Nate. His face was blood-red as he vacated his desk and reluctantly left the classroom. I felt sorry for him.

No sooner had the captain resumed his lecture when the inspector's shrill voice, although indistinct, penetrated the classroom walls. Nate was getting nailed.

FUNERAL MANEUVERS

A respected captain had passed away and at his funeral the honor guard came under Thor's scrutiny. Thor was outraged!

"They made a mockery of their maneuvers; they were a disgrace," Thor agonized, "they were out of step and didn't execute anything in unison," he complained.

The following morning before classes, we cadets were assembled in front of the precinct for, "Funeral Maneuvers". Thor paraded our small formation in front of the station for several minutes.

"Column halt. Left face." Our two ranks faced the street. "At ease," he ordered.

Standing before us, he proceeded to lecture us on the importance of military protocol. When he had finished, he abruptly commanded, "Right face. Forward march."

To Thor's utter amazement, several of the cadets who tried to execute the commands stumbled into the majority of the cadets, whom stood fast. Chaos followed.

Thor realized that he had done something incorrectly, but had no idea what it was. Finally, in total bewilderment, Thor, cried, "Halt!"

We cadets quickly re-grouped into two ranks.

I knew that I was sticking my neck out, but someone had to set the ol' man straight.

One of my favorite activities in the Marines was close order drill. I actually enjoyed it.

"Sir," I addressed the inspector, "When the men are at ease they have to be ordered to attention before another command can be executed."

"Humph." Thor sputtered. He obviously was embarrassed.

He then called: "Attention!" The men snapped to.

Apparently unwilling to risk further humiliation, he directed Captain Gladieux to, "Take over." Thor then headed for his office; so much for funeral maneuvers.

REPRIEVE AT A PUB

The Friday we shot for record we finished early on the pistol range and to our surprise Thor dismissed the class. Although we were sweaty and tired we were relieved that after one more week we would be free of the academy for the summer. We also were excited about working the streets.

"Hey, Guys." Tom Kolinski commanded the attention of a small group of us leaving the pistol range. "A cold beer would really hit the spot right now and I think a little celebrating is in order; what-da-ya-think?"

"Sounds great," Greg Norris answered and the rest of us agreed.

"I know just the place not far from here," Tom continued, "and my car is near by."

So, Nate Taylor, Greg Norris, Frank Ostrowski, "Swede" Rasmussen and myself climbed into Tom's car and away we went. Rasmussen was stocky and of medium height with platinum hair and an alabaster complexion. Because of his Swedish accent he was good-naturedly called "Swede"; a quiet fellow, everyone was surprised that he joined us.

Kolinski parked across the street from a bar in a North-Polish neighborhood. We threw our gun belts on the rear seat and made sure that Tom locked the car.

The bar had only two patrons as we settled at a table and ordered a round of beer. We were just about to order another round when a police officer entered, briefly scanned the interior and came directly to our table.

He spoke in a low voice, "Do one of you own a green Dodge parked across the street?"

"Yeah, officer," Tom's face paled, "is there anything wrong?"

Lowering his voice to a whisper, the officer asked, "Are you fellows police cadets?"

When we all nodded affirmatively, he continued, "I want all of you to leave slowly and I'll see you outside." He then left the bar.

The officer stood beside a police cruiser parked behind Tom's car. He took the police radio's microphone in one hand while conversing with his partner, who was seated behind the steering wheel. "I told you they'd be rookies from Thor's 'House of Horrors' wetting their whistles."

"Scout 6 to Dispatcher," the officer spoke into the 'mike', "do you have a complainant on our call?"

"No, Scout 6. No further information."

"Dispatcher; all's normal here. You can put us back in service."

"Scout 6 in service."

The officer then addressed us: "You fellows were asking for trouble displaying your guns in plain sight. Someone called in reporting you as suspicious armed men."

"Will Thor know about this?" I asked.

"Not unless you tell him. We're not making any report, but I suggest you guys get out of here pronto!"

We all thanked the officers profusely; jumped into Tom's car and left.

"Any more bright ideas, Tom?" Nate asked, as we got under way.

Before Tom could reply, Greg, chimed in: "Hey, don't blame Tom, we all wanted to stop remember?"

"Well, that proves one thing," Swede, remarked, "you can't fart in a windstorm without someone bitching about it."

The quiet Swede surprised us again.

CHAPTER 3

THE ARM-BAND TOUR

EPISODES

1. STREET ACTION

2. BABY NEEDS NEW SHOES

3. EMERGENCY TREATMENT

4. HOUSE CLEANING

5. THE SURVIVORS

View of the garage attached to the Safety building, along Jackson Ave.;
containing 3 large doors and an apron for limited time parking. Circa 50's.

Front of Safety Building, at 525 N. Erie St., as it appears today.

TRAFFIC OFFICER CLIFF WARNER AND TWO UNIDENTIFIED ROOKIES CONVERSE AT THE CORNER OF N. ERIE STREET AND JACKSON, NEAR THE SAFETY BUILDING. THE ROOKIES ARE WEARING ARM BANDS AND WILL RIDE-ALONG WITH A PATROL CREW FOR AN EIGHT HOUR TOUR OF DUTY, AS PART OF THE TOLEDO POLICE ACADEMY PROGRAM. CIRCA 1950'S

STREET ACTION

On Friday, a hot, muggy July day of the week before we were to fill- in for vacationing officers, our class met at the Safety Building for the 3 PM shift to ride with scout-car crews.

We were all hoping to see some action. Dressed in civilian attire, each cadet wore a white arm-band on his left arm bearing the word "police" in black letters. Each cadet carried his badge and was armed with his Colt, .38 cal. revolver. It was too warm to wear jackets, so our gun belts and weapons were readily visible.

My assigned unit was 11 Scout with Officers Harold "Hal" Wright and Eddie Scofield, both veteran Negro policemen, weighing about 240 pounds each. They were both reputed to be no nonsense, top rated officers and despite their bulk, were agile and no one to fool around with.

They had an impressive arrest record and many commendations on file. Hal was the senior officer, laid-back and deliberate under stress, while Eddie was quick-tempered and emotional.

Eleven Scout covered the heart of the inner city; a "hot" district.

After introductions and checking the equipment in the trunk of the cruiser, Hal drove directly to the Big Boy Drive-In on Summit near Clayton where we all ordered coffee and hamburgers.

"You see," Hal, explained, "a good cop takes care of his needs first, because if he waits, he may get busy and not have time later."

"After we finish here," Eddie, broke in, "We'll try to pick up a couple of 'movers' to keep the sergeant off our backs,"

"What's a mover?" I asked, eager to learn police jargon.

"That's a moving-traffic-violator," Hal answered. "The command expects a crew to get about 30 a month, which isn't always possible, so we try to keep ahead by knocking off one or two when we first hit the street. That way if we get busy, we won't have to play catch-up at the end of the month."

When we finished eating, Hal drove to the intersection of Indiana and Division, which was controlled by a four-way stop. He parked in a no- parking zone on Division so they could observe the traffic flow on Indiana, the busier street, and watch for drivers who failed to stop.

About three minutes passed when Eddie announced, "There goes one."

"Nah," Hal disagreed, "that was more of a rolling-stop."

Then a car traveling West on Indiana sped right through the intersection. "Here we go." Hal cried, pulling away from the curb with a fast start. He caught up to the violator, flipped the red-light on and sounded the siren just enough to direct the errant driver to pull over.

Eddie approached the car as Hal informed the dispatcher of our location and activity. Returning to the cruiser with the operator's driver license, Eddie proceeded to run a check on him and the vehicle: "Eleven Scout to Dispatcher."

"Go ahead eleven."

"Request a check on a blue, '47 Ford, Ohio license 5504 J- John and on one, Marvin F. Mc Coats, Negro male, DOB: 5/12/22, present address: 1224 Lincoln."

"Stand by eleven." The Dispatcher then had to relay the information via phone to the Record Bureau and await the clerk's finding.

Several long minutes elapsed until the dispatcher called back: "Eleven Scout, that car is clean, but there is an active warrant on file for McCoats for armed robbery; use caution, he may be armed and dangerous."

"Bingo," cried Eddie, as both officers sprang from the squad car. With drawn service revolvers they ordered the man from the car. The driver submitted meekly. He was placed under arrest, frisked, handcuffed and placed in the rear of the squad car between me and Eddie. Hal searched the car for a weapon, to no avail, and locked it.

The prisoner was taken to the men's jail on the fifth floor of the Safety Building. While being booked, I accompanied Eddie to the Record Bureau on the second floor to obtain a copy of the warrant.

After the necessary paper work was finished, Eddie called the Dispatcher and informed him that we'd be in service, but in and out of the car for awhile.

"Well," Eddie said to Hal, "What do you say we give our young cadet the grand tour?"

BABY NEEDS NEW SHOES

The first stop was a red brick building at 901 Washington Street. Entering an open door, the three of us walked in on several men who were yelling and chattering around a crap table.

The "shooter" had his back to the door and was unaware of our presence. Shaking dice in one hand and clutching a wad of paper money in the other, he yelled: "Come on! Baby needs a new pair of shoes."

The building, as it appears today, with the shop on the left end
where a man smashed the showcase. (Chapt. 17).
The door to the right is where the gamblers were shooting craps.

The other gamblers, upon seeing us, became statuesque. Sensing that something was amiss as he threw the dice, the shooter turned, saw the uniforms and let our a wail tossing his handful of bills into the air. The money floated in every direction descending to the floor as Hal and Eddie roared with laughter.

Hal picked up some of the bills and held them towards the group of men, "These belong to anyone here?"

"No, no," they all cried.

"Huh," Hal grunted, "Must be mine then." He stepped towards the door, but stopped in front of the man who had flung the money. The frightened man stood motionless with his mouth agape. Hal stuck the bills into the man's mouth and said: "Here, buy yourself some baby shoes."

The three of us departed, still laughing.

Returning to the cruiser, I had a question for the duo: "Why didn't you make an arrest?"

"Hell," Eddie answered, "we don't fool around with that petit ante stuff; we don't have time. Besides we're giving you a tour."

Hal stopped the car by the Cold Spot at Avondale and Division; a notorious bar.

"You'll find this place very interesting," he promised.

We entered and found the place jammed shoulder to shoulder with customers standing about drinking, mostly from bottles. There wasn't a vacant space in the tavern. Hal directed my attention to the back bar and the ceiling above it. "See those holes?" he asked matter-of-factly, "from a shotgun." Pointing at the front bar he continued: "there's also a few bullet holes there, too."

As we elbowed our way to the end of the bar I was in awe. Then I heard a voice from the crowd say: "They's lookin' for someone, they's got a white dude with them. Someone's in trouble."

Standing at the end of the long bar Hal ordered three sodas. The bartender, a huge Negro with a wicked scar across one cheek, set three bottles of pop in front of Hal. The two officers each took one, but neither made an effort to pay for them. Hal handed the remaining bottle to me; it was cold and refreshing.

"How's it going?" Hal asked the bartender.

"Same-oh, same-oh, you know, but it's still early," he replied.

"How true," Hal agreed. We finished our drinks, thanked the big bartender and threaded our way to the front door.

EMERGENCY TREATMENT

We just got seated in the cruiser when we received a call: "Eleven Scout. Mercy Hospital Emergency Room, disturbance; a disorderly patient."

"Eleven, O.K." Eddie acknowledged over the "mike."

In record time, Hal pulled into the small parking lot near the hospital's emergency entrance. We were met at the door by an anxious nurse, "He's in room A, down the hall. He's quieted down some now," she informed us.

"Is he drunk?" Hal, inquired.

"Either that or he's on something." the nurse ventured, "the doctor's on his way."

We walked into room A through swinging doors like those depicted in western bars. A small, dark Negro male, propped up on one elbow, was sprawled on an examining table. He was fumbling with a crumpled pack of cigarettes trying without success to extract one. His clothes were dirty and unkempt. He had a nasty abrasion on his forehead and several cuts on his face.

"No smoking in here!" Eddie, barked and snatched the cigarettes from the man's trembling hands.

The man erupted. "Hey! What-da-ya-think you're doin', ya fat pig!"

Eddie ignored the remark and sat in an optical examination chair. "Don't you know better than to smoke around oxygen?"

Hal looked out a window to check the scout car oblivious to his partner's concerns.

"If ya didn't have that gun I'd whip yore ass." the man spat out.

In one fleet movement Eddie was on his feet. His gun belt dropped into the chair as he sprung to the table, pulled the man to his feet and punched him in the face. The poor wretch was catapulted through the swinging doors and across the hallway where he splattered against the wall and then slowly crumpled to the floor in a sitting position.

Eddie then grabbed the man by an ankle, slid him across the polished floor under the swinging doors, picked him up bodily and slammed him back down on the examining table.

"Now what-a-ya-gotta say you son-of-a ..."

"What do we have here, gentlemen; an unruly patient?" the doctor uttered as he fluttered into the room.

"Not any more," Eddie murmured.

The man was now bleeding from his nose and mouth, besides his original wounds.

"Well let's take a look here," the doctor said, looking into the patient's eyes with a small flashlight. "It appears he may have a slight concussion, however I believe he can be patched up and be on his way."

Fifteen minutes later with a large bandage on his forehead, his nostrils stuffed with cotton and several band aids on his face, the disheveled handcuffed man was slumped between Hal and me in the rear seat of the cruiser. Hal had insisted that Eddie drive to make sure that he didn't have any further contact with the prisoner. The subdued man was booked for: Drunk and Disorderly; Creating a Disturbance and Resisting Arrest. But he did receive emergency treatment before being booked!

HOUSE CLEANING

When Eleven Scout went back in service a call was waiting. We were sent to 1112 Wabash on a disturbance call. When Hal parked in front of the given address we could hear loud voices reverberating inside the modest house.

As we approached the home a small, elderly Negro woman with her gray hair worn in a bun opened the door for us. Several young men were arguing and using profane language in the dining room.

"What's the trouble, Ma'am," Hal asked.

"Trouble? Dere's no trouble here officers. I jest want yo' to get 'dem niggers out-a ma house."

"Are they relatives," Eddie inquired.

"No, Sir. 'Dey's jest no good friends o' ma grandson. I ast them to leave, but 'dey's not doin' it quick 'nuf, so I calls yo' to hurry 'em up."

Hal raised his voice over the din: "Listen up you people; all of you clear out of here right now."

The group of jabbering youths became silent, looked at the huge officers, looked at each other, then started for the door.

"You better not come back after we leave," Hal warned, "or you'll spend the rest of the night behind bars."

As the last of the group left, Eddie asked the old lady, "Do you think your grandson will come by?"

"No, Sir. The laaz time he was here he done stole some money from me, so he done knows better ta show his face 'roun' here."

"You have any more trouble, you give us another call, Ma'am" Eddie advised her.

"I surely will, officers, an' thank yo' for all yore help."

THE SURVIVORS

"Eleven Scout. 1924 Oakwood; shots fired. Twelve Patrol is en route."

Eddie acknowledged the call as Hal burned rubber ratcheting the cruiser into high gear with the red lights and siren penetrating the night air.

"Man! I'm sure glad we had those burgers when we did," Eddie remarked.

An ambulance was in front of the given address and Twelve Patrol was at the scene, when Hal and company arrived. A large Negro woman was being carried on a stretcher; she was drenched with blood. "We're taking her to Mercy," the ambulance attendants said.

"She's been shot several times by her ol' man," Twelve 's crew informed us. "He's still inside and just before you came we heard a single shot, but don't know where in the house it came from."

The four uniformed officers entered the house to find the suspect with me behind them; all of us with drawn revolvers. The search was futile until a moan was heard sounding from a bedroom.

When the wounded man was finally located, Hal swore: "Well, I'll be damned." The shooter was lying between a bed and the wall. "He must have tumbled there after shooting himself."

Twelve Patrol placed the bleeding man on their stretcher and rushed him to Mercy Hospital, too.

"Well," Eddie lamented, "It looks like a double homicide for sure. We'll have to wait for the dicks to get here and I'm stuck with the report."

"Yeah," sighed Hal. "This should finish our shift. I'm sure glad we had those burgers when we did."

It was late when our three-man crew returned to the Safety Building. Hal made a phone call.

"Well, I'll be damned!" he exclaimed as he set the phone aside.

"What's the matter?" Eddie and I wanted to know.

"I contacted a nurse I know at Mercy. She told me that the woman from Oakwood was shot five times, but nothing vital was hit and she'll be O.K. The woman's ol' man shot himself in the head and lost a lot of blood, but he'll survive, too. Can you figure the odds on that?"

"That's really amazing," Eddie, commented, "but I'm not re-doing my report; as far as I knew they were both headed for the morgue and that's the way it's going to stay!"

After salutations, Hal, Eddie and myself parted. While walking to my car I reflected on the long, exciting day. I felt drained, but I was engulfed with a feeling that I was a part of something important and meaningful which would afford me a future and fulfill my desire to help my fellow man.

How little did I know!

CHAPTER 4

ROOKIE EXPERIENCES

EPISODES

1. UNEXPECTED GREETINGS

2. FIRST ALMOST ARREST

3. TEMPTATION

4. FIRST AMBULANCE RUN

5. ONLY ONE PAIR OF HANDCUFFS

6. THE FURTIVE APPROACH

7. ONE FOR THE BEAT

8. A SAD ENDING

UNEXPECTED GREETINGS

After graduating from the Toledo Police Academy one of my first assignments, working the second shift, was a traffic post at the downtown corner of Madison and Superior.

One Fall afternoon I was standing on the corner by the then, Edison Building, monitoring the traffic. I was wearing a pair of mirrored sun glasses. Suddenly, a young, attractive woman walked up to me and without a word kissed me fully on my lips. She stepped back, looked at me, then exclaimed, "Oh, my God! You're not, Kenny!" She then hurried off.

Awhile later at the same location I observed a fellow whom I knew in high school named Jack Wilfred. He was scurrying down the opposite side of Madison. I crossed the street and caught up with him in front of the Ohio Building. I grabbed his arm, spun him around and said, "Hey, Jack. How are you doing?"

He jerked away from me. His face went pale and he blurted: "Don't ever do that again; you scared the living hell out of me!" He abruptly turned away and hustled down Madison without another word.

In retrospect it may have been a shock to him to be grabbed by a uniformed police officer without warning. Than maybe **he had a guilty conscience,** who knows? I did learn that it takes time to get use to wearing a police uniform and to realize the impact it may have on some people . . . and I did get rid of the mirrored sunglasses.

Looking West on Madison Ave. at Superior St. Notice the call box behind the
white sign on the right; also the throngs of pedestrians. Circa 50's.

View of the Northeast corner at Madison & Superior St. and what was called the Edison Bldg. as it is today. The author was standing by the large corner-column of the building when the unknown woman kissed him. The call box is missing; they were removed throughout Toledo about three years after the author retired.

Madison at N. St Clair St.
The photo on page 33, shows heavy traffic moving West on Madison Ave. at N. St. Clair St. In downtown Toledo in the 50's, Patrolmen had to stand in the intersections on week days to direct the flow, from 4 PM to 5:30 PM, without a break. The Ohio Building towers on the left, where the author accosted and startled a man he knew. Circa, 50's.

LOOKING WEST ON MADISON AVENUE AT THE INTERSECTION OF HURON STREET.
MADISON WAS ONE-WAY WEST AND HURON WAS ONE-WAY SOUTH. THE
BUILDING ON THE LEFT, FAR CORNER IS WHERE THE HEART PATIENT WAS
TRANSPORTED IN THE FREIGHT ELEVATOR, TO THE MAIN FLOOR. CIRCA 1950'S.

FIRST "ALMOST" ARREST

Working the third shift, I was walking the upper 50 beats: 50 to 53 from Water St., West on Madison Ave. to Huron St., South to Monroe Street and East back to Water St.

There was a chill in the night air so the first thing I did was to grab a cup of java at the White Hut at Jefferson and Superior Streets while I could take the time.

After my respite I casually strolled to Monroe Street from where I observed a woman sprawled on a bus bench at the corner of Summit Street, two blocks East. In checking I found a large Negro female sleeping. I suspected that she had been drinking because I couldn't arouse her and there was the odor of alcoholic beverages about her. Next to the bench a purse was sitting which was undoubtedly hers.

An arrest was mandatory. She was in no condition to care for herself and someone could take advantage of her. I used the call box directly across Monroe Street.

"Moore on 50 to 53. I need a wagon at Monroe and Summit."

Suddenly a car stopped near the woman. Three Negro men jumped out, loaded her into the car and sped away. It happened so fast that I hardly realized what had actually occurred. When I contacted the box operator again, he asked:

" Why do you want to cancel the wagon?" I replied, "She got a ride."

TEMPTATION

Working the third shift, a sergeant dropped me off on a West end district just before midnight. Buddies Lunch, a business place on the beat that prepared food to be delivered to factories the next day, was still open. After enjoying a free sandwich and coffee I hurried to Collingwood and Delaware where I had my raincoat stashed in a Traffic Control Box; it had began to sprinkle.

Collingwood was lined with small businesses on both sides. North of Delaware on the West side of Collingwood was a dressmaking shop, a bakery, a florist and a shoemaker. There was large residences between the last store and The Rosary Cathedral at the corner of Islington.

The rain was light so I decided to check the rear of the stores, beginning with the dress shop. The dress shop and the bakery was secured but when I tried the rear door of the florist shop, expecting resistance, it gave easily and I almost fell through the doorway.

A dim light in a small room to the right of entry afforded ample illumination to see the interior of the store. A larger room to the left also had a light which shown upon a large safe like the kind seen in Westerns; black, about six feet tall, made of solid steel with two large doors that swung open.

My eyes widened; the doors of the safe were standing fully open revealing numerous stacks of paper currency on the shelves . Some of the stacks were quite high. I stood silently in the dim light trying to gather my senses.

I never entered the room the safe was in because an evil thought penetrated my mind: the hour was late, the night was dark and rainy without a soul around and I was sure that no one had seen me enter the building.

My raincoat had large pockets as well as my uniform under the raincoat. All those pockets could hold a lot of bills. Chances were that no one would discover the missing money until late morning with the rear door unlocked just as I had found it. I had no idea how much money was in the safe as I couldn't determine the denomination of the bills from where I stood; It may have been thousands.

Then I remembered what Inspector Thor had said in one of his lectures in the Academy: "Whenever you are faced with temptation, ask yourself : Is it worth trading your badge for?"

I ascertained that the rest of the store was secure, set the lock on the rear door and slammed it tightly behind me. I filed a Sergeant Report before going off duty stating what I had found and what action I had taken. I never regretted it!

FIRST AMBULANCE RUN

Bill Mather finished his breakfast, stood up and brushed his short, dark hair back with his hand. "Well, Honey, I gotta run, but I sure don't feel like going in."

"Just take it one day at a time, Dear," Bill's wife advised.

"Did I tell you who I'm working with all week? A stupid rookie not even out of the academy yet. That Sgt. Hastings has got it in for me."

"He has to learn the same as you did Bill."

"Yeah, what a louse of a first partner I had."

"You better run or you'll be late."

"O.K. See ya when I get home." Bill yelled over his shoulder.

After roll call and checking the gear in the rear of the wagon Bill and I got into the cab. While Bill leisurely patrolled about the East Side the interior of the cab was soon sweltering; police vehicles had no air conditioning then. Opening the windows didn't help much either on hot and humid summer days like that one.

Bill hadn't said a word all morning. There was little radio traffic and the dull morning seemed to have slipped into a time-warp. I became amused by my reflection in the windshield. The convex glass distorted my image making me appear larger than I was. My gun-belt appeared to be twice its width with a huge buckle. It reminded me of the large belt and buckle always depicted on Santa Claus.

Bill finally parked in the lot of a restaurant on Front Street and broke the silence for the first time: "If we get a call, Kid, let me know."

He left the wagon and entered the small eatery. The motor had to be left running so the police radio wouldn't wear the car battery down. Thus, the hot air poured in on my legs causing my calves to break-out with a prickly rash and soon that rash began to itch. I was miserable.

Suddenly the radio came to life: "Two Patrol. 800 block of Oak, a girl struck by a car. Accident Investigation on the way."

"Two Patrol O.K." I answered, wondering if my excitement could be detected in my voice. I hurried into the restaurant and summoned Bill, who was slugging down the last of a frosted milk shake.

Under way it concerned me if a stretcher would be needed. I wasn't exactly sure how to extract it. Over the wail of the siren I shouted to Bill: "Do you think we'll need a stretcher? The reason I'm asking is because I'm not sure how to get it out."

"Look, Kid," Bill yelled, "I told the command that the next time they gave me a rookie that I wasn't telling him a 'freegin' thing and I ain't telling you a 'freegin' thing."

I felt as if Bill had struck me across my face. I was stunned. My cheeks burned and I felt dejected as we careened onto Oak Street.

A teenage girl with red hair, wearing a thin, green dress was sitting in the middle of the roadway. A severe gash had been inflicted in her left cheek. There was congealed blood on the front of her dress and a small pool of it on the simmering street. It looked like red gravy.

I felt like I was in a daze; I didn't know what to do. I saw a rear-vision auto-mirror lying by the curb and I absent-mindedly picked it up. It was smudged with blood.

Faintly, I heard my partner's voice calling: " get the stretcher, get the stretcher," but it didn't register. Finally I heard him say in disgust, "Hell, I'll get it myself."

I saw Bill enter into the rear compartment of the wagon and then I heard a "thump" and Bill's voice cursing. He emerged with the stretcher in one hand and holding his other hand over his right eye.

Suddenly, I came to my senses as I helped Bill spread the rubber sheet over the stretcher and then gently lay the victim on it and cover her with the police blanket. We carried her to our vehicle and placed our human cargo inside. I then slid onto a seat in the rear of the wagon, as Bill slammed the doors shut and we were off to St. Charles Hospital.

The hospital staff attended to the sixteen year old girl in one examining room while Bill was being treated in another for a cut above his right eye.

The Accident Investigation Squad arrived to complete their report. Bill greeted them with a conspicuous bandage over his injury.

"Some meathead didn't bother to fold up one of the legs of the stretcher; left it sticking out," Bill explained.

The A.I. Squad related that the injured girl wasn't struck by the car, per se, but that she had stepped out from between parked cars and the outside mirror of a passing car struck her face. The force was so severe that it broke the mirror off of the car's door.

Later when I was going off duty I overheard Sgt. Hastings chortling as he was relating Bill's injury to the command officers of the next shift: "The funny thing is that when they were finished working on Mather, he looked worse than the poor girl who was hit by the car."

A "PADDY" WAGON; THE WORKHORSE OF MOTORIZED UNITS. USED FOR PATROL, TRANSPORTING SUSPECTS, PRISONERS AND PROPERTY; THEY ALSO DOUBLED AS AMBULANCES, UNTIL THE CITY CONTRACTED FOR PRIVATE AMBULANCE SERVICES SOME TIME IN THE '60'S. THE WAGON PICTURED IS A 1967 FORD. THEY WERE TOP-HEAVY AND NOT DESIGNED FOR CAR-CHASES.

ONE PATROL WORKED OUT OF THE GARAGE (BARN) FROM AN OFFICE AND RECEIVED THEIR CALLS VIA PHONE. THEY WERE CONSIDERED THE "FIRST LINE OF DEFENSE" IN CASE OF AN EMERGENCY IN THE SAFETY BUILDING. CIRCA 1950'S.

ONLY ONE PAIR OF HANDCUFFS

The city equipped each paddy wagon with one pair of handcuffs.

When I reflect back I can't help but realize how many police officers placed themselves in jeopardy because they couldn't afford the price of a pair of handcuffs. Peerless handcuffs (the best on the market) cost $ 10.00 and a leather case was $3.50. A total of $13.50, yet it seemed like a small fortune at the time.

"Scout 11; 1223 Palmwood, a 918. Use caution."

A 918 is a demented person. When we heard the dispatch my partner and I working 12 patrol, an adjacent inner-city district, headed towards Palmwood.

Officers Hal Wright and Eddie Scofield arrived at the Palmwood address in record time. A woman was standing in front of the house waving at them. "Hurry officers, he's wrecking the house and threatening to kill everybody; he's gotten off his medicine again."

The berserk man was large, muscular and out of control. He confronted the officers at the front door and the policemen, weighing 240 pounds each, met the deranged man head on. While the three men were grappling on the front porch my partner and I arrived and joined the fracas. It took the total effort of all four of us to subdue him.

While the other three lawmen held the man down I got the stretcher and the one set of handcuffs from the wagon. We managed to get the struggling man on to the stretcher and handcuffed his right wrist to the right side-rail, then strapped his left wrist to the other side-rail with a restraining strap. We placed the mad man into the rear of the wagon with both Hal and Eddie literally sitting on him.

I drove the wagon and my partner drove the Scout car to the Mental Health Center. We hardly got rolling when I heard a commotion in the back of the wagon. The crazed man had managed to free his left arm; the strap wasn't able to keep him contained. Hal and Eddie had their hands full all the way to our destination.

Upon our arrival, an attendant gave the psycho a shot which calmed him down and he was admitted with a lot less trouble than what it took to get him there.

"Yes, Sir," Eddie exclaimed as the four of us cleaned up in a washroom. "I'm buying a set of handcuffs tomorrow no matter what the cost."

"I think each wagon should have two sets instead of one," I ventured.

"Actually," Hal said, "each officer on the whole department should have his own set and furnished by the city."

"Amen to that. We sure could have used them today," Eddie concluded.

It wasn't long after that when I saw a set of Peerless handcuffs with a leather case displayed in the window of a pawn shop on Monroe Street for a bargain price. Although I couldn't really afford them I made the sacrifice; the need was too great.

THE FURTIVE APPROACH

Nick Farley was appointed to the Toledo Police Department only a couple of years before me but he seemed much older. He was friendly and easy to get along with.

Four Patrol was his regular assignment and I was filling in for his vacationing partner on the second shift. We had a few minor calls during the afternoon but I was surprised that the radio was so quiet since nightfall; a moonless night.

"While we aren't busy let's check the Ackerman Coal Co.," Nick suggested. "The coal yards are off of Lagrange down near the railroad tracks and the office is way in back." Nick turned onto an unpaved road and drove around and between large dunes of coal while heading for the office. Although the area was pitch black Nick turned the headlights off.

"Hadn't you better leave the parking lights on?" I suggested.

"Not really," Nick replied, " If anyone is snooping around that'll give us away."

Nick continued to proceed slowly on the winding road in total darkness when suddenly the entire wagon lurched forward and stopped with a bang. Nick tried to go forward but the wagon wouldn't budge. Turning the headlights on, we were agast; Nick had driven into a construction ditch. The front wheels were suspended over the ditch and the frame of the wagon, behind the wheels, was resting flat on solid ground. It was private property and the company wasn't required to place any guards near it or warning signs which we wouldn't have seen anyways. We sat there for an hour before a tow truck arrived and pulled our wagon free. So much for the furtive approach.

ONE FOR THE BEAT

During my first year as a police officer I overheard the shift captain conversing with a lieutenant while en route to roll call on the second shift:

"All I know captain is that Brady's district sergeant suspects him of drinking on duty because he has had the odor of liquor about him at times. Sergeant Anderson said that he's followed Brady around on his beat but has never seen him go in a bar or take a drink. He can't figure it out."

"Has Anderson talked to Brady about it?" the captain asked.

"Anderson told me that he confronted Brady, but Brady denies it and the sergeant has no proof. Brady's a good cop, captain, but he's also a known boozer."

After roll call I was in the lavatory off the patrolmens' locker room when John Brady, a twenty-year veteran, entered and stood at the urinal next to me. He calmly pulled a pint bottle of whiskey from a trousar leg via a cord attached to his pant belt. He removed the cap, took a swig, re-capped the vessel and lowered it back to its hiding place. He then left without saying a word.

Why did he reveal his secret to me? Was he sending me a message that he trusted me or . . . was he testing me? I never found out. To my knowledge he was never caught drinking on duty.

A SAD ENDING

Beat officers, especially rookies, were "spare parts". At roll call one never knew what his assignment would end up being. Even if you called the Desk Sergeant and he told you, by roll call time that could be changed.

The auto pound, jail, tax office, court bailiff; all were possible assignments when a regularly assigned officer called in sick.

Also, unexpected situations could arise demanding foot officers: large fires or explosions, guarding a prisoner at a hospital, strike duty, traffic jams and the list goes on.

What was most annoying was when a foot officer was expecting to walk a beat in the winter season and dressed accordingly, like wearing long-johns, then being assigned to an inside job. I've been there and have done it all.

Patrolman "Skippy" Johnson was the regular booking officer on the second shift and Patrolman "Big Ben" Williams was the Turnkey. Whenever Skippy was off, Ben would take over the booking and the officer filling in would be the Turnkey.

One side of the mens' jail had three large "bull pens" each sparsely furnished with wooden benches bolted to the brick walls and a single toilet. The other side contained about nine single cells on each side of an aisle and three cells across the rear wall; each had a small barred window, a bunk and a toilet.

Two of the cells nearest to the Booking Room were called "blind" cells, because instead of bars they had four, solid steel walls. The door was solid steel, too, with a small aperture allowing the Turnkey to view the interior. There were no facilities: no benches or plumbing. These cells were used for either prisoners who were violent or who were so intoxicated that they couldn't stand or were liable to roll off a bunk and be injured.

The end cell across the back could be viewed all the way from the Booking Room and was reserved for any prisoner with suicidal tendencies.

The Turnkey's duties included fingerprinting the prisoners when booked and he was required to make a round every quarter-hour to check each prisoner's welfare.

The Turnkey on the first and second shifts also fed the prisoners.

Skippy was a small, friendly man in his 50's with a good sense of humor.

Ben looked older than he probably was; a large, gruff, slow-moving uneducated person who didn't say much except to gripe. It seemed that he didn't care much for the younger officers; to him they were all smart-alecks.

Vividly, I remember one second shift tour in the jail. Skippy was off, so Ben was in charge. The number of prisoners was low, but it was a tour I'll never forget.

About 7 P.M. a uniform crew brought John Brady in to be booked for Assault & Battery. He had been drinking and struck his wife.

Brady had retired and I hadn't heard much about him. He looked awful; he was thin and pale, his clothes were soiled and he had a severe cough.

I placed him in the "suicide" cell so I could keep an eye on him; he didn't look well.

During my rounds I observed that Brady's cough was getting worse.

"Ben I think you should send Brady to Maumee Valley Hospital; he looks bad and his coughing is terrible."

Ben glared at me. He remained mute and puttered around behind the booking counter. Finally he spoke in his gruff voice: "He'll be all right, don't worry about it."

But, his facial expression told me: "Who in hell are you to tell me how to run this place. All you rookies think you're smarter than me."

Making my 9 o'clock round I discovered Brady coughing up blood. I ran to the booking desk: "Ben, you've got to do something, Brady is hacking up blood."

Ben ambled to the rear cell and slowly returned to the Booking Room. He hesitated a moment, as if he was studying a chess move.

"Ben, if you don't call for an ambulance I will." I started for the phone on the desk, but Ben was closer and reached it first.

"Dispatcher," he muttered into the phone, " Yeah, send a police ambulance to the fifth-floor jail. I've got one to go to Maumee Valley."

In record time One Patrol's crew arrived with a stretcher and strapped Brady's gaunt body on it and disappeared into the fifth-floor elevator. That was the last I saw of him.

John Brady expired that night in Maumee Valley Hospital.

At least he didn't die in a jail cell.

CHAPTER 5

THE WAY IT WAS

EPISODES

1. VETERANS AND ROOKIES

2. THE ESCORT

3. WAITING IT OUT

4. ANOTHER DAY OFF?

5. ONE FOR THE ROAD

6. A SUNDAY RETREAT

7. THE RUN-A-WAY

8. THE PICNIC

9. THE PORK CHOP RUN

10. THE LAX DECISION

11. DOG GONE

12. WORKING SOLO

VETERANS AND ROOKIES

During the mid-fifties there were many veteran officers on the Toledo Police Department; some with more than 30 years seniority. Most of them were not concerned with being promoted; after all, sergeants were only paid $40 more a month than patrolmen and charged with much more responsibility.

However, among many of the senior officers there seem to be an uncanny dedication to the job, to the point where many would rather work than be on a day off. Although, it was also common knowledge that many of the old timers didn't enjoy a happy home life and that many of them were alcoholics, who drank on duty as well as off duty.

I don't mean to imply that all the veteran officers were in that category, but I worked with many who were and the following true incidents support my statements.

Furthermore, there was an uncommon loyalty among the senior officers and they went to extremes to protect one another.

If any of them worked a day off they were certain to be assigned to a vehicular district instead of walking a beat even if the desk sergeant had to add an extra squad car to make that possible. If that was the case a beat officer, usually a rookie, had to be pulled from a walking beat and be partnered with the veteran on the additional car; as at that time all patrol units had two-man crews.

(As a point of interest, no female officers were assigned to the patrol division at that time. Upon graduation from the training academy they were immediately assigned to the Crime Prevention Bureau as detectives of juvenile-involved crimes, sex crimes and missing persons.)

There was also no such position as: "Training Officer." Actually, the veteran officer substituted as a training officer whether he chose to be or not and some did not relish that responsibility, as my experience with Bill Mather illustrated.

A real negative aspect of this policy was that whatever attitude the older officer held was impacted upon the younger officer, whether it was good, bad or indifferent. This also applied to whatever bad habits the veteran officer had, like drinking on duty.

The rookie, in turn, if he was eager to learn the job, had to depend upon the veteran officers to "show him the ropes." If the older officer committed a breech of departmental rules or an act outside of the law, a rookie was absolutely intimidated not to expose him. This was for two valid reasons:

One: The rookie depended upon the veteran for an "unofficial evaluation" of what kind of person and officer he was, which he knew would be shared with every officer the veteran would come into contact with. In brief, the veteran could "make or break" him.

Two: The rookie knew whatever action he took against the veteran would be known throughout the ranks of the department within two days (cops are terrible gossipers) and he feared that he would be branded as a "fink" and be ostracized by the entire police force and no one would want to work with him. Whether this was a reality or not, it was feared beyond belief and the young men were afraid to risk it. The following incidents, which all are true, should hear me out.

Patrolmen Archie Best and R. Chisholm, bantering outside of the Safety Bldg.,
while bringing in their gear after a tour of duty. Circa 50's.

Patrolmen Bart Connelly, Pat Bruen and Bill Callanan enjoying a light moment, before roll call.
Circa 50's.

THE ESCORT

Working the third shift (11 pm x 7 am) I was assigned to Scout 14, the South End District, with fellow rookie, Greg Norris, who was appointed with me.

When we "hit the streets" I was driving. Before we could even get coffee we were ordered by the dispatcher to meet Sgt. Morgan in the 400 block of Crittenden, just East of Maumee Avenue.; four blocks from where I lived at the time.

When we arrived we observed the sergeant in his vehicle parked behind another car, which was partially over the curb with the driver slumped over the steering wheel.

Sgt. Martin Morgan was a large man: 6' tall and about 250 pounds; overweight to be sure, but no one to fool with. He was very friendly and helpful to the rookies and usually worked the sergeants' desk at The Safety Building. This night he was on the street and was our district sergeant.

He approached my side of the car, " Do you know where Wiley Street is?"

He gave us a disgusted look when Norris and I both replied negatively.

Maintaining a scowl, he gave us an order: " Norris, you help me move the guy from behind the wheel and you follow me in his car. Moore, you follow us."

When everyone was ready to roll the three-car parade took off. Upon arrival at a house on Wiley, Norris parked the man's car in the driveway and helped Sgt. Morgan lug the incapacitated person into the house.

"You guys go back in service and keep your mouths shut," was the sergeant's last instructions. He never told us who the man was or how he came across him and we weren't about to ask. Eventually, I learned that the man, whom the sergeant aided was a police officer, who obviously didn't make it home. I never spoke of this incident until now.

WAITING IT OUT

When the municipal courts were located in the Safety Building, Toledo Police officers served as bailiffs. Their duties entailed bringing the prisoners from the Toledo Police Mens' Jail, on the fifth floor to the holding cell (bullpen) located below the court rooms.

When a prisoner's case was called up, that individual would be escorted to the court room and kept under guard until his case was disposed of. If a prisoner was remanded to jail, he was returned to the bullpen until court was adjourned and then all such prisoners would be taken back to the fifth floor. When prisoner's cases were resolved without further incarceration, such as fines, they were processed through the clerk of courts and released.

Female prisoners were handled by women matrons whom worked in the women's jail located on the fourth floor; their cases were processed in a like manner. There seldom was more than three women prisoners where by contrast, the men numbered anywhere from a dozen to twenty or more.

Court began at 9 am and usually lasted until late afternoon. Court assignment was good duty: clean and not too physically demanding. Most court officers were over forty and many were nearing retirement. It was a good way to finish ones career.

On more than one occasion when a court officer became ill on duty, he would absolutely refuse to go home. One such case was Officer Vince Becker, Sr. He was one of the older court officers and was in his 60's.

One day when Vince felt ill, he was advised several times to take the rest of the day off. He refused and sat in the rear of the court room until court ended about 2 pm. Then he quietly put on his jacket and left.

Personally, I've always given these officers credit for loyalty to duty and the police department. However, it was common knowledge that some of them didn't have ideal marriages and some went on record that they'd rather work than be at home.

ANOTHER DAY OFF ?

A court officer I'll call "Pappy" was next to being the oldest officer assigned to the court. He was spry, slim, articulate and always wore his silver-gray hair in a crew-cut.

At that time, the Toledo Police Department was working a 48 hour week. The patrol shifts worked four days on with one day off. To maintain this schedule on an annual basis every patrol officer had to give up one- day- off per month and thus work nine consecutive days each month. This was bad enough on the first and second shifts, but it was worse on the third shift.

For most officers the third shift was most inconvenient, because everyone was use to sleeping nights and found it most difficult to rotate from the day shift to the third shift and have to start staying awake all night. Also, because the three shifts rotated every month, officers on the third and second shifts had to "double-back". The second shift got off at 11 p.m. and had to return to duty at 7 a.m. the following morning; a mere 8 hour reprieve. The third shift quit at 7 A. M. and had to report for duty again at 3 P.M. that same day; which also was only 8 hours later.

The Toledo Police were fighting for a 40 hour week and negotiating with the city through their bargaining unit, The Fraternal Order of Police. the city offered us a 44 hour week and it was under discussion prior to being voted on.

During that period I had to appear in court one morning and was with a small group of patrolmen waiting for the doors to open at 9 A.M. Pappy was in charge of opening the court and was standing in the hall with us just prior to starting time. Our small talk turned to the issue of voting for a shorter work week when Pappy, in a serious tone of voice, had this to say:

"You know fellows I've been thinking that if we go to 44 hours, that would give us another day off." Then in the same solemn tone Pappy added: "Fellows, what would you do with another day off?"

We were amazed, because he was absolutely serious.

It happened that the police voted down the 44 hour offer and remained working 48 hours. The following year the offer of 44 hours was accepted and it was yet another year, 1960, before the work week was reduced to 40 hours.

The Lakeside Café (Now named The Mayfly Café) is still located on Summit St. near 101st. St.

ONE FOR THE ROAD

On the second shift of a summer day, Officer Mike O'Grady had to work a day-off. I learned at roll call that I would be his partner on the Point Place car: Scout 5.

I had worked with Mike before. He was 5' 10" tall, stocky with salt and pepper hair. His rugged complexion complimented his bland 50 year old face and mild manners. Mike was a quiet man until someone or something irked his Irish temper; then get out of his way.

Mike was well connected with the brass and got away with a lot of things that other officers would have been reprimanded for. He did his job, but wasn't overly ambitious.

On two-man patrol cars, the veteran officer was designated #1 and his partner #2. It was the #1 officer's prerogative to drive for the entire 8 hour tour or he could split that chore with his partner. The majority of the officers shared the driving, but there were an isolated few who drove the entire time.

After checking the gear in the trunk of the scout car, O'Grady took the wheel and drove directly from the Safety Building, straight out Summit Street to 101st. Street, where he parked the cruiser in front of the Lakeside Cafe.

Leaving me sitting in the warm afternoon sun, O'Grady said, "I'll be a couple of minutes, Kid. If we get anything let me know." He entered the saloon and disappeared.

About twenty minutes later a call came over the police radio: "Scout 5. See complainant; 2811 Summit; all we know is that someone wants to talk to the police. You will be out of service."

When I entered the cafe there was O'Grady, bigger than life in full uniform, sitting at the bar with a bottle of beer in front of him.

"We got a call," I announced from the door; there was no other patrons in the place which I was glad of.

O'Grady lunged behind the wheel moments after I had returned to our cruiser. I gave him the particulars of the call and he proceeded towards the location. After resolving that complaint the rest of our tour was quiet, listless and boring. O'Grady offered no explanation for his conduct and I didn't question him. He was the senior officer and if he wanted to put his welfare on the line, so be it. I had a gut feeling, though, that O'Grady was very certain that if he was reported or if a command officer had seen our squad car and checked on us, nothing would have been done about it.

However, I was slightly miffed that O'Grady would pull a stunt like that, knowing that I was still on probation. On the other hand he must have trusted me. However, all this was conjecture and only the Lord knows what his reasoning was.

THE SUNDAY RETREAT

On a quiet Sunday morning I reported for duty at the East Side station. At roll call I was assigned to walking a beat on Main Street, but Officer Grant Gibson was late, so I replaced him on two patrol with his partner Gary Ryan and Gibson had to take my beat.

Officer Ryan was less than 6' tall and hefty, with sandy hair and a matching moustache. He was a congenial fellow with a ready smile.

"They call me Sandy," Ryan greeted me at the wagon. "We'll pick up a paper and get some coffee first thing. Sundays are usually quiet, but you never know."

"Glad to know you, Sandy. Call me Jim. I'm sorry your partner will have to walk."

"Serves him right, but it's no big deal. On a Sunday he's better off than we are."

After a coffee stop, Sandy coasted around our tranquil district until almost 11 o'clock. Then he drove up an alley and stopped in front of a garage door in the rear of a brick building in the 500 block of Main St. He tooted the horn and to my surprise the door was opened by Officer Grant Gibson

"Where the hell have you been?" Grant inquired. "I've been waiting all morning to read the paper."

Sandy drove the wagon into the building, got out and closed the overhead door.

"I gave the kid a look-sy at the district. Here, catch." Sandy threw the paper towards Grant, but it fell short.

"Damn, you can't do anything right today, can you?" Gibson grumbled, as he grabbed the paper off the cement floor. "What was so important to show the kid, anyways?"

Ignoring Grant's question, Sandy asked, "Is Kelly around?"

"Yeah, she's up front," Grant replied, as he flopped on one of several worn, leather chairs along one wall and opened the paper.

"Tell her to scoot across the street and get us some hooch."

"Tell her yourself. She thought you weren't coming. And again, what was so important to show the kid?" But Sandy had gone to the front of the building.

Seconds later he returned with an attractive, young lady dressed in tight jeans, a loose blouse and a bandana. "What'll you guys have?" she smiled.

"The usual; Jack Daniels." Grant replied.

"That O.K. with you, kid?" Sandy looked at me.

"No, none for me, thanks," I said, but seeing the alarm in Sandy's face and Grant looking up from his newspaper, I quickly added, "I don't drink whiskey."

"How about something else?" Sandy persisted.

Fearing to jeopardize the veteran officers' trust, I asked: "How about a beer?"

"Make that two pints of Jack Daniels and two beers, Kelly," Sandy ordered, "And tell Matt to put that on my tab," he added with a wink.

When Kelly returned she set the bottles on an old end table; there were no glasses. Obviously the building was used for auto repairs. There were oil slicks on the floor and jacks, tool chests and motor hoists along the wall across from the leather chairs.

"Doesn't Grant have to hit a box pretty soon?" I inquired of Sandy.

"Nah, he's got a fix in with the box operator; not to worry."

We lounged around the ol' garage reading the paper and imbibing until two o'clock when a call blurted from the wagon's radio: "Two patrol, 1233 Front Street, see complainant, boys. In service."

Grant opened the garage door as Sandy got behind the wheel of the wagon and I got in beside him. Sandy backed out and abruptly braked, got out and retrieved his cap from the hood of the wagon, got back in and gunned the motor. The wagon didn't budge. Sandy neglected to shift from park to drive.

"You want me to drive?" I offered.

"Nah, I'm fine. Almost lost my hat, that's all."

The caller was waiting on her porch when we arrived. "Look, Jim," Sandy instructed, "just see what the beef is, pacify her and let's get the hell out-a-here; it's almost hitting-off time."

I greeted the woman; listened to her complaint; assured her that we would do all in our power to find the boys involved; returned to the wagon and we sped off.

THE RUN-A-WAY

Scout 14 was my favorite patrol district. It covered most of the old South end where I was raised. I not only knew the streets, but also the alleys; the businesses and even many of the residents.

Basically the district boundaries were from Clayton Street on the North, to the railroad viaduct on Broadway, it's South border, to the Anthony Wayne Trail, the West border, to Erie Street and back to Clayton.

At roll call on the second shift the "dope" included a report of a run-a-way girl, age 7, from 802 S. Erie Street. This was not the first time she had run away from home and she was known to hide around St. Peter and Paul's Catholic Church and School compound on S. St. Clair Street, about two blocks from her home.

St. Peter & Paul Church and School viewing the crossway where the little run-a-way girl was found.

These locations were on 14 Scout's District which I was assigned to that day with a veteran officer named Donald (Duke) Harris. He was in his forties, just under 6' tall, medium build with a "beer belly". He was a "no nonsense" officer with an attitude.

Upon hitting the streets, the first thing Duke did was to check St. Peter and Paul's, but there was no sight of the child run-a-way.

However, after dark Duke drove down a byway between the church and the school and a young girl ran across the beam of our headlights. Duke jumped from our cruiser and confronted the child, shining his 3-cell flashlight directly on her face.

"Come here, Kid," he ordered in a gruff voice.

She was wearing a thin summer dress and was obviously chilled from the cool night air. She also was obviously frightened by the large, looming uniformed figure of Duke and his harsh flashlight.

I walked up to her and said, "Don't be afraid, Honey, we're not going to hurt you."

Taking her small, trembling form into my arms, I tried to reassure her and said, "We have to take you home."

" I don't want to go home." She cried.

"You have to," I replied, "you can't stay outdoors all night."

Placing her on the rear seat of the squad car, I got in beside her and Duke drove us the short distance to her home.

Her Mother was delighted and relieved to see her, but her Step- Father was irate and course.

"What's the matter with you?" He shouted, " how many times have we told you not to run away?

Honestly officers, I don't know what to do with her. We give her everything she wants and all we get in return is a lot of sass.

You know what she did last week? She said a bad word, so I told her that if she says another bad word I'll wash her mouth out with soap. You know what? I find her in the bathroom chewing on a bar of soap . . . I ask her what she thinks she is doing and she told me: 'I wanted to see what it was going to taste like.' What do you think of that?"

" I think you've got your hands full, Mister." Duke answered, "but, we have to get back in service."

I wanted to tell the jackass that instead of thinking up ways to punish her, he should find ways to show her that he loves her . . . but, it seemed doubtful that he would.

I didn't voice my sentiments aloud because I didn't think that Duke would approve. While I was trying to console the child, when we found her, I saw a look of disdain on his face, so I thought it best to play it cool. When we got back on the street, Duke proved that my line of thinking was correct.

"You know," Duke began, " the instructors in that candy-ass police academy try to convince the cadets that police officers are social doctors, when in fact we don't have time for that bullshit on the street. We don't have time to hold hands and hear sob stories. Some days we go from one call to another without a break. You answer each call, do what you can and move on; you seldom ever see the same people twice."

" I'm sure you're right, Duke." I replied, not wanting to argue. I figured that I'd probably work with Duke again sometime and I wanted to stay on his good side.

However, I felt that cops with attitudes like Duke displayed, deterred any efforts toward professionalism. It's true that some days crews are extremely busy and do go from one call to another. I've experienced that scenario myself, many times. But, in some cases it has made a big difference when an officer took a few minutes to explain what's going on; to show an interest in a complainant's problem; to comfort someone or to show empathy. And with the majority of the public . . . it pays off.

To this day I wonder how that little, defiant child fared in life. God bless her.

THE PICNIC

Another tour on 5 Scout, this time with 15 year veteran, Officer Ed Burton; who was working a day-off. Ed was in his mid-forties, only 5'10" , but stocky. His hair was graying and receding over pale blue eyes.

Ed drove 100 per cent of the time and was assigned to 12 Patrol, a very active wagon district, which covered a large portion of the inner-city.

After checking the gear kept under the two bench-seats in the rear compartment of the wagon, Ed always spent several minutes wiping the steering wheel with a paper towel. After all, someone had driven the truck for eight hours before him.

Ed was headstrong, independent and a teetotaler with a reputation on the department for hating drunks. He was known to park in secluded places near busy bars and when a patron would leave, whom appeared intoxicated, Ed would wait until that person got into his car and follow him until he observed the driver maneuvering erratically, then pull him over and arrest him for driving under the influence.

Ed's regular partner went along with him on these arrests, but if Ed was working with a different partner and that officer disapproved, Ed would still make the arrest and simply sign and file the affidavit on his own.

We barely finished our coffee, when we received a call to check the police pistol range for trespassers. The shooting range was noted among law enforcement agencies as one of best in the country. It was located at Detweiler Park on a large piece of land at Suder Ave. and running along Summit Street for nearly a mile. Only a small portion of the park was available to the public and furnished with a couple grills which were seldom used.

As Ed drove up the entrance way and passed the range house, we observed several men and women playing softball on the shaded, grassy area near the center of the police facility. Others were using the grills and preparing for a picnic.

A couple of the men looked familiar to me, but before I could say a word, Ed bounded from the cruiser and said, "Stay here, I'll handle this."

After a brief moment, Ed turned from the trespassers and signaled for me to join him. As I approached the group, Ed began to introduce them to me. Lo and behold! They were all patrolmen from the traffic bureau and their wives. All of them obviously had been imbibing and were loud and giddy; the men more so than the women.

Traffic personnel only worked the first and second shifts and no weekends, with exception of special events, such as parades. The bureau was an elite entity of its own, with its' own command and I learned for a fact that a patrolman had to have connections to become a member of the Toledo Police Traffic Bureau.

Then came the real shocker: apart from the group playing ball, the inspector in charge of the traffic bureau was standing inside the small metal structure, at the 25 yard firing line of the paper-target range. The small booth was used for a Range Master to stand in while supervising pistol shooters. The inspector was nursing a beer and I dare say, that if it wasn't for the booth, he would have fallen on his face; he was crocked!

I had never met him, so Ed introduced us. The inspector's words were so slurred I could hardly understand him. I tried to conceal my reaction to his condition, but I'm sure he was well aware of it.

We didn't know who called in and we certainly weren't going to take any action. In fact, I told them I was glad to have met them; Ed wished them all a good time and we got the hell out of there.

THE PORK CHOP RUN

Patrolman Ronald Bebeshimer, known as "Bebe", was a policeman less than three years. He was only 28, but most people took him for much older because of his receding hair, which was already turning gray. He was thin and lanky with a weak chin. His only positive feature was a crooked grin.

His uniform was usually unkempt and wrinkled. He had removed the wire band from the inside of his eight-point cap, which caused the sides to flop down in a "ninety-day-wonder" look. His shoes were scuffed and in need of polish.

To say he was frugal was an understatement. Bebe sought free newspapers, coffee, meals and anything else he could mooch. He only parted with money when he had to and was constantly looking for bargains.

On an afternoon shift we were partners on 2 Patrol, the East side wagon. We finished booking a prisoner at the Safety Building and were going back on the street.

Bebe was driving. " Where are you going?" I inquired, when I realized that he was not headed for the East Side.

"They've got pork chops on sale at Kroger and I thought I'd run into the one on Broadway and get some on the way back to district," Bebe, replied matter-of-factly.

"Broadway!" I exclaimed. "that's in the South End way off district. What if we get a call?"

By now, Bebe had driven down Michigan to Washington, South of the downtown area , over to Summit and was nearing Broadway.

"No sweat, good Buddy," Bebe, answered as he sped South onto Broadway. "Depending on where the call is, we can either zap over the High Level bridge or the Fasset Street bridge and be there in no time."

Bebe swung into the Kroger lot, parked and jumped out from behind the wheel, "Be right out," he called as he hurried towards the store.

Thirteen anxious minutes crawled by until Bebe returned to the wagon with a package. He started the motor, pulled out onto Broadway and turned West onto South Street, instead of East.

"Where in hell are you going now?" I yelled excitedly.

"We're close by the Anthony Wayne Trail and I live right off of it a short ways. I want to put these chops in the freezer. It'll only take a minute," Bebe, explained.

"You know I'm still on probation and I could lose my job for this," I spat out, " if we get caught, believe me you're going to be the sorriest bastard on earth!"

"Don't worry so much," Bebe consoled. "Everything is going to be fine; you'll see."

The wagon screeched to a stop in Bebe's driveway and he ran into his house. More apprehensive minutes dragged by as I prayed that we wouldn't get a call.

Finally, we were racing over the Fasset Street Bridge, across the Maumee River and were safely back in East Toledo.

"See!" Bebe beamed, "I told you we'd make it O.K."

"Pure luck," I sighed aloud.

A LAX DECISION

Working two patrol on the East Side with Officer Ronald "Bebe" Bebeshimer again, I was driving on a day tour when we observed a car traveling at an excessive speed on Woodville Road. When we pursued, with lights and siren, the errant motorist increased his speed. Bebe radioed the dispatcher.

The subject careened onto East Broadway towards a railroad crossing. The speeder ignored the lowered gates, flashing-red-signals and clanging bells as he swerved around the barrier and throttled across the single track to beat an approaching train. We were right behind the reckless fool in hot pursuit and I held my breath as we also cleared the track before the roaring train rushed by. The fleeing auto swung around the gate on the other side of the crossing and charged up a side street. As we continued the chase, the wayward driver unexpectedly gave up and coasted to a stop along the curb. Bebe approached the law breaker as I apprised the dispatcher of our disposition. I expected Bebe to return to the wagon with the operator's driver license, but to my astonishment the culprit began to drive away as Bebe got back in our vehicle.

"What in hell's going on?" I asked.

"Well," Bebe explained, "The guy said that if he gets one more ticket, he'll lose his license, so I gave him a break."

Railroad crossing, with gates raised, on East Broadway at Hexler, where author pursued errant driver across tracks, while a fast train was approaching.

"You what?" I gasped. "He's the kind of nut you want to take off the street!"

Putting the wagon in motion, I caught up with freed driver and signaled for him to stop again. Alighting from the wagon, I nonchalantly approached him, not wanting to spook him into another chase.

"What's the matter now, officer?" he asked suspiciously

"I have to see your driver license again, Sir. My partner missed some data," I explained with a smile.

At that time it was the policy of the Municipal Clerk of Courts to stamp on the back of operators' licenses each violation a driver was convicted of. The man handed me the document and when I turned it over I was shocked. The entire back was completely stamped, including the margins along all four edges.

"Wait here," I ordered and upon my return the erratic driver's face paled as I handed him five citations: Two for speeding; one for disregarding railroad signals; another for reckless operation and a fifth for attempting to elude police officers. I was still upset over the close call with the train, but decided not to book him.

Bebe spent the rest of the day trying to justify himself.

"Forget it." I told him, "It's history."

However, I hoped that I'd never have to work with Ron Bebeshimer again.

DOG GONE

Officer Leo Dominski was a veteran officer with nearly twenty years of service and it was common knowledge that he had a fondness for booze. Frequently, regardless of what shift he had worked, he would come home inebriated.

One day after working the third shift, he arrived home about noon intoxicated as usual. His dog began barking incessantly and would not cease, so Leo took his service revolver and shot the dog dead!

Leo's wife was horrified and called the police. A crew responded, but insisted that there was nothing that they could do about it. It was Leo's dog and killing it was no crime. They made a report of the incident and left.

However, the chief of police looked at the matter in a different light. The chief summoned Leo to his office and suspended him for thirty days without pay for violation of a departmental rule: The unnecessary discharge of his issued firearm.

WORKING SOLO

One evening on third shift I was assigned to work with Leo Dominski. After roll call we got into our squad car with Leo driving. He traveled exactly two blocks from the Safety building, turned into an alley and parked near the rear door of a dark building. There was a dim light above the door, but no signs.

" I'll be right out," Leo promised.

Two hours later, Leo emerged from the door with his cap sitting sideways on his head. He was soused. He opened the passenger door where I was sitting and in a very slurred voice said: "Move over, Kid, you're driving."

I climbed behind the steering wheel as Leo fell into the seat I had occupied. Before I could drive the cruiser out of the alley he was snuggled down in the seat loudly snoring with his cap over his eyes. I was tempted to return to the Safety Building and summon the shift captain to witness Dominski's condition, but I honestly had no clue as to what the captain's reaction would be. Would he try to cover for him or relieve him of duty and assign another officer to work with me.

What was worse in my mind was if the captain did take the latter action, what would the consequences be for me? What would the other veteran officers think? What would any of the other officers think?

I truly feared that I would be ostracized, not only by my fellow patrolmen, but by the members of the entire department. I simply could not take the risk of being branded a fink! So I drove with the drunken lout throughout the tour; checking buildings and known trouble-spots as best I could, while Dominski was in slumber-land. Fortunately, our unit did not receive a single call and I didn't come across anything that I couldn't handle alone. It was an unusually quiet night.

About 5 A.M. Dominski's binge wore off and he wanted to get some coffee. We took turns having breakfast and soon after it was time to re-fuel the car and hit off. I made a promise to myself that I'd never work a squad car with him again.

Years later a Los Angeles police officer published a book featuring the ten most deadly mistakes police officers make while working. One chapter was about an officer sleeping on patrol while his partner "worked solo." Without arousing his sleeping partner the alert officer stopped a car in a residential area and when he approached it alone he was shot dead for his efforts. The shots awakened the second officer, but it was too late.

The suspect car was gone and his partner was sprawled on the street dead. When the errant officer radioed for help, he didn't have the slightest idea as to where his location was.

After reading this book and reflecting upon my experience with Dominski, I literally shuddered. Only by the grace of God, something as tragic didn't happen to me.

CHAPTER 6

LIFE IN THE BIG CITY

EPISODES

PIPED ABOARD

Working the day shift, my partner Larry Peters and I answered a brief "Call for Police" dispatch. No details were given. The address was in a modest, quiet neighborhood. That may have been the reason we didn't take our billy clubs with us or it may have been a simple quirk of fate.

In response to my knock, a man answered from within, "come in". The door was unlocked and we had barely entered the dwelling when it slammed shut behind us. The man had been waiting in ambush behind the door. He was small in stature but the pipe wrench in his hands was huge.

"If you guys came in here with those baseball bats, I was going to knock your heads off." His voice was angry and he appeared hostile.

"Someone called the police and we're just answering the call," Larry informed the man in a calm voice.

I observed two empty beer bottles on the kitchen table. "Why don't you have another beer and tell us what your problem is?" I suggested.

The man's disposition immediately changed. "That's a good idea, officer." Placing the wrench on the floor, he strode to the refrigerator and cheerfully added, "Will you gentlemen join me?"

"Sorry, we can't, we're on duty." I offered, trying not to offend him.

"You see," he said, as he opened a beer, "I'm seeing a 'shrink'..." and he spent the next ten minutes pouring out his troubles to us.

We ended up persuading him to seek further treatment and he even agreed to let us take him to the State Hospital ... under one condition: that we brought the wagon around to the rear gate so the neighbors wouldn't see him leave with us. Larry was driving, so he went to move the wagon and I waited with the man alone for several l-o-n-g minutes. I just made sure that he didn't need a wrench!

A U.S. MARINE TACTIC

My first steady riding assignment was on a patrol wagon with a four-year veteran, Larry Peters. At that time the wagons also served as ambulances and were equipped with among other items, a folding stretcher and two blankets.

One afternoon we were dispatched to a residence to take a woman to a hospital. She was bedridden in an upstairs bedroom, so we brought in the stretcher and blankets, but there was several problems: one, she weighed at least 300 pounds; two, the staircase had a sharp turn at a landing, making it impossible to negotiate an open stretcher and three, we lacked the brawn to carry her. Larry was 5'9" and 160 pounds and I was 6'2" and 175 pounds.

We were baffled until I recalled the "blanket-carry", which I had become acquainted with when I was in the U.S Marines. There was no other way, but we needed an additional crew, which arrived shortly after we called the dispatcher.

Using both blankets for good measure, we rolled the woman on her side and placed the blankets under half of her. Then, we rolled her to her other side and pulled the blankets under her whole massive body. This alone was a chore.

Next, two officers gripped the blankets on either side to carry her. We got her to the edge of the bed on the first lift; on a second effort we lowered her to the floor. After two more lifts we were positioned at the top of the stairs. My fingers were aching. We made another sortie to the landing and a final move to the living room floor. My fingers were numb. We then placed her on the stretcher and the four of us carried her to the wagon. The second crew had to follow us to the hospital to help carry her inside. The moral of this story is: "Where there's a will, there's a way."

A NAÏVE FEMALE

"Scout One; meet the Rescue Squad ; 1400 block of Southard, the Southard Apartments; you'll be out of service," the dispatcher informed us.

"Scout One, O.K." My partner Bob Skinner answered.

"Wonder what's up with them?" I mused.

"We'll know in a minute, they're just around the corner."

As we parked behind the rescue vehicle a fire captain approached us.

"Sorry to have to bother you guys, but this calls for an investigation. In apartment two-ten we had to patch up a guy with three knife wounds. His common-law wife got him pretty good with a butcher knife; twice in an arm and once in the buttocks. He refused to let us take him to a hospital . . . so they're all yours.

"O.K. captain, we'll take care of it,"

The door of apartment 210 was standing open, so we entered. A small, dark, black man, about age 25 with processed hair was sitting in a lounge chair with a pillow under his posterior. He was wearing an undershirt and black pants. His left forearm was bandaged heavily with a second bandage wrapped around the bicep of the same arm. What I'll never forget is how closely he resembled Sammy Davis, Jr., the actor.

Before anyone could say anything a very young, attractive, white female walked out of a bedroom. A crib containing a tiny infant was in view through the bedroom doorway.

"You want to know why I hurt him? I'll tell you why: I was in the hospital for several days to have our baby. Not long after, we began having sexual relations again and I caught a venereal disease. He told me that I probably got it from a toilet seat. I went to the City Health Clinic for treatment and a doctor told me that it's almost impossible to get Gonorrhea from a toilet seat; that you get it from having sex with someone who has it.

He's the only one I've ever had, so I had to get it from him. That means he was fooling around while I was in the hospital . . . the lousy son-of-a-bitch."

"Do you want to prosecute her?" Bob asked the man.

"No, but she's got me all wrong. I didn't do nothin' Baby." he pleaded to the blond.

"Is everything going to be peaceful if we leave?" I queried. "Because we don't want to have to come back here."

"Yes." the blond replied. "I haven't made up my mind . . . I don't know what I'm going to do, yet . . . but I'll let him be."

"If you should need it for any reason, our report will be on file," Bob added.

As we left I remarked: "How much you want to bet she doesn't leave?"

Ignoring me, Bob said, "She's the most naïve and stupidest broad I've ever seen."

THE BRIDE WORE WHITE

Working 13 Patrol in South Toledo, Larry and I were sent to 537 Jervis on a wagon call for the vice squad. It was 11:00 P.M.

The interior of the house, which featured lacquered Chinese furniture, was decorated beautifully. There was also balloons and streamers suspended from the ceiling. Members of the vice squad had raided a wedding.

The groom was a small, skinny man wearing a tuxedo. The bride, holding a large bouquet of flowers, wore a full white gown with a veil. The bride weighed about 300 pounds and was completely b-a-l-d; the bride was a man, too!

Same-sex weddings and all homosexual acts, whether in public or private, were strictly illegal in the fifties. Their one consolation was that they were both booked in the mens jail, but placed in separate cells.

BEATING THE CLOCK

She had a good time and she felt good all over. She knew she had too much to drink but she had to get home. It was past 3:30 A.M. and her husband would be home from work by 4:00 A.M. She didn't dare to drive any faster; it was too difficult to see the road. What was that up ahead? "Oh, my, God!" **CRASH!**

Working 13 Patrol in the South End, Officer Bill Marsh and I received an emergency run to a train-auto accident. We rushed to the scene with our siren blaring and red light flashing in the misty pre-dawn air.

A speeding car had smashed through a railroad-crossing gate and struck the thirty-seventh boxcar of a freight train. The auto was dragged along the track over a hundred yards before the engineer could halt the train.

Although we could only view the car from the roadway, we were certain that it was an injury accident, so we ordered an ambulance. An accident investigation unit also responded.

Then Bill and I decided to take our stretcher to the wrecked car. We could check for injuries and possibly carry someone to the road while the ambulance was en route. It would save some time and maybe a life.

The driver was a hefty blond in her mid-forties. The frothy blood on her mouth indicated that she had a pierced lung. She complained of pain in her right knee, the patella was obviously fractured.

We extracted her from the mangled vehicle and placed her on the stretcher as gently as possible. We carried her along the track, reaching the roadway just as the ambulance arrived. She was placed into the ambulance and transported to Maumee Valley Hospital.

The emergency room doctor ascertained that a broken rib had punctured her right lung. Besides her fractured patella, she also suffered a slight concussion and some minor bruises and abrasions. She was a very fortunate woman.

She admitted that she had been speeding to get home before her husband and didn't see the railroad signals in time.

Returning to duty, I remarked to Bill, "She was really lucky not to have been injured more seriously."

"She isn't out of the woods yet," Bill replied. "Wait 'til her husband gets here."

WHAT'S IN A NAME

Ted Curtis jammed his 6'3" frame and 250 pound body behind the steering wheel of our patrol wagon. His "reefer", a Mackinaw-type uniform coat, didn't help matters. We were working Unit 17 in West Toledo.

It was after noon when we were dispatched to an apartment building on Douglas near Berdan to take a report of a burglary. It was a nicely kept, better than average neighborhood with numerous brick-veneered buildings, each containing four apartments.

In answer to the chimes a very attractive woman opened the door of a lower apartment. She was about 5'3", not over 105 pounds, in her mid-twenties, with long brunette hair and dark eyes to match; with a creamy complexion. She was wearing a knee-length, ivory-colored kimono trimmed with gold lace. Apparently she hadn't been up for very long.

"Your apartment was burglarized, Ma'am?" I inquired.

"Yes, officer. Someone broke-in through my bedroom window. Follow me and I'll show you."

The spotless, white carpeting was plush and complimented the brocaded sofa and two club chairs in the living room. Genuine oaken tables topped with Italian marble and lamps with white satin shades completed the ensemble. The furnishings were lavish and expensive.

She led us down a hallway and into a bedroom where she pointed to a window, but while doing so she placed a knee upon the bed causing her kimono to part, revealing a slender thigh. Suddenly, the room temperature increased.

"The screen was removed and the window forced," she informed us.

"What was taken?" I inquired.

She glided to a closet before replying: "A mink-trimmed blouse, a Minolta camera and case and a genuine ostrich leather purse are missing. About a thousand dollars worth of stuff."

"You'll need to obtain the serial number of the camera and the brand of the other items, if you can, for the detectives."

"I'll try." she promised and twitched her cute nose.

We started back to the front room with Ted in the lead. Where the hallway met the living room a throw rug covered the telephone cord which ran from a wall to where the telephone was stationed on an end table. Somehow, Ted managed to snag the cord with one of his huge shoes, pulling the phone to the floor with a "clang". Embarrassed, Ted quickly gathered up the phone and set it back on the table.

The young woman reclined on the sofa crossing her shapely legs which raised the hem of her kimono well above her knees. Ted and I sat in the chairs across from the sofa which afforded us both an excellent view of her underpinnings. The temperature in the apartment was soaring. I unbuttoned my reefer but it didn't help much.

"Do you have insurance?" I asked. She turned towards me and although I was writing in my notebook, I observed Ted ogling her bare limbs.

"No, not really. At least I don't believe those items would be covered." she replied.

"Why not?" Ted asked, allowing me a discreet view of her smooth, attractive legs, as she looked towards him.

"Well, they were gifts from a suitor, using the word loosely, and I just don't think the insurance company will make restitution." She shrugged her dainty shoulders for emphasis. "In fact, I was going to mention him as a suspect," she added, now addressing me and allowing Ted to feast his eyes again.

"Well, the detectives will follow this up from our report. By the way, I'm sorry, but I didn't get your name when we came in."

"Shelby," she cooed.

"Sharpy?" I exclaimed.

"No, Shelby." She raised her voice a trifle.

"Okay, and your surname?"

"Hacker," she murmured.

"Hook . . . what?"

"Hacker," she repeated more distinctly. The room felt like the inside of an oven.

"Fine. Well, our report will be on file and we'll make a special effort to get the detectives out so you can have that window repaired," I assured her.

When Ted and I left the torrid apartment the outdoor air felt more frigid than ever and we shivered with every step to our wagon.

The next morning after roll call Ted and I got into our wagon. I couldn't help but notice that Ted was sporting a big grin which broke into a chuckle and then escalated into a full belly-laugh.

"What in hell's so funny? I asked, bewildered.

Ted forced himself to calm down to a giggle, then related to me: "Last night I was telling Judy about our curvaceous complainant."

"You told your wife about her?"

"Sure, no big deal." Then with another giggle he added," I don't know when she laughed more when I told her I almost ripped the phone out of the wall or when I told her you put the gal's name on the report as, "Sharpy Hooker."

A FAILURE TO COMMUNICATE

Patrolman Bill Marsh and I were summoned out of roll call on a bleak winter morning to respond to a suicidal situation at a residence on Glendale, just off the Anthony Wayne Trail.

Our destination was a long way off. We didn't have any details, but we assumed the situation was life-threatening for us to be dispatched in such a rush and to miss roll call.

We wanted to make time but it was starting to snow and the streets were slick with ice; the Anthony Wayne Trail was no exception. Our wagon zigzagged at oblique angles as we struggled to make progress on the glassy roadway.

After a harrowing thirty-minute trip, we skidded to a stop in front of the address. A distraught woman let us in. "He's upstairs, first room to the right," she cried.

Bill and I clambered up the steps in tandem. The door to the room was ajar but something just inside the doorway impeded our entry. We pushed our way in; the obstruction was a man's body lying on the floor. He looked to be in his fifties, with dark wavy hair and graying sideburns; dressed in beige pajamas, a maroon silk robe and Romeo slippers.

His right hand clenched a chromed, semi-automatic pistol and there was a bullet wound in the man's right temple. He was dead, in fact, he was stone-cold-dead.

We had just jeopardized our safety to rush to the side of a person who had been dead for hours. We had questions for the woman.

Yes, he was her husband. Yes, she heard the shot about 2:00 A.M. No, she didn't call it in immediately; she just couldn't bring herself to do it. Yes, she did finally call the police between 6:30 A.M. and 7:00 A.M.

We filled the dispatcher in and waited until the coroner arrived. We took possession of the gun and when relatives came to care for the woman there was nothing more we could do, but to file our report.

We went to a coffee shop, but we could have used something stronger . . . it was a hell of a way to start a cold winter day.

THIS IS AMERICA

For the second time I was breaking-in Patrolman Paul Richards. First, as a patrol officer and now as a detective in the Juvenile Bureau. It was a pleasure though, as Paul was a sincere young man, a six-footer with a sharp mind and eager to succeed.

On a summer morning in June of 1966, my beige police car wouldn't start so we had to take a car from the motor pool. A black sedan was the only vehicle available. Nothing is as obvious as two men wearing suits and ties, riding in a black sedan. We might as well have taken a marked car.

Paul was driving west on Adams at 16ᵗʰ Street, a "honky-tonk" area, dominated by cheap bars. There was a supermarket on the corner of 17ᵗʰ Street with a parking lot sandwiched in between the store and a house on the corner of Southard Avenue. Paul turned North on 17ᵗʰ Street when I observed a group of boys walking through the parking lot. Several of them were struggling to carry a large cardboard carton; others were following. They all appeared to be adolescents, except for one obvious teenager.

"Stop the car, Paul, I want to see what those kids have in that box."

"Probably just pop bottles," Paul ventured, but as he steered our car to the curb the boys dropped the box and all of them began running toward the parking lot exit on Southard.

I jumped from the car in pursuit, glancing into the carton as I ran by. It contained lots of CB radios. I passed two of the youngest boys to go after the oldest one. He was almost to Southard Avenue.

Meanwhile, Paul drove around the corner onto Southard and the youth I was pursuing actually ran into the side of the unmarked police car. I caught him, but it took both Paul and I to get him handcuffed and placed into the back seat of our sedan; by then the rest of they boys had disappeared.

"Paul, you'd better drive back around the corner so I can get the contents of that carton before our evidence disappears," I advised.

That done, we began to question the seventeen-year-old youth. He readily admitted that he and the other boys looked for CB antennas on roofs and then entered the houses and stole the radios.

"Some of those houses had unlocked doors and windows," the youth protested. "They deserved to lose them!"

"This is America," I said, "People shouldn't have to lock their doors or windows."

We booked the youth at the Child Study Institute. He gave up the names of the others involved and we cleared 24 burglaries. Not bad for Paul's first day in the bureau.

THE MISSING WOMAN

My partner Bob Skinner acknowledged the noon call: "12 Patrol OK."

We proceeded to 1410 Woodland where a black male was waiting.

"My name is Nelson and I called about my neighbor, Mrs. Harlow; no one has seen her for a couple of days. We're pretty close, I have a key to the place so I checked the house, but she isn't there. She hardly ever leaves her house and certainly not for this long."

"All right, Sir, we'll check it again." The three of us entered . . . what a shock: there were cats all over the place; lounging on the floors; walking on the furniture; several were on the dining room table and they all appeared hungry and unkempt. The house smelled like a pig sty.

"Oh, yeah," Nelson spoke up, "I forgot to tell you about the cats. I think there are twenty-seven or twenty-nine; I forget.

The last place we looked was in a summer room attached to the rear of the house. Bags of garbage were piled against the walls up to the ceiling and the entire floor was cluttered with more of them, two or three deep.

Apparently the woman was missing. We called the Humane Society to take custody of the cats. After the cats were removed, Nelson focused our attention on a huge oil painting hanging on the inside wall of the front room. It was in a gigantic ornate frame.

"Mrs. Harlow told me that if anything ever happened to her that I could have that painting," Nelson informed us.

"Well, until we know her disposition that painting better remain where it is," Bob advised Nelson. We then went back in service.

The next morning we were dispatched again to Mrs. Harlow's address. Detective Brian Snyder was waiting. "I've had some dealings with Mrs. Harlow and I know her well enough to know that she'd never leave her cats. Let's check the place again."

When Snyder got to the summer room, he exclaimed, "Here she is."

When Bob and I reached the room, Snyder was holding her dead body up amid the heaps of garbage bags. "She must have suffered some kind of ailment and collapsed into the piles of bags," the detective deduced. I spotted the suede stole around her neck or I may have overlooked her too."

THE TARGET ZONE

During the summer months patrol crews working the day shift would be sent to the Toledo Police Pistol Range for shooting-practice; a couple at a time from different sections of the city.

Practice consisted of shooting at various targets; stationary, pop-ups, a running man, an anatomical man and shooting from a police car. All the targets, made of steel and painted black were shaped like human silhouettes. They were coated with oil so the "hits" could be obliterated with another coating, providing each shooter with a clean target.

One day while I was at the range a black Councilman, who was usually negative towards the police, visited the facilities. Although he seemed impressed with the operation, he did voice one concern.

"Ah realizes that you has to practice, but does you always has to hit the target in a vital spot?"

Major Thor, a veteran marksman and instructor patiently took time to explain to him why officers are trained to shoot at the widest area of a target. "Once a bullet leaves the barrel of a gun there is no calling it back. If a bullet misses an intended target it will continue until it strikes something that will stop it; that could be an innocent person.

Aiming at the widest area of a target allows the most margin for error. In the event an officer's sight alignment is slightly flawed there is good probability that the bullet will still strike the intended target." When he left the Councilman seemed satisfied.

The one thing that I thought he would challenge, but didn't, was the fact that all the targets were black.

Close-up of the Anatomical Target with Officer Leo Stasiak. Note the six apertures. Circa 60's.

PATROLMAN FRANK PERZ CHECKING THE "RUNNING MAN" TARGET AT THE TOLEDO   CIRCA 1960'S
POLICE PISTOL RANGE.

Another view of The Running Man Target. It was electrically powered.

NO FRIENDS WHEN IN NEED

Officer Chris Myers, working foot patrol on the East Side, was patrolling on Main Street anticipating the end of his shift. Dawn was breaking, indicating that it would be about two more hours.

He was in the 700 block when he observed a man stooped over in the doorway of a store. As Chris approached the suspicious man straightened up, holding a long, heavy screwdriver. He obviously had been trying to pry open the door.

Chris tried to draw his service revolver, but the culprit attacked Chris with the sharp tool and they began to grapple in the doorway. Every time the officer attempted to draw his gun, the crook would menace him with the screwdriver. They wrestled across the sidewalk and rolled into the street. Chris managed to clear his revolver from its holster, but his adversary had a grip on Chris's wrist and was trying to force the gun from his hand.

It was getting daylight and people were going to work; cars passed by the two men as they fought for possession of the firearm. A semi-tractor-trailer roared by and more autos; one even slowed down to maneuver around the uniformed officer struggling in the street with the man.

Finally, the revolver was dislodged from Chris's hand and the felon snatched it from the pavement and aimed it at Chris. The policeman stood up, as the hood escaped on foot leaving Chris standing in the street stressed and unarmed..

About a week later the police revolver turned up in a West End hock shop where detectives retrieved it. Although Chris searched for the thief's identity from "mug books," as far as I know, the culprit was never apprehended.

THREE FOR CONGREGATING

On a hot, mid-July day of 1965, an order was issued directly from the chief's office: The district crew was to terminate the carousing and gambling taking place in front of the Tally-Ho Club at E. Woodruff and Vermont Street. A report was to be submitted daily on what action the crew took and if any arrests were made.

Before the area was integrated the café was a chic neighborhood bistro with quiet, law-abiding customers. As the cultural transition changed the area from all white to all black the place became a constant source of complaints to the police by the distraught citizens of the neighborhood.

The day the order was issued I was working second shift with a rookie named Eric Johnson; who was fresh out of the academy. My regular partner was on vacation. About 4 P.M. we checked conditions at the Tally-Ho Club; all was quiet and there was no activity in front of the tavern.

After we responded to several minor calls, we checked the nuisance location again and observed a large multitude of people on the sidewalk in front of the bar. Many of them were drinking bottled beer and several were playing craps. A vender had left a cart near the front door.

Officer Johnson and I alighted from the squad car and ordered the crowd to disperse; to go inside or leave the corner. Everyone began to comply except for four light-skinned black men; they stood side-by-side in front of the building, in defiance. I reached into the police car for the "mike" and ordered a wagon.

Just then a young woman emerged from the front door of the structure and walked towards the corner. One of the four men broke ranks and started after the woman.

"Hey, Baby, where ya all going"?

When I started after him the other three men ran away in the opposite direction. I grabbed the man, who had followed the woman, and spun him around. We were of similar height, weight and build.

"Where do you think you're going? You're under arrest," I informed him.

Meanwhile the entire bar emptied and formed a ring around us about four to six persons deep. I had no idea where my partner was. My adversary and I were standing toe to toe and I thought, " With this hostile crowd I'm going to get the hell kicked out of me for sure."

The confrontation seemed eternal as if time was standing still. I was surprised, but relieved that the crowd remained passive, except for one loud fellow, whom was urging the arrested man to resist. Finally, I slowly moved my right hand to my slapper in my back pocket. I thought: "If he starts swinging I'm taking his front teeth out."

The man's eyes followed my right hand. Suddenly, he relaxed and when he did I pushed him onto the top of the vendor cart and said, "Now stay there until the wagon gets here."

The wagon finally arrived and the rookie re-appeared at the same time. I informed the wagon crew: "The man on the cart is going for Congregating and Resisting Arrest," and then I grabbed the big-mouth fellow, "and this guy's going for Interfering with the Lawful Duties of a Police Officer."

An elderly man had just emerged from the bar and was standing near the doorway when Johnson grabbed him and said, "He's going too."

I had no idea what he was arresting the old man for, but I didn't dare to question it at that time with a crowd of unfriendly people milling around. Again, we ordered the crowd off the corner; they complied and peace was restored. The wagon left and Eric put us back in service.

When we resumed our patrol I asked Eric: "What on earth did you arrest that old man for?"

"Well, you need three for congregating, don't you?"

The main defendant pleaded not guilty to congregating. When we went to trial the judge found him guilty, but practically implored him to appeal the ordinance. He did just that and in due time the ordinance prohibiting congregating was rescinded and the elements of the ordinance prohibiting loitering were so drastically altered that it was nearly impossible to enforce.

CHAPTER 7

PROJECT EXPERIENCES

EPISODES

1. MEL'S DINER

2. THE MIRROR BALLROOM

3. THE LION STORE

4. THE LOOP THEATER

PROJECT EXPERIENCES

In Toledo Police jargon the word "project" was synonymous with "extra job", whether it was in or out of uniform. Considering the meager pay police officers earned in the '50's and 60's, most of the younger officers worked a multitude of projects.

According to departmental rules officers could work about any type of job with the exception of tending bar or driving a taxi. Prohibiting tending bar I could understand, although this rule was ignored to some extent, but the only reason I could ever entertain about not driving a taxi, although I never knew of a Toledo police officer doing so, was that the power brokers of the city didn't want police officers learning the locations of the whore houses and gambling joints in the city. The reasons for this should be obvious.

Officers who rotated shifts each month usually shared projects with officers on other shifts, whom they were buddies with. Obviously, if an officer was working the 3 P.M. to 11 P.M. shift, he wouldn't be available to work an evening project unless it was his day off. The same rational applied for a day shift project.

MEL'S DINER

One of my first projects was working the parking lot at Mel's Diner, a drive-in restaurant at Cherry and Delaware. It was owned by the Joseph's brothers, of Joseph's Supermarkets. It only paid $5.00 an hour, but that was the going rate for most projects, at that time, unless there was something extraordinary about the job.

Mel's was an easy task as it was usually a quiet and orderly place. However, one Friday evening about 9:00 P.M., several youths were cutting through the parking lot on foot. They appeared to have been drinking, but were orderly; except for one of them. He was about 19 years old, tall and thin, with a loud mouth and was staggering heavily.

When he saw me, he began to shout in a high voice, calling me some choice names. When I approached him, he began yelling: "Shoot me! Shoot me!"

The other youths ran off. The tall fellow became even more belligerent, so I spun him around and slapped a pair of handcuffs on him. I led him to a small office from where I phoned for a wagon and he was taken to jail.

About a half hour later I received a phone call from the jailer. "Jim, this guy you sent in went zero on the balloon test."

"What did you give him a balloon test for? He wasn't driving."

"Well, for crying-out-loud; why didn't the wagon crew say so?"

"Apparently they screwed up. Go ahead and book him for Intoxication and Disorderly Conduct, he's high on something. I'll make out the paper work when I get off here."

The next evening I was working again at Mel's and I learned that the youths I had encountered the evening before were coming from a "pot" party at a house near by.

The youth, in question, apparently pleaded guilty and I never saw him again.

THE MIRROR BALLROOM

The Mirror Ballroom was a large, rectangular, one-story building on the Old Dixie Highway in North Toledo. The interior was one huge room with mirrored walls, thus giving the place it's name. No less than ten bars lined the outer walls The middle of the gigantic room was one open dance floor with tables and chairs bordering it.

Another officer and I worked this project on Saturday nights over a long period of time. One week the dance crowd would be blacks and the following week it would be Mexicans. We most always earned our money.

When a problem arose among blacks there was usually a commotion; shouting, perhaps a stand-off. Many times the rift was resolved without further ado. But, if one of the participants left in a huff there was always the possibility that he'd return with a weapon; for this we had to stay alert.

It was a different situation with the Mexicans. When there was a scuffle or disturbance somewhere in the bar, by the time an officer got to the area, everything would be calmed down.

The officer would be assured that everything was all right. A few minutes later a fellow would be writhing on the floor with a knife wound. No one had seen or heard anything and the perpetrator would never be known; at least not to us officers.

At one of the dances, which happened to be a Caucasian affair, there was a rumble at the front door which spilled outside. My partner and I went out to try to quell it. One of the participants got behind my partner and I thought he was going to hit him. I raised my nightstick, when a young punk near me said, "No you don't", and tried to grab my club.

Out of reflex I flicked my club and the tip of it glanced off the punk's chin propelling him backwards until he fell near the side of the highway; a good distance away. I couldn't believe the force of that slight contact.

I threw the fellow aside, who was behind my partner, but before I could get to the punk I had struck to arrest him, a car pulled up and two fellows grabbed him, threw him into the car and sped away.

At the next Caucasian dance I intercepted that same punk at the front door. "You're not getting in Sonny, so take off," I admonished him.

"Aw, come on, officer, let me in. I won't cause any trouble; I promise."

"All right," I relented, because I knew that he knew what he'd get if he didn't behave.

THE LION STORE

For almost two years, I worked a couple evenings a week at the Lion Store on Summit St. downtown Toledo, as a store detective. "Lawsuit Laura" was a notorious shoplifter. Whenever she came into the store I not only followed her, but stood right next to her at every counter, with my hands clasped behind my back, so I could get as close as possible, without touching her. She was usually discouraged in a brief time and would make some snide remark to me, before leaving. She knew all of the store detectives and we knew her.

When a store department wanted a detective, a code was sounded throughout the store via bells ringing in sequence. A detective would call the phone operator and she would connect him with the department seeking his aid.

The main entrance of the Lion Store on Summit St. Notice the
two large lion statues by the curb. Circa 50's.

One day I was summoned in this manner. "The dress department wants you right away," the Operator informed me. At the second floor department, a clerk was waiting for me by the dressing rooms with a young, black woman, in her early 20's.

"This woman entered a dressing room with two dresses and a suit, but came out with only the dresses," the clerk explained. "There is nothing in the dressing room and she insists that she doesn't have the suit," the clerk concluded.

The woman was very thin and I couldn't observe any bulges on her person.

"Do you mind if the clerk searches you?" I asked.

Surprisingly, the suspect consented "I don't mind," the woman replied. The two women retreated to the dressing room and in a very brief time, they emerged. The woman was looking sad and the clerk was holding a very wrinkled, two- piece green, suit with mink trim. Although the garments were of quality material, they had been twisted as tightly as possible, distorting them into two, long, thin rolls thus, making it possible for the two pieces to be concealed about the body of the suspect.

After the thief was identified and on the way to jail the clerk asked me about how she could get the suit back. "Well," I explained, "the suit will have to be held as evidence and presented at the woman's trial. Afterwards, it would be kept in the property room until claimed."

"That's very interesting," the clerk said, "I'll keep that in mind."

About a month later, I was working and saw the clerk wearing the green suit with the mink trim. She observed me staring at her. "You wouldn't believe what the Lion Store sold this suit to me for;" she related, "after we got it back from the city, the store considered it as used property and I got it for a fraction of the retail price." One woman's crime was another woman's gain.

Some shoplifters are very bold. One dark and rainy evening I was walking through the Lion Store basement, when I observed a well- dressed, middle-aged fellow walking ahead of me at a rapid pace. Without missing a step, he grabbed an umbrella from a display, as he passed it. I followed him up the steps to the main doors, where he exited to Summit Street.

Observing him leave the store without paying for the umbrella, I now could charge him with shoplifting. I stopped him and asked to see a receipt for the umbrella. Of course, he could not produce one. I arrested him and took him into custody.

Store detectives use many devises to observe thieves among the shoppers and also to conceal the fact that they are detectives. At the Lion Store, for instance, I had employed binoculars, while stationed in a balcony, and had stationed myself behind two-way mirrors, installed in doors.

One strategy I liked to use was to carry a gift-wrapped empty carton, to make me appear as a regular shopper in the store. One day, while I was carrying a beautifully wrapped carton, another detective was assaulted by a shoplifter, whom he had placed under arrest. I immediately dropped the box and ran to his aid, a short distance from my location. When the skirmish was over and the thief was subdued and handcuffed, I went to retrieve my 'merchandise', but it was gone. A clerk at a counter near-by called to me: "The second you dropped that box, a fellow scooped it up and ran out the door as fast as he could," she informed me. To this day, I wish I could have seen the look on his face, when he opened it.

THE LOOP THEATER

In the 400 block of Superior Street, between Adams and Jackson, the Loop and the Royal theaters were side by side.

The Royal served as a shelter for bums and had its own usher/bouncers.

The Loop was mostly attended by low-income persons and during Saturday matinees by a multitude of their children; the majority of whom were black.

A uniformed officer was hired on Saturday afternoons to keep the peace. This project was worked for a long time by a veteran officer, who I'll call Buck. He had a solid relationship with the black community through an athletic program sponsored by the Police Athletic League.

During the mid-sixties the theater changed ownership and acquired a new manager and for reasons unknown to me, Buck wanted to give the project up and offered it to me. The pay was good and it was only a five hour commitment per week on Saturday afternoon.

There was only one major problem: the kids attending the matinee were rowdy, rude and undisciplined. They talked constantly during the movies; ran up and down the aisles; jumped up and down on their seats and in general caused a constant commotion.

Adult patronage was nil, because of the conduct of the kids and the few adults, who did attend were almost as bad as the kids. What I didn't understand was why Buck condoned this behavior. The new manager and I was on the same page: the stated situation had to be corrected.

Of course the patrons were allowed to yell for the good guys and to boo the bad guys, but only as required and for a limited, reasonable duration.

During the first several weeks I was constantly on my feet the entire five hours patrolling the aisles; admonishing the kids for putting their feet on the seats in front of them; for talking out loud; for running in the aisles and grossly misbehaving. I ejected kids left and right, all with the same message: they could return the following week, if they behaved.

After approximately six weeks they got the message; they were in a sense, trained. I began to sit in an end seat in the last row where I could keep an eye on the audience. If I was needed the staff knew where to find me. Occasionally, I'd make a round of the aisles, walk through the lobby, check the men's room and observe how things were going, in general.

The manager was pleased, because patronage had increased and more adults were attending the matinee, thus ticket sales were higher. And as a bonus I got to see some very good movies with a minimum of interruption.

The view is South on Superior St. at Jackson Ave. Notice the Loop Theater on the right. Also, the Jackson Bar on left corner; the Dental Lab was located next to the bar (Chapter 15, Episode 1)

CHAPTER 8

YOU HAD TO BE THERE

EPISODES

1. HEART STOPPER

2. MACHO MAN

3. INSTANT RESULTS

4. BEST LITTLE BIKE THIEF IN TOLEDO

5. THE CLOSET CASE

6. THE ONE THAT GOT AWAY

7. THE HILLCREST HOTEL FIASCO

8. BRUTE STRENGTH

9. A BARE SITUATION

10. A PROUD MOMENT

HEART STOPPER

The Old West end of Toledo encompasses many large Victorian- style houses which were occupied by rich families in the past. Then, in the 1960's a "cultural transition" occurred; in brief: the whites moved out and the blacks moved in.

About five years later, the latter occupants found it more and more difficult to maintain the huge dwellings, so they re-sold the mansions. Many of the next owners converted the upper floors of the homes into apartments for added income.

Officer Marvin Meyers was my partner, working 10 Scout in the Old West End on second shift. One late afternoon, we received a call to meet a complainant and check for the safety of the occupant in one of the large houses on Parkwood, which had been remodeled and converted into apartments.

The owner of the house met us and stated that she hadn't seen the elderly tenant of a second floor apartment for two days; that she tried to reach her by phone to no avail.

When she let us in with a key, we found nothing amiss in the living and dining rooms and began to check several rooms off a long hallway.

One door opened to reveal the woman in the middle of a large bed; only a tuft of her white hair was visible under a pile of quilts covering her to the top of her head. She didn't appear to be breathing.

"She's in here. I think she expired, " I called to Marvin.

Instantly, the woman popped up in bed and exclaimed, "What's the matter officer?"

I was so startled by her "coming to life" that my senses were shocked; my heart raced and I gasped for breath.

"Your landlord was worried and let us in to check on you," I explained after I regained my composure. "She called you on the phone but you didn't answer."

"I've been ill with the flu," she replied, "and too weak to go to the front room to answer the phone."

All's well that ends well, but I was sure glad I didn't have a weak heart.

MACHO MAN

In the mid-sixties, Toledo contracted for private ambulance service, so our patrol wagons were no longer used as such, except in extreme cases.

One morning while working on the day shift in the South end on 13 patrol, Bill Marsh and I were dispatched to a vehicular accident at South Detroit and Arlington Avenue.

Near that location, on Arlington Avenue, we discovered a lone motorcyclist lying in the street. He had lost control of his bike, struck a curb and was tossed onto the street. His right ankle was obviously fractured, so an ambulance was summoned.

At the scene, the ambulance attendants explained to the injured man: "We're going to apply an air-bag to your ankle, which takes the place of a splint; you can expect some pain, while we're applying it, but it shouldn't be too bad."

The victim was about 35 years old, with a dark beard and long sideburns; his hair was braided into a pony-tail. He wore Levis and Jack-boots and a black leather jacket with silver studs along the sleeves, a skull and crossbones was depicted on the back.

Just as the attendants were about to apply the airbag, the patient saw a man walking across the street and called out to him, "George! George! Is that you?"

The man came over and knelt by the prone man's side.

"George, hold my hand." The injured rider pleaded.

His friend took the injured man's hand while the air-bag was being applied and the biker kept crying, "Harder George. Squeeze harder!"

What a touching scene: a macho biker having his hand held by a male friend while enduring a little pain.

INSTANT RESULTS

A man wanted on warrants barricaded himself in his house and refused to surrender. The lieutenant in charge decided to use tear gas. The fugitive peeked out of a door just as a shell was fired. The projectile struck the edge of the door and ricocheted around the interior of the room. The law-breaker ran out of the house with his hands raised, screaming, "What the hell are you trying to do, kill me!"

THE BEST LITTLE BIKE THIEF IN TOLEDO

Bobby Smith was seventeen years old and had a long police record. He was a suspect in many cases involving stolen bikes or bike parts. The modus operandi was always similar: while complainants left bikes unattended at stores, parks, etc. parts such as seats, pedals, even handle bars and wheels would be stolen off them.

I went to Bobby's house to talk to him and found him in the driveway spray-painting the stripped frame of a bicycle which he had sanded down to the bare metal. All of its parts were lying in a heap near-by on the cement.

In answer to my questions, he replied: "You got me wrong, man, this bike ain't stolen. No! I ain't been takin' no parts from anybody's bikes. I'm jus' paintin' this for a friend o' mine."

"If I find out you're lying to me, I'm coming back to arrest you," I warned him. I made a note of the serial number on the partially painted bike frame.

The serial number o' this bike is already registered," he assured me.

"I'll see," I said as I returned to my unmarked car.

The bike in question had been registered and was on file at the police Record Bureau. However, there was no report on file that it had been stolen. Not satisfied, I called the registered owner and learned that the bike Bobby was painting was indeed stolen the day before from Woodward High School. The owner of the bike, a teen-ager, thought that his Father had reported it and his Father thought that his son had made a report of the theft.

I kept my word and arrested Bobby and had a wagon crew take the stolen bike, with all of its parts, to the Toledo Police Property Room.

The next morning, I received a frenzied call from the property sergeant. He was very upset about the bike being left in the property room in pieces. I assured him that I would resolve the matter as soon as possible.

Bobby was still in custody so I brought him to the property room and told him that the sergeant didn't believe that he could put the stolen bike back together. Bobby accepted the challenge and I returned to my work. I figured it would take him at least a couple of hours.

I was hardly gone when the property sergeant had me summoned. When I returned, the bike was fully assembled. I asked the sergeant how Bobby had accomplished the task so rapidly.

He replied, "You had to be there."

UNIDENTIFIED OFFICER CHECKING BICYCLES IMPOUNDED AT THE TOLEDO POLICE PROPERTY ROOM. THE POLICE HANDLED SO MANY BIKES THAT A POLICE AUCTION WAS HELD TWICE ANNUALLY. CITIZENS WITH "AUCTION FEVER" USUALLY BIDDED MORE THAN WHAT THE BIKES SOLD FOR NEW.

THE CLOSET CASE

Working 4 Patrol with Steve Evans on the afternoon shift, we were dispatched to a house in the 1200 block of Huron Street on an ambulance call; we weren't given any details.

When we arrived a woman let us in. " Officers, my daughter just had a baby." She then led us to the front room of the small house and there squatting in a closet was a thin, young woman, holding a newborn infant in her arms. The umbilical cord and the placenta was still intact.

Before we could say anything the young woman spoke: " My Mother and I were washing the dishes at the kitchen sink when I felt funny and the next thing I knew I gave birth. I didn't want to get blood all over, so I stayed in the closet while Mom called for help." she paused, then added: " I didn't even know I was pregnant."

I obtained the stretcher from the wagon and unfolded it near the closet. Steve helped me spread the rubber sheet over it and then pointed to a basket of clothes in the room.

"Are those clothes clean?"

"Yes, they were just washed," the Mother assured him.

Steve took a sheet from the basket and we spread half of it over the rubber sheet, then placed the young mother on the stretcher and folded the other half of the sheet over her. The new Mother placed her baby on top of the sheet and Steve placed a clean towel over the infant. The umbilical cord was left intact for the hospital staff to deal with. We then transported the Mother and newborn to Riverside Hospital. Another strange, but true incident.

THE ONE THAT GOT AWAY

David Freeman was one of the best partners I had the good fortune to work with. Although we were virtually opposites, we got along famously on and off duty. Dave was laid back and I was aggressive; he was quiet, I was talkative; he was under 6' tall, I was over 6' tall; he was stocky with a muscular build, I was thin all over and I could go on and on. One thing we both liked though, was to go fishing.

One day Dave called me: "Hey, I need your help."

"What's up?"

"I bought a small fishing boat and I need help getting it home."

We met where he had bought the boat. It was on a trailer, which came with it. I hitched it to my car and we parked it by his garage. We both lived in Point Place, so it was no big deal.

"I can't wait to use it," Dave said, "When can we get together?"

"How about when we get off Friday morning, we go right out?" I suggested.

"Great, we can pick up bait and ice after work and I have two large, metal tubs to pack the fish in."

"I'll furnish the most important item…the beer," I volunteered.

I thought Dave was being very optimistic with his two tubs, but it didn't matter. My idea of fishing after working all night was to lounge in the stern of the boat and drink beer; letting the sun warm me into a state of utopia.

That was exactly the state I was in, awhile after we were afloat on Lake Erie, Friday morning, when suddenly our fishing poles began to jump up and down. Dave and I grabbed the rods and pulled out a perch on each of the two hooks tied to our lines. Apparently, we were upon a school of perch. We didn't take time to re-bait our hooks; we simply cast them back into the water and pulled more fish out. Dave and I were delighted. This kept up for what seemed a long time and then just as suddenly ceased.

It didn't matter, both tubs were completely filled with fish. When we got back to Dave's place, we each took a tub. Mine contained so many fish that I had to call my wife's parents to come over to help clean them. I never had such an experience again.

I related this story to showcase how Dave and I got along. However, there was one area of police work, which Dave and I differed on: Stopping cars for traffic violations. Dave just deplored "getting movers," while I considered such action an opportunity to check on vehicles and their occupants.

The commission of a traffic violation furnishes a police officer probable cause to stop a car legally. It also allows a cursory inspection of the interior of the car. Furthermore, it affords the answer to a lot of concerns: Is the driver licensed? Is the car registered to the driver? Is the car and driver compatible?

Example: A driver looking like a hobo in an expensive auto. Is the car stolen? Does the driver have a record; is he wanted? If there are passengers, how do they appear? Who are they? Are any of them wanted on warrants? What objects are inside the car in plain view? Are any of the items contraband?

Because an officer stops a car doesn't mean that he has to issue a citation. Many times when the offense was minor and there was nothing amiss, I simply gave the driver a verbal warning, after informing said driver of what offense was committed. Thus, the incident became an occasion for good P.R. (Public Relations). Why so many officers failed to realize this always amazed me.

Working 13 Patrol on a summer evening in the early'60's, Dave was slowly driving South on S. Detroit Avenue. We had just passed the intersection of Airline, where the Kitchen Nook restaurant was located, when a speeding car ignored the stop sign and with screeching tires headed North on S. Detroit at a high rate of speed.

"Dave, did you see that guy? He just busted that stop sign and is driving like a bat-out-of-hell; let's get him!" I shouted.

The paddy wagon just kept crawling in the opposite direction, as Dave ignored my concern.

"Thirteen Patrol, the Kitchen Nook restaurant at S. Detroit and Airline was just robbed. Suspect is a white male armed with a handgun; no further description," our dispatcher informed us.

"Damn, Sam!" I exploded. "We could have had that S.O.B."

Dave made a U-turn and drove to the crime scene to take a report. I was mad as a wet hen. And as much as I liked Dave and as well as we got along, it took me awhile to get over, "the one that got away!"

Two nights later the same robber was arrested by another crew, as the felon was sitting in his car at a closed gas station counting a large sum of money.

THE HILLCREST HOTEL FIASCO

Chet was a rookie, small in stature, but with plenty of moxie. We were working 10 Scout on the second shift during a warm day in July of 1964. Our tour was slow, we even had time to eat a decent meal, but that wasn't to last.

About 9 P.M. we were dispatched to the Hillcrest Hotel on a complaint of a disturbance.

The Hillcrest was a dignified, established hotel in Toledo located on 16th. Street at Madison Ave., just West of the downtown area. I was hoping that we could handle whatever the problem was in a professional manner.

There were several cars parked along 16th. St. and we had to park some distance from the main entrance. (This would prove to be a hindrance later on.)

We entered the spacious lobby and was directed by the Manager to a fellow standing near the entrance to the "Grape Room". The man appeared to be in his late fifties, over 6 feet tall, slender, wearing glasses, a yachting cap and a suede, buckskin jacket, trimmed with fringe along the sleeves. He obviously had been drinking and showed symptoms of intoxication.

"What seems to be the matter?" I inquired.

" I'm Buck Frank," he announced, " and I want a drink. The manager is denying me that pleasure and I don't think he has the right to do so. I'm a respectable citizen and I own a resort in Michigan. We certainly don't treat our customers this way."

We had moved towards the center of the lobby as we talked. "Well, Sir," I replied, "You're in Ohio now and there is a policy adhered to of not serving alcoholic beverages to anyone who appears to have had enough to drink and is impaired."

As I talked to him I placed an arm about his shoulder to guide him towards the door.

" I suggest we go outside if you want to discuss it further."

A woman standing near by was thumbing through a magazine. She was wearing a shimmering, silver dress, which clung closely to her body and she held a matching handbag. Her hair was white and perfectly set; complimented by her pearl earrings and necklace. Suddenly, she knocked my arm off the man's shoulder.

The Hillcrest Hotel where "Buck Frank" and his wife were arrested.

"And whom might you be?" I asked, surprised by her actions.

"That's my husband and I'm backing him up," she averred.

"Well, lady, I advise you not to do that again, because you're interfering with the lawful duties of a police officer and are subject to arrest."

I took Buck Frank's arm again, to maneuver him towards the door and again his wife knocked my arm away.

"That's it lady; you're under arrest," I declared, when suddenly Buck Frank grabbed me around my neck from behind. We struggled and both of us fell to the floor; then his wife jumped on me.

Chet came to life and pulled her off of me and I got to my knees. I was incensed and as Buck Frank got to his knees, I grabbed my slapper from my pocket and swung at his head; the lenses of his glasses shattered into bits as he fell back. I grabbed Buck Frank under his arms and half carried and half dragged him towards the door.

I could see that Buck Frank's wife had entered a phone booth and had blocked the door from within, so Chet couldn't open it; she was telephoning someone. A man in a tuxedo was taking Chet's badge number.

As I was taking Buck Frank outside, the tuxedoed man approached me with a pad and pen.

"Badge 348." I informed him. I laid Buck Frank on the sidewalk and went to the police car to call for a wagon. The police radio was busy and I couldn't break in. When I finally contacted the dispatcher, Frank Buck was crawling on his hands and knees back into the hotel lobby. He was bleeding profusely from a small cut above one eye and by the time it took me to come from the cruiser to the lobby, he had smeared blood on a brocaded settee and the floor was a bloody mess.

Then Captain Moser and Lieutenant Haskins, my shift command, walked in. I was horrified as I lugged Buck Frank out of the building for the second time, passing the two astonished command officers near the doorway

A wagon arrived and Buck Frank and his wife were loaded into it and sent to jail.

What I wanted to be an uneventful incident turned into a bloody fracas. The only thing that helped the situation was that the hotel manager backed me up.

"The officers did nothing wrong," he told the command officers. " The man and his wife were the aggressors and I will swear to that." The manager was true to his word and accompanied us to the Clerk of Courts office and filed a charge of Disturbing the Peace against the Michigan couple.

Buck Frank Evers was charged with Drunk & Disorderly, Resisting Arrest and Assault & Battery on a Police Officer. His wife was charged with Interference with the Lawful Duties of a Police Officer, Assault & Battery on a Police Officer and Resisting Arrest. As stated, the Hillcrest Hotel Manager had filed a Disturbance of the Peace charge. The Evers pleaded not guilty to all charges and demanded a trial by jury. However, the drunk charge was a misdemeanor with a maximum penalty clause of $50 and could only be tried in a Municipal Court, where Mr. Evers was found guilty. For the other charges, a jury had been selected for trial in Common Pleas Court.

Everyone was present on the court date: the hotel manager as well as the bartender of the Grape Room, Chet and myself and Buck Frank Evers, his wife and any witnesses they may have had subpoenaed. Just as the trial was to begin, the Evers attorney persuaded them to change their pleas to guilty, which they did, but they still had to pay court cost for a jury trial because the jury had been impaneled.

I had no intentions of making an arrest, when Chet and I encountered the Evers and if they had left the hotel peacefully, all would have been well. As it was, they paid a high price for a drink they were never served.

BRUTE STRENGTH

"Thirteen Patrol: Westwood railroad tracks off of Airport Highway, a train-auto accident; check for injuries," the police dispatcher advised.

"Thirteen Patrol O.K.," Officer Dave Freeman responded.

I turned our aging wagon towards Westwood while Dave activated the red lights and siren.

The dispatcher's voice cut through the screech of the siren: "Thirteen Patrol, there is no Accident Investigation Squad available; you'll have to take the report."

"O.K.," Dave replied somberly; he hated making reports.

A car had been struck by a train which was switching tracks. There was less damage to the car than we expected, but the elderly driver was trapped in the driver seat. The steering wheel had been bent and was against the old man's chest, pinning him against the back of the seat. No matter what Dave and I did, we couldn't get the man out of the car.

Finally, Dave got into the rear of the auto behind the driver seat and placed his right knee against the middle of that seat. Then gripping the top of the seat with both hands, Dave pulled mightily and actually broke the back of the seat down. I couldn't believe my eyes. I knew Dave was strong, but not that powerful. You had to be there.

The driver was freed and sent to a hospital to be checked for injuries.

"Dave," I said, "In appreciation of your splendid endeavors on this occasion, I personally will relieve you of the task of making out the report."

"Aw, shut up and order a tow," Dave replied, with a big grin.

A BARE SITUATION

Rose Lopez and Raul Dominguez were not married, but had been living together, off and on, for several years. They made an odd couple: Rose was several inches taller than Raul and out-weighed him by 115 pounds. Their relationship was a stormy one, with many arguments punctured with accusations and sometimes with physical violence.

I had just finished directing traffic at Cherry and Superior Streets about 5:30 P.M. on an afternoon shift, but couldn't leave the intersection until 6 P.M. I was waiting by the large pawn shop that dominated the corner building, which had apartments overhead.

Suddenly, I heard a faint hissing sound: " Pssst; pssst." It was coming from a doorway next to the pawn shop, which was the entry to the apartments above. Upon investigating, I saw Rose standing behind the partially opened door and to my astonishment, she was entirely nude.

"Jim, you have to help me; Raul threw me out of our apartment."

She opened the door to me and started climbing the stairway. What a sight: The bare rear of a 250 pound woman, quivering like Jello, while ascending the stairs ahead of me.

When she reached her apartment door, she turned to me revealing her total, frontal nudity. Her breasts were massive. I tried to keep my eyes focused on her face.

"This is our apartment," she said, as she banged on the door. "Let me in Raul, I have Jim the policeman with me." There was no response.

"Come on Raul," I called. "Let us in, Rose will catch her death of cold."

The door opened and we entered. "What the hell's the matter with you?" I admonished the small, thin man.

"She pisses me off," Raul exclaimed. "The apartment's a mess and she didn't make dinner."

"That's not true," Rose called from the next room, where she put on her panties and bra in full view of Raul and myself. "Every time I fix a meal you make an excuse not to eat it. All you want to do is drink, have sex and argue."

"See what I have to put up with?" Raul complained.

"Raul you can't evict Rose from your home. Ohio is a common-law state and you have a common-law marriage; what's yours is half hers and vice-versa.

Now I have to hit on my district and I don't want any more trouble here. If I have to come back, you're not going to like it. Do you hear me Raul.?"

"Si. Si. Officer Jim, everything will be all right. I have to work at the Dixie Club tonight and I will not bother Rose. Come in later for a drink, Si, Amigo?"

And that ended another episode where, you had to be there, to believe it.

A PROUD MOMENT

Excellent marksmanship, with either rifle or pistol came naturally to me and the U.S. Marines taught me well. It was a talent that I carried over to the Toledo Police Department, with enthusiasm.

For many years I was a National Rifle Association (NRA) Certified Pistol Instructor and a Classified Expert, with either type of weapon.

However, I did do one thing contrary to their teaching: I've always kept my service revolver loaded when off duty. It was kept holstered on the top shelf of the hall closet with my leather gear.

Being an avid pistol shooter, I also had several unloaded target pistols locked in a case in the same closet.

Of course I knew that the service weapon was accessible to my children, but I believed that because of the discipline and the training I afforded them that they wouldn't violate my trust.

One afternoon my son, Tim, age seven at that time, entered the house with a pal. The boyfriend had a cap pistol. While Tim got drinks for the two of them the friend said:

"Why don't you get a gun before we go back outside?"

My son agreed and obtained a toy clicker-gun from his bedroom.

"No, not that," cried the boy, "I mean one of your Dad's real guns."

I was shaving in the bathroom off the hallway and I could hear them. I held my breath, as I waited to see what my son's reaction would be.

"Oh, no," Tim firmly replied, "No one touches my Dad's guns."

The boy was obviously disappointed, but said nothing more as they went outside.

That was a very proud moment for me.

CHAPTER 9

UNEXPECTED INCIDENTS

EPISODES

1. OVER EXPOSED

2. NOTES TO YOU

3. TO SIR WITH LOVE

4. THE SEAT BELT JIG

5. A SILENT ALARM

6. PISTOL RANGE COMEDY

7. THE TRAFFIC STOP

OVER EXPOSED

My partner was Ronald "Bebe" Bebeshimer and we were working 2 Patrol on the East Side, when we received a call: "2 Patrol, man-down at 111 Euclid".

Our destination was off Front Street and one street South of Main. A crowd had gathered and when we pushed our way through, we found an obese, middle-aged male passed out in the doorway of a closed bar; an empty liquor bottle was on his lap.

We labored to get the intoxicated man to his feet. He was about 250 pounds of dead weight. We finally got him upright, facing away from the people, when his trousers fell down; he had no underpants on. There was a loud guffaw from the crowd.

By holding his shoulders on each side, Bebe and I managed to pull his pants up, thus ending the show. We managed to get him into the rear of the wagon and take him to jail for his own safety. He was booked on the charge of Drunk and Disorderly.

The bar at 111 Euclid (As it appears today) where the drunk was passed out in the doorway.

NOTES TO YOU

The day shift could be very boring with no activity calling for police action for long periods of time. To kill boredom while working 13 patrol, my partner Bill Marsh and I would sit in our patrol wagon just inside the gates of Ohio Medical College at Arlington and S. Detroit Avenue and scan the morning newspaper.

The campus also housed an institute for the mentally ill and some of the patients were allowed to walk about the grounds. On occasion, a small elderly woman, looking very profound, would approach the wagon and give Bill a hand-written note on a full sheet of paper folded down to a small square. She always chose Bill to give her note to. Bill, as usual would thank the woman, unfold the note and dutifully read its contents. The note would usually predict a world crisis, such as a meteor collision with the Earth or an invasion from Mars.

One morning the woman came up to Bill and before she could offer him a note, Bill handed her a note folded into a small square. The woman was taken aback but took the note, unfolded it and then began to read it as she wandered away.

I was as surprised as the woman, because I had no idea that Bill was going to do that. He never revealed what the note contained, but we never saw the woman again after that.

TO SIR, WITH LOVE

The Toledo Zoo is located in South Toledo on Broadway, which was within the old 13 Patrol District. The late Dan Danford,* was the curator at the time and a personal friend of mine.

The reptiles were fed on Monday at 6:00 A.M., which was an hour before 13 Patrol's hit-off time on the third shift. I, with my partner, was allowed in the reptile house to watch the spectacle.

One Monday morning, after watching the feeding, Officer Ted Curtis and I were returning to our patrol wagon. A building we were parked near had open-air cages. The outside perimeters were barred but permitted a closer proximity to the animals by spectators. The end cage held an orangutan.

"See that orangutan?" Ted asked. I nodded affirmatively.

"Well, if you give him a lit cigarette, he'll actually smoke it."

Ted could see that I was skeptical. "You don't believe me? Watch this:"

Ted threw a lit butt into the cage. The orangutan picked the cigarette up and began to puff on it. He held it Russian style, between his thumb and forefinger, with his palm held upwards.

"See, I told you," Ted boasted, " I better warn you, though, sometimes when least expected, he'll reach behind himself and fling a handful of excretion at you."

As we approached our vehicle, Ted yelled, "Watch out!"

I ducked and "smack", monkey feces splattered across the windshield. We drove to a gas station on Arlington St. and hosed the substance off the wagon.

The owner, whom we knew, asked what we were doing, so we told him the story.

He laughed, then remarked, "That monkey may have the right idea throwing shit at the cops." But he quickly added, "Hey! I'm just kidding."

But my partner and I weren't laughing.

THE SEAT-BELT JIG

One evening I was walking a beat downtown when a lieutenant picked me up to transport me to the Safety Building. He was in his fifties, with graying hair. He was tall, but had a prominent stomach. Although he was usually easy going, he could be a stickler at times. I climbed into his marked car and as he proceeded to drive to our destination; he observed that I didn't use the seat belt.

"Why don't you have your seat belt fastened, officer?"

"Well, Sir, I don't usually wear them, because if I get an emergency call I want to be able to get out of the car quickly. Seat belts have been known to jam and to delay an officer from getting out of the car; such a delay could be critical at the scene of an important call."

"They can also save your life, young man," he reminded me.

A few minutes later, he stopped the car in front of the Safety Building and I readily exited. When I reached the front steps of the building I realized that he wasn't with me. I halted and looked toward the car and saw that the lieutenant was still sitting behind the steering wheel; he was gyrating to and fro. He appeared to be moving in a rhythmical jig; undoubtedly in an effort to get his seat belt unhooked.

Finally, his efforts succeeded and he alighted from the car; obviously embarrassed.

I entered the Safety Building well ahead of him, not wanting to embarrass him further, and refrained from making any comment, like: " What took you so long?"

A SILENT ALARM

When you had walked a beat as long as I had you picked up an array of little gimmicks to make life easier for yourself. Like I learned that I could stash my raincoat in a Traffic Control Box, which contained the controls to the traffic lights at intersections. It beat carrying my coat while not wearing it. The boxes were kept locked, so they were safe. I can't recall how I obtained a key to them.

A smart beat officer made friends with the merchants on his beat. It was not only good public relations (PR) but good insurance. If a beat officer needed help, they could usually be relied upon to summon assistance for you; there was no walky-talky radios back then. If there was no call box near-by or a private phone available, a beat officer could be in for a rough time.

The third shift was the toughest, especially in the wee hours of the morning; there was seldom anything going on. If a beat officer could find an "open door", providing it wasn't due to a burglary, it could afford him a refuge until he had to hit his next box. The greatest problem was falling asleep and miss reporting-in on the allotted time. To prevent this I carried a small, portable alarm clock on my person.

One evening during roll call, I had the clock in the left pocket of my coat. Suddenly, the alarm sounded. I squeezed the clock with my left hand with such force that it stopped the ringer mechanism from functioning; to my amazement no one else had heard it. But I had to keep my firm grip on the clock all through the remainder of roll call, which was about ten minutes; by that time my hand was numb.

Unidentified police officers practicing at the Toledo Police Pistol Range. Circa 50's.

PISTOL RANGE COMEDY

During the summer months police crews, on the day shift, were sent to the Toledo Police Pistol Range to practice while they were on duty. Usually, two or three units were dispatched at a time, drawn from districts distanced from one another, so no one area of Toledo would be completely unprotected. However, when it came to shooting practice, except for officers who were serious marksmen, it was an exercise in futility. Also, when it came to their revolvers, even though they were inspected weekly, many officers neglected to clean them properly.

Some officers had enough lint, dust and other foreign matter encased around the hammer, cylinder and in the barrels of their service revolvers to cause me to speculate if any vegetation could be cultivated in those areas if they were exposed to daylight more frequently.

Some veteran officers with much seniority had worn out their leather gear and some replaced those items with inferior and/or unsuitable equipment. I had a partner I'll call Steve Wexler. I don't know what happened to his original holster, but he obtained a replacement for very little cost. The problem: it was designed for a .45 caliber pistol, which was much larger than our issued .38 caliber revolvers. Also, it had a large flap which folded over the holstered firearm and snapped shut. When the flap was open, all that was visible of his holstered .38 was the very tip of the grip. Steve had to draw his revolver by grasping the tip of the grip between his thumb and forefinger; a precarious maneuver at best. I still chuckle when I recall this 34 year old, 210 pound husky specimen of manhood, extracting his undersized weapon from that huge holster in such a delicate manner. Fortunately, he realized his plight and bought a regulation holster.

On one occasion I recall an officer about to shoot at a bulls eye target. When he drew his revolver it stuck in his holster and his entire gun belt, with the holstered gun was raised to the level of his armpits.

The opposite predicament occurred to another older officer, whom had lost weight. When he cleared his revolver from his holster his entire gun belt slipped down to his knees. If it wasn't such a serious matter it would be a riot.

Keeping one's revolver clean and leather gear in good condition, to me, was essential. Also, that target practice should have been a priority with all officers, especially those with young families; however, it just wasn't so. I understood that the majority of officers held second jobs and some were involved in sports; it was a matter of their priorities.

To me, being proficient with a pistol was tantamount to a good life insurance policy. My mind set was: it's either me or the other guy and I was prepared to do whatever necessary to make sure it would be me, who came out on top.

If the hundreds of hours I spent practicing shooting on my own time by myself; at pistol club sessions; at registered pistol matches, both civilian and police, is what it took than so be it. It was time well invested and it always gave me confidence in my ability to defend myself or someone else, if need be. That much I owed to my family.

To illustrate my point, I and about a dozen other Toledo Police officers at 21 feet from a silhouette target, could draw and fire 6 rounds from the hip, reload and fire an additional 6 rounds from the hip, in just 25 seconds and place all 12 shots within a 6 inch circle located at the center of the target. Some of the other officers I recall were: Lynn Paquette*, Larry Przeslawski*, Robert Burgard*, Dave Bush*, Robert Pitzen Sr.*, P.J. Moore,* (No relation) Frank Martin*, Fred Neipp* and Lee Stipes*.

Personally, I carried my service revolver in a Jordan River fast-draw holster which was designed by Bill Jordan, a Border Patrol Officer. It differed from most issued holsters in its featured cut-away design which enabled an officer to clear his weapon from the holster quickly. I'm positive that I was the only officer on the Toledo Police Department to wear that type of holster in 1959 and throughout the 1960's.

(Bill Jordan instructed pistol marksmanship at Camp Perry, in conjunction with the National Pistol Matches sponsored by the U.S. Army and the National Rifle Association.)

THE TRAFFIC STOP

For a dozen years I was a proud Scouter with the Toledo Area Council of the Boy Scouts of America. I earned Scouter Keys in Cubbing, Scouting and Exploring. Each key required a minimum of three years service as a leader in each respective level of scouting.

During the summers of 1971 and 1973, I was appointed a Crew Leader with the TAC of BSA for excursions to the Philmont Scout Ranch, at Cimarron , New Mexico. Each trip was for a period of two weeks, consisting of camping in the wilderness with a crew of seven to ten Boy Scouts from various troops within the Toledo Area Council.

All equipment: tents, sleeping bags, clothing, food and water was backpacked by members of each crew; including the Leader. All tents were erected, meals cooked and camp sites set up, torn down and cleaned up by crew members during the two week hiking trip through pristine country; with side trips to the summit of several mountains. Believe me, they were no excursions for the weak-hearted.

In September of 1972, my Troop 434 of Meadowvale School, in Northwest District was participating in a Camporee at Put-in-Bay, an island in Lake Erie. The Scout Troops would be ferried across the lake come rain or shine.

I was driving a borrowed pick-up truck with a camper-shell. Several of my senior scouts were riding in the back, traveling from Toledo, Ohio, to a Ferry Landing near Port Clinton, Ohio. We were carrying supplies and equipment to set up a campsite. The rest of the troop would arrive that evening with other leaders via a later ferry. The weather was misty with sporadic rain. Visibility was limited.

Driving through Monroeville, Ohio, I was negotiating a curve in a 50 mph zone when the speed limit suddenly dropped to 35 mph. What alarmed me more was the police radar car sitting by the sign. It reeked of a speed trap to me.

The officer pulled me over and I was hoping he wouldn't become aware of the boys in the camper shell. I didn't want any more problems than I already had. As the officer approached I alighted from the truck and we met near the side window of the camper shell.

Except for my navy-blue baseball cap, I was wearing a regulation scout-leader's uniform: a short-sleeve shirt with earned medals and patches; shorts, neckerchief, belt, knee-stockings, green garter tabs and hiking boots.

Compared to me, the officer was short but his appearance was sharp. His dark blue uniform was neat and spotless. Instead of a tie he wore a light-blue dickey. The name etched on his nameplate was William Williams.* I thought that was unique. Looking up at me, he spoke first.

"Should I salute you?" he asked.

I couldn't imagine why he said that. He seemed to admire my uniform and was very respectful, as if I out-ranked him. I couldn't help but be amused.

"No. I don't think that's necessary," I replied, trying to conceal my amusement.

Then to my dismay I observed the window of the camper being cranked open. I surmised the boys wanted to hear the conversation.

At the officer's request I showed him my driver license and informed him of my destination and purpose for driving there.

"Your speed was excessive when you entered the 35 mph zone." He informed me.

"The speed limit changed rather suddenly." I replied.

"Perhaps, but you have to consider that the pavement is wet." He countered.

"I don't want to argue, Sir, but if I don't make the ferryboat on time my trip is for nothing."

He released me with a verbal warning and wished me good luck.

He never knew that I was a police lieutenant, or that I intended to write a letter to his superior commending him for his professionalism and courtesy.

I have procrastinated too long, Officer Williams, but for the record, "I salute you."

CHAPTER 10

NO TIME FOR SERGEANTS

EPISODES

1. THE WAYWARD WIND

2. TO OBEY OR NOT TO OBEY

3. WORDS OF WISDOM

4. ALL'S FAIR IN LOVE AND POLITICS

5. A DIRTY BIRD

THE WAYWARD WIND

A phone call awakened me at 4 A.M. The desk sergeant ordered me to come down to the station immediately; there had been an explosion in the downtown area.

From the station I was transported by a patrol sergeant to the site of the disaster. The Hy-Grade Meat Packing Company, at 21 Superior Street had blown up from a gas leak causing severe damage to the building and three fatalities.

February 13, 1956 was a cold day with a sleeting rain. The sergeant posted me at Superior and Monroe Streets to assist another officer with traffic. I assisted the officer for about twenty minutes, when a second sergeant told me that he was making me the relief officer and that I was to give the officers at each of four intersections ten minute breaks.

The Red Cross had set up a trailer in the area and was dispensing hot coffee and doughnuts to the firefighters and police at the scene. I was a rookie, but I knew enough to get refreshments for myself before giving any relief.

I had just finished my coffee when Sergeant Forest ordered me to go with him to Huron Street in the warehouse area two blocks over. Tom Forest was a veteran officer who recently received his stripes. He was in his mid-forties, about 5'10" tall, stocky with salt and pepper hair. His concerned face gave me the following information:

"Most of the plate-glass windows in the two story buildings here have been shattered, leaving shards of heavy glass dangling from the window frames. I want you to keep anyone coming into this area from walking near the buildings; we don't want anyone injured."

"Sergeant, I already have an assignment."

"Never mind that, I need you here." His voice rose in volume. He was known to have a quick temper.

I was a little exasperated. Three assignments by three different sergeants within thirty-five minutes and the last assignment was dubious.

"How about if I clear the windows with my nightstick instead?"

"What'd I just tell you to do?" the sergeant looked perturbed.

"I know, but it'd be better to eliminate the hazard than to stand around and watch it." I told him.

"Damn it! It isn't your job to eliminate anything, but to do as I say," the sergeant bellowed. He then strode angrily away.

Dawn was breaking and workers would be coming into the area soon. I saw another rookie officer near by and asked him to watch out for pedestrians, then I proceeded to knock out all the broken windows from each building with my club. It took me about a half hour.

When I was finished, I walked to the command post where Sgt. Forest was standing with the shift captain and a lieutenant; they were poring over a map of the area.

"A strong wind blew those broken windows out, sergeant," I reported, "there's nothing more to watch. What do you want me to do now?"

Sergeant Forest's face reddened, as I observed the captain suppress a smile.

"Traffic officers are taking over," the lieutenant intervened, "you'll be taken back to the station for roll call and your regular assignment."

When I reached the station I discovered my partner and all the veteran officers lounging and playing cards in the gym. Only the rookies had been rousted from bed at an ungodly hour and ordered to report for duty.

The bottom line is that Sgt. Forest was on my case for a year because of that "wayward wind".

TO OBEY OR NOT TO OBEY

The building at 234 N. Erie where the author and his partner entered through the roof. Circa 50's.

Working the third shift, my partner Larry Peters and I were ordered to call the dispatcher, via phone, at 11:30 P.M. We were informed that a call for help was received from a man who said he was the custodian at a brokerage firm located at 232 N. Erie , in downtown Toledo, and that he was being held captive by a gunman.

We parked down the street from the business firm and went to the rear. There was no back entrance but the edifice directly behind the brokerage firm had a fire escape, from which we leaped to the roof of the target building.

On top of the brokerage firm we discovered a large air vent through which we could gain entrance by removing a metal hood.   I looked down from the roof over the front walk and saw Sgt. Forest arrive. I called to him and told him that we found a way into the building.

He gave me an explicit order: "Do not go in."

However, my partner had already removed the hood and had entered the dark opening. Now I had to make a decision: Stay on the roof as ordered, or enter the opening to back-up my partner. Fearing that Larry could run into trouble, I chose to go in.

The vent was over a small lavatory. I dropped down and joined Larry. We could neither hear nor see anything. With revolvers drawn, we searched the darkened second floor in vain.

I cautiously descended a staircase to the main floor. A large window loomed on my right and when I reached it, I was startled by the angry face of Sgt. Forest glaring at me from outside.

"I told you not to go inside," he shouted, "now stand by this window and don't move; do you understand me?" His voice was shrill.

My silhouette in front of the window made a perfect target, I reasoned, so I ignored him and took cover in the dark interior, among the first floor furnishings.

Lieutenant Haskins and the owner both arrived. The owner unlocked the front door, shut off the alarm before it could activate and turned on the lights. He informed us that there was no janitor employed there, the building was empty and the call was phony.

Sgt. Forest, appearing very agitated, began to say something when the lieutenant interrupted, "See!" he boasted proudly to the owner, "my men found a way in here and they didn't even set the alarm off."

The owner acknowledged his gratitude; the lieutenant was happy; the sergeant was disgusted, but apparently, I was off the hook and my partner never knew how close we came to being in trouble.

WORDS OF WISDOM

With his complexion he could have come from the South Sea Islands or the West Indies. He was a very large man; tall and erect with graying hair. He seldom smiled and remained aloof from the patrolmen.

This aptly describes Sgt. Ira Mongona. The first thing he told new officers under his command was not to call for him unless it was absolutely necessary and if it wasn't necessary, they could expect a well polished shoe up their backside. Rookies took his word for gospel.

Experienced officers like my partner Bob Skinner, a veteran of ten years, could handle about anything that came their way. However, there are exceptions and this was the case one Fall day on the first shift in 1964.

A fellow brought his car into an upholstery shop and arranged to have the entire interior of the car re-upholstered. The shop was located on Monroe Street near Collingwood Avenue between a gas station and the Toledo Art Museum.

Apparently, after making the arrangements, the customer had reservations, so about noon while the employees were eating lunch, he crept into the shop and pushed his car out to the street. He got it as far as the gas station when a shop worker saw him and alerted the shop owner. The work hadn't been completed, there was a hassle and the police were called.

Bob wasn't sure what to do about the mess so he called for a sergeant and Sgt. Mongona was dispatched.

Sgt. Mongona towered over everyone, including Bob and myself. After listening to both parties concerned, he asked the shop owner and the customer: "Do you know what I think?"

Both of them shook their heads negatively.

Bob and I were standing by waiting to hear the sergeant's words of wisdom in case we should ever have a similar dispute.

Sgt. Mongona stuck a large forefinger into the chest of the customer and said, "I think you're full of shit."

He then turned towards the shop owner, jabbed him in the chest and said, "And, I think you're full of shit."

I was mortified. I wanted to disappear but there was no way to do so or to avoid the humiliation of the moment.

Just then a shop worker called out that the shop owner's attorney was on the phone. Apparently, the shop owner had put a call in to him. Sgt. Mongona told us to detain the customer and went into the shop with the owner.

They both came out within a few minutes. The sergeant informed everyone that the car owner could take his car. It was his property and that the shop owner would bill him for the amount of work that had been done. If the customer failed to pay the bill, then the shop owner would have to pursue the matter through the courts, as it was a civil case.

Obviously, the sergeant was quoting the attorney. However Sgt. Mongona looked pleased with himself and left. Neither of the two principals in the case looked as pleased but had no choice. Bob and I were glad that the matter was settled so we could go to lunch.

"Well," Bob addressed me, as we returned to our cruiser, "I learned one thing from this."

What constitutes a civil case?" I ventured.

"No!" He said emphatically. "The reason Sgt. Mongona doesn't want any crews to call him."

"And just why is that?" I was curious to know.

"It's because he doesn't know his ass from a hole in the ground."

ALL'S FAIR IN LOVE AND POLITICS

My partner and I clocked her speeding on Front Street at 70 mph in a 35 mph zone. It was after 3 A.M., traffic was light, but that was way too fast. Besides, she was arrogant and even denied that she had been speeding. When she was issued a citation she warned us: "You'll be sorry."

Thirty minutes later, Sgt. Forest called for us to meet him. Apparently our lady speeder had friends in high places.

The sergeant asked us to drop the charge. We refused. He explained that the woman lived in Birmingham Terrace, a low-income housing project off Consaul Street, next to St. Stephen's Church. He also subtly implied that the shift captain was interested in the case.

We agreed to a rare concession: we changed the ticket to read 50 mph in a 35 mph zone. The sergeant wasn't completely satisfied but went away.

We were low on fuel so we obtained permission from the dispatcher to gas at the police service station. Afterwards, we went to the Safety Building near by, which housed the Toledo Police Department and the Municipal Courts. At the Clerk of Courts office we filed the speeding ticket, which in essence is an affidavit. Once an affidavit is sworn to, it becomes an official document of the court and no one may dare tamper with it.

We just returned to our district when Sgt. Forest called to meet him again. He came right to the point, " Captain Miller wants you to drop the speeding charge that we discussed earlier."

"Can't do it, Sarge."

"Why not?"

"We already filed it at the clerk's office."

"You what?"

"Yeah, we had to go for gas so we stopped at the clerk's office before returning to district."

"Damn." Sgt. Forest gasped, "The captain's going to be mad as hell."

After the sergeant left, my Polish partner had a final comment, "Tough, Shitski."

A DIRTY BIRD

Until the late sixties, police officers had only their police car radios for contact with police dispatchers, it was their lifeline. Only one officer of a two-man crew could leave the car at any one time to assure they would not miss an assignment or other radio communication.

There was a way however to circumvent this situation which some officers deployed. An electronic receiver, such as those used at drive-in theaters, could be modified by attaching two extension wires with "alligator" clips at the ends. A small bit of insulation on each of two wires of a police car radio would be scraped off and the alligator clips clamped onto the bare wires. Thus, a transmission on the police radio would be transmitted to the extended receiver which could be placed as far from the police car as the extension wires allowed; most were about twenty feet long.

Officers Brown and Schefield, assigned to 14 Scout, had such an extension devise. One evening they hooked up to the fire station at Orchard and Broadway to eat dinner with the firemen. The extended receiver was placed in the kitchen where it could be monitored while they ate.

While thus occupied, Sgt. Bricker rode by and observed the empty squad car by the fire station and quietly disconnected the alligator clips. He drove a short distance away and radioed the dispatcher to have 14 Scout meet him, knowing that the crew would not hear the call.

When it was obvious that the officers were not going to respond, the sergeant told the dispatcher that he would look for them. He then went back to the fire station and informed the crew that they had missed a call to meet him. He ordered them to report to the captain's office.

Captain Billings was highly respected by the officers on his shift. He was a fair and reasonable man and also was known to be very religious; never using swear words. The men showed their respect by not using such language in his presence.

The trio walked into his office and Sgt. Bricker explained the situation, concluding that he thought the crew was guilty of neglect of duty. Of course he omitted the fact that it was he, whom caused the problem.

"What do you officers have to say?" the captain asked.

"Well, Sir, we did have a radio hook-up at the fire barn," Brown admitted.

"We were invited to eat dinner with the firemen, Sir," Schefield added. "However, if some son-of-a --- I mean, "dirty bird" hadn't tampered with it, there wouldn't have been a problem."

"Sir, we do our job and we've never been in trouble before," Brown concluded.

"Who do you think the dirty bird was who tampered with your radio?" the captain asked the crew.

"We don't know, Sir," the officers said, but their eyes shifted towards the sergeant.

"Who do you think the dirty bird was, Sgt. Bricker?" the captain looked directly at the sergeant.

" I have no idea, Sir."

"Well, Gentlemen," the captain said, donning his cap at the door, "while such radios are not official equipment, I have received no orders to ban them. In fact, in some instances they can be of help to a crew. I think what we have to do is to be on our guard. Now sergeant, I want you to be especially watchful and to protect your crews from such dirty tactics. Can I count on you?"

"Absolutely, Sir." The sergeant's voice was hoarse and his face crimson.

"So, let's get back to work everyone," the captain concluded, "We have a job to do."

The Fire Station at Orchard and Broadway, as it appears today. It is vacant and no longer in use.

CHAPTER 11

STRANGE BUT TRUE

EPISODES

1. FRIGID MUSI C

2. THE LAST PLACE YOU'D LOOK

3. OBJECT DE ART

4. A RARE INCIDENT

5. A NEIGHBOR'S INTEREST

6. EASING THE IMPACT

7. CURB SERVICE

8. THE MAN WHO WASN'T THERE

FRIGID MUSIC

One of my earlier experiences on patrol was a call to a pond on the East Side. It had snowed and the roads were icy. A teenager lost control of his speeding car and sideswiped a telephone pole propelling the careening car into the pond. Miraculously, he and his passenger managed to jump from the car before it hit the freezing water and swam to shore. Both of the shivering boys went to a near by residence where a family took them in and called the police.

When we arrived we wrapped the boys in police blankets and placed them in our squad car with the car heater turned on high.

An hour elapsed before a wrecker could get to the scene and winch the vehicle from the pond. When the car was pulled to the shore, it was full of water and silt but what was most surprising, after being submerged in icy water all that time, was that the head lights were still shining brightly and the radio was playing dance music.

THE LAST PLACE YOU'D LOOK

Officer Bob Skinner and I were working 7 Patrol on third shift when a businessman, Mr. Joseph, reported that his late model Cadillac had been stolen from in front of his Joseph's Store at Cherry and Delaware earlier that evening.

My partner and I searched all over our district and because it was a quiet night we even checked adjoining districts throughout our tour with negative results.

When I arrived home from work about seven in the morning there was a Cadillac parked almost in front of my house. My wife told me that at about eleven-thirty the prior evening a man parked it and walked away. It was the stolen car.

OBJECT DE' ART

A man reported that the entire front of his car had been stolen: the bumper, radiator, fenders, headlights and the hood. Unbelievable.

Several days later two crews and I forcibly entered a large Victorian type house in the same area. We were in direct pursuit of a wanted fugitive running from the law.

After we found the culprit hiding upstairs and arrested him, we made a startling discovery in the large front room. Standing upright, intact, like an Object de' Art, was the missing car front. I can't imagine how it was brought into the house; if the parts were taken from the car separately and re-assembled in the house, or what. Of course the arrested fugitive knew nothing about it.

A RARE INCIDENT

As a police officer and a civilian, I participated in numerous pistol matches in a tri-state area of Ohio, Michigan and Indiana. While shooting at a registered match at Jackson, Michigan, there was a commotion on the firing line during the .45 caliber Timed Fire stage. When one of the competitors fired a shot at his target, simultaneously a round went off in the magazine of his pistol.

Surprisingly, the shooter was not injured. The explosion cracked the left pistol grip of his .45 cal. pistol and left an outline of the butt of the gun on the marksman's shooting hand in burnt gun powder, but the pistol grip next to his hand was not damaged. I don't know the extent of damage, if any, to the magazine.

The shooter was too upset to continue competing in the match. I had never seen anything like that before, or since. It was a very rare incident.

A NEIGHBOR'S INTEREST

Working 12 Patrol, Bob Skinner and I were sent to "See the complainant, at 1510 Klondike." A man was waiting for us at the curb.

"What's the problem?" Bob asked.

"She's been sitting there for a real long time and hasn't moved." he answered.

"Who are you and who are you talking about?"

"Sorry; I'm Ivan Schmidt. I've been watching my neighbor, Mrs. Kelly, for over an hour; she's reading but hasn't turned a page. I think she's dead.

The front room of the large house next to Schmidt's was well lit. The three of us observed the woman through a side window. She was sitting upright in a lounge chair holding a book in her lap. Her head was bent forward and she appeared to be reading. However, she was completely motionless and there was no indication that she was breathing. And as Ivan pointed out: she was not turning any pages.

"You know, officers, I have a key to her house . . . I've been putting up her storm windows in the Fall and screens in the Spring for years. If she's dead I hope she remembers me in her will.

We gained entrance to the house with Ivan's key. Mrs. Kelly was no longer among the living. The Coroner's Office was notified.

During the entire time it took the Coroner to arrive, Ivan kept verbalizing about all he had done for Mrs. Kelly over the years and what he hoped she might have bequeathed to him in her will.

When we got back in service Bob said, "That nut was driving me up a wall. He better not go back and help himself to anything either."

"The only way he can get back in is to break in," I stated, as I flipped Ivan's key in the air and caught it. "Wouldn't it be a shame if she didn't leave him anything?"

EASING THE IMPACT

In response to a call: check the safety of the occupant, the landlord let my partner and I into an apartment with a key.

The elderly man occupying the suite was lying dead in the middle of the front room. He had knelt on the floor and shot himself in the chest, but before doing so, he had placed a pillow in front of him so that when he fell over - - - he wouldn't hurt himself?

CURB SERVICE

Early in my career, I was walking a beat in a honky-tonk district at Summit and Cherry Streets. There was numerous bars in the area.

A tall thin man piqued my suspicious nature. I observed him repeatedly frequenting bars but staying only briefly in each one. I discovered that the man was "taking orders" for stolen merchandise. You want a television set? A tape recorder? Whatever; he'd get it for you - - - just allow him a day or two.

One morning I saw him on my beat carrying a gallon-size wine carton. I observed that the top of the carton had been cut open. I stopped him and checked the contents; twelve new percale sheets were stacked perfectly inside of the box.

When he was brought to the detective bureau for questioning, a problem came to light: none of the sheets had labels indicating where they had come from. Without a complainant the thief could not be prosecuted, so he was released. However, I never saw him on my beat again.

Along this area of Cherry St. the man was "taking orders" for merchandise. At the Seville Café the author arrested a man with a concealed hunting knife on his person; there were stabbings reported in the area, at the time. Circa 60's

THE MAN WHO WASN'T THERE

It couldn't have happened at a more appropriate time…Halloween night. Officer Bob Skinner and I, working 12 Patrol, were summoned to an address on Nebraska Avenue near St. Anthony's Church: "To see the complainant."

When we arrived, an elderly woman bid us to enter her home and informed us: "He's upstairs."

When we followed her to an illuminated bedroom there was no one in the room. Although there was a pair of mens' shoes neatly set on the floor near the bed, the bed was empty.

The woman pointed to the empty bed and said, "There he is. I want him removed from my house."

Bob and I looked at each other, shrugged our shoulders and went through the motions of taking a man from the bed and escorting him downstairs and out the door.

The woman thanked us and locked her door behind us. Is that strange, or what?

CHAPTER 12

BEHIND THE SCENES

EPISODES

1. DIAL 'A' FOR ARREST

2. PING-PONG AND THE SAILOR

3. CONCEALED WEAPONS

4. THE CREATION OF A MONSTER

5. BUMPER TAG

6. IN THE NAME OF CHIVALRY

7. GUN DEAL

8. THE WARNING SHOT

DIAL 'A' FOR ARREST

"Thirteen Patrol, robbery in progress. Wayne's Bar. Westwood and Airport Highway. Two white males in black leather jackets; both armed with handguns. Considered armed and dangerous. Use caution."

"Thirteen Patrol, O.K." Officer Bill Marsh responded. It was just 11:00 P.M.

"At least we're not very far away," I remarked; coaxing the ol' wagon to 70 mph while streaking down Airport Highway. We stopped a short distance from the café leaving the car doors ajar as we approached the building with revolvers in hand. Nothing seemed amiss or unusual to indicate a crime in progress.

We cautiously opened the front door and eased in, keeping our guns inconspicuous. The café was well attended with patrons sitting at a long bar to the right of the entrance sipping their drinks while other customers were sitting at tables. Several persons turned towards us, surprised to see police officers. There was no sign of any gunmen.

Holstering our revolvers, Bill and I went to the far end of the bar to talk to the barkeeper. He looked to be in his forties, stocky with a beer-belly and chomping on a cigar stub. His hair was parted down the middle and he resembled the bar tenders of yester-years. He looked up in surprise.

"How's every thing going?" Bill inquired.

"Yeah. It's a little noisy, but peaceful, officers. Yeah, is there anything wrong?"

"Have you had any trouble with anyone tonight?" Bill inquired.

"Yeah, well, now that you mention it, yeah, I did have to cut one guy off - - - Marty Johnson. He was getting rowdy and, yeah, he had more than enough booze, so I told him to leave. Yeah, come to think of it, he used the pay phone before he left."

"Do you know where he lives?" Bill persisted.

"Yeah, just north a block or two. Yeah, he's a regular, I've got a tab on him."

While the bartender located an address for Bill, I radioed a 10-4 from the wagon to the dispatcher and informed him that there would be a follow-up on the case.

We parked in front of a shadowy house on Dunlap; a front room light was lit. A man with an unsteady gait came from the darkened part of the house in answer to the doorbell. He was about fifty years old, average height, overweight, balding, with a bushy salt-and-pepper mustache.

"I thought I heard the bell." His words were slurred as he opened the door and beckoned us to enter.

"Are you Mr. Johnson?" I calmly asked while stepping inside.

"That's me, gents. What can I do for you, officers?" He swayed, almost losing his balance.

"We understand that you called the police from Wayne's Bar and we'd like to know what you wanted," I improvised.

Johnson studied us for a moment. He appeared apprehensive, then stammered, "I- I, ah, did make a call officers." Then gaining confidence he loudly proclaimed, "That bartender there is crooked! He's watering the whiskey and I saw him do it!"

"What about the armed robbers?" I demanded to know.

"Robbers? I-I-I don't know anything about robbers." Johnson waxed nervous and began to lick his tongue along the bottom of his mustache, "He's serving watered whiskey," he repeated meekly.

"I want you to know that we responded to that call at 70 miles an hour!" Bill was adamant. "and that we jeopardized our safety and maybe other's too, for that phony call? You're under arrest Mr. Johnson, for intoxication and for making a false police report."

"Y-Y-You can't prove anything," Johnson pouted.

"Yes we can, Mr. Johnson," I replied, "Every call received at the Police Alarm Building is taped. It will be a simple matter to get a copy of that tape and present it in court as evidence."

Johnson pleaded guilty and was convicted of all charges. It was the extra effort behind the scenes that made it possible.

PING-PONG AND THE SAILOR

Roll call was held in the police gymnasium at the Safety Building. A regulation boxing ring dominated one side of the huge room with numerous marred, wooden chairs scattered along the walls. An ancient, ping-pong table set at one end of the gym by itself. Like the chairs, it had seen better days.

Several officers usually arrived early and gave the old table a workout before roll call. Quite a few patrolmen were very proficient at slamming a little white ball back and forth over a net; I was one of them.

Joe Watkins was a rookie, six months out of the Toledo Police Academy. He was 24 years old but when he took his cap off he aged ten years; he was prematurely bald. He stood 5'10" and weighed 165 pounds with a muscular build. His dark eyes always seemed sad though, in contrast with his ready smile.

I was breaking him in on 4 Patrol, one of the smaller districts which covered part of the honky-tonk area along Cherry Street from Summit as far West as E. Bancroft, then North to Columbus via Stickney Avenue and back East to Summit Street.

The area contained many businesses including the New Yorker Bar on New York Street which was, for most part, a quiet neighborhood bistro.

One evening, about 8 P.M. our unit was dispatched there in answer to a complaint about a disturbance. Joe stuck his nightstick into one of his back trouser pockets as he emerged from the wagon. I carried a "slapper", which is two pieces of flat leather sewn together, affording a grip at one end, with a round piece of lead sandwiched in the other end. . It is very effective for subduing unruly persons and usually causes less trauma than a nightstick.

Everything was peaceful as we entered the front door but the place was a mess: tables were tipped over, chairs broken; a back bar mirror smashed; even the cash register was damaged.

The only occupants were a young, sickly-thin woman sitting at the far end of the bar, a sailor sitting at a table with his head in his hands, a waitress sweeping broken glass into a pile and the bartender who was trying to get the cash register to open.

The bartender motioned to us, "I'm the owner and everything's going to be all right," he gushed. "The young sailor had too much to drink and went wild. He is going to pay for everything."

"Is that right?" I queried the sailor.

His white uniform was mussed; sweat stains showed under the arms of his blouse and his bell-bottom trousers were dirty. He was calm but sweating profusely. He was about 25, with sandy hair and a good physique.

"Yes, Sir," he replied as he lifted his head, revealing a baby-face." I'm stationed here at Bay View Park and I'll take care of everything." His face was flush, his speech slurred; He was obviously intoxicated but remorseful.

"I don't know how you're going to pay for anything out of your measly pay, you fathead," spewed the skinny woman at the end of the bar. She actually resembled "Olive Oyl", she was so thin.

Hey! You keep out of this," Joe admonished her.

"You can't talk that way to my wife," the sailor sneered. Newly energized, he leaped up and grabbed Joe in a bear-hug. The two men began wheeling about in a circular pattern. Joe's arms were pinned to his sides and it was all he could do to keep his balance and awkwardly move with the sailor, gyrating in a sort of dance. There was no way that he could reach his club or break the sailor's grip.

I pulled out my slapper as they whirled around but feared I'd accidentally strike Joe. However, as the two figures rotated near me, I gauged an opening and smacked the sailor along-side his head. He went down like a sack of grain. We quickly handcuffed him and hauled him out to the wagon.

The frail female followed us outside shouting obscenities and calling us vile names. We got the sailor into the rear of the wagon, then Joe corralled the lean woman, handcuffed her and placed her into the wagon also.

"She's going in for interfering," he declared. I nodded in concurrence.

The anxious owner ran up to us, "Does this mean he won't pay for the damages?" he sputtered.

"You'll have to go through the prosecutor's office, " I informed him. "As soon as we book these two, we'll be back to explain everything to you and do a follow-up for our report," I assured him.

Later, I couldn't help comparing my slapper with a ping-pong paddle. In retrospect, it seems that playing ping-pong before roll calls proved to be a veiled training exercise.

CONCEALED WEAPONS

Working 12 Patrol. with Stan Novotny was a pleasure. He was a husky, robust, good-natured fellow; senior to me in age as well as on the job. He was a very good role model.

"Twelve Patrol: Alberta Brown Homes, number 168. See complainant. Disturbance." The dispatcher's voice was monotonic.

"Twelve, O.K.," I replied into the mike.

The Alberta Brown Homes was a large apartment complex built for low income families in the inner city. The many apartments were numbered in such a confusing arrangement, along with multiple parking lots and entrances from several streets, that all police crews serving the area carried a map of the compound.

"I don't like disturbance calls," Stan remarked as he headed our wagon towards the A.B.H. "They can involve anything from a minor disagreement to a homicide."

"They can be dangerous." I agreed.

"I'd rather answer a gun call," Stan continued, "at least you know what you're up against before going in."

Even with the map we had to hunt for the apartment. We reached the green-painted front door, identical to all the other apartments , just as a teenage girl emerged.

"Be careful, he's got a gun," she warned and hurried on her way.

"Come in," a masculine voice responded after our knock.

The voice came from a man sitting on a couch smoking a cigarette. He appeared to be about forty, medium height and build, wearing a white tee shirt and jeans. The couch was covered with a blanket.

A heavy-set woman was prone in the middle of the floor sobbing.

"What's the problem?" Stan asked the man.

"Let her tell ya," the man offered, "I ain't got no problems."

Stan helped the woman to her feet.

"Where's the gun?" I asked the man directly, keeping both of my hands in the pockets of my leather jacket, while gluing my eyes to his hands.

"What gun?" the man countered, "I don't have no gun."

"Yes, you does," the woman spoke between sobs in a high pitched voice, "He done got it mail-ordered and was down by the creek shooting it earlier." The woman paused to get her breath, "Then he was playing around with it, loaded, in the house." She continued, "All I did was ask him to put it way until afta' the kids was in bed and he done hit me." The woman began to cry again.

"Do you want to prosecute?" Stan asked her.

"I'm not sure, what's I gotta do?" she sniffled gaining her composure.

Stan escorted the woman into the kitchen to talk to her.

I stayed in the living room to watch the man. I freed my left hand but kept my right hand pocketed.

The man casually stood up, opened the door and flipped his cigarette butt outside.

I sprang to the couch and ran my left hand about the area where he had been sitting. I felt something hard and metallic under the blanket: a colt .38 caliber revolver. I swung the cylinder open; it contained six shells, three empty and three charged.

The man returned to his seat appearing dejected.

I held the gun near his face and said evenly, "You don't know what a gun looks like, do you?"

Stan re-entered the room with the wife.

I held the gun up for Stan to see. "Let's take him in," I said.

"No," Stan replied. "We'll just confiscate the weapon. His wife knows what to do." I respected Stan's judgment, so I said nothing more.

Stan turned to the man, "If you cause any more ruckus after we leave and we have to come back, you will go to jail – and you might have to go to a hospital first. Do you understand me?"

The man looked down but nodded his head in acknowledgement.

"Twelve Patrol, back in service," I spoke into the mike. "Confiscated gun, no arrest." I informed the dispatcher.

"Twelve Patrol, in service," the dispatcher echoed.

As we drove off, Stan knew that I was waiting for an explanation.

"Why should we waste our time taking that meathead to jail?" he began. "He didn't do us any harm so let the complainant do her part and swear out a warrant if she wants him arrested."

"You're right. I never thought of it like that," I admitted.

"By the way," Stan glanced at me, "I'm sure glad that joker didn't pull that gun on you."

"That would have been his last act on Earth," I said, as I pulled an automatic .32 caliber pistol from my right pocket, "I would have shot him right through my jacket."

"Well, I'll be damned," Stan exclaimed, "I wondered why you kept your hand in your pocket."

"Check this," Stan said, revealing a snub-nose .38 caliber revolver holstered under his left shoulder. Neither of us had been aware that the other had a second piece. The two of us were armed with four guns.

THE CREATION OF A MONSTER

Of all the rookies I had broken-in I never had one like Patrolman Brian Metzger. He was listless and wasn't interested in enforcing any laws or doing anything else that was productive. I really don't know why he became a police officer; certainly not for the money.

Working second shift, we stopped a car with a Michigan plate for a minor traffic violation at Ashland and W. Bancroft, about 6 PM. The driver was a black male with a black female passenger. He had no operator license. According to our Record Bureau he was clean; the car belonged to the woman. Because he was from Flint, Michigan, and he was black, Metzger wanted to let him go.

"No way," I objected. "We don't even know if his I.D. is legit. Besides, if he should cause an accident we'd be morally responsible for letting him drive."

" If we book him we'll have to tow the car," Metzger protested.

"Not so; it's his girlfriend's car, so she can drive it."

The man was booked on the original traffic violation to establish "probable cause" for stopping him and for Operating a Motor Vehicle Without A Driver License. When we left the Safety Building I told Metzger: "He's the one who disregarded the law; If he's legit he can get out on bond . . . we did our job.

When we got back in service a call was waiting for us: a disturbance in the Delight Bar at W. Central and N. Detroit. Upon our arrival the action was over, but a brawny bartender was holding a small, struggling, white male.

"He was the cause of it all," the barkeep informed us. "He shot his mouth off to two of my regular customers and they were gonna clean his clock for him when I stepped in and broke it up."

"Where are the other guys?" I asked.

"They took off."

"He told them to beat it," the small man shouted, "I could have creamed 'em."

"What do you want us to do? Metzger queried.

"I just want this punk out-a-here and I don't wanna see 'im around here again."

We escorted the man outside. "What's your name?" I asked.

"Barney Carson and I'll tell ya' somethin' fuzz . . you couldn't arrest me if you wanted to," he boasted.

"Yeah? Why not?" I asked out of curiosity.

"Because I'm a star witness for the Vise Squad in a big drug bust, that's why. Without me they don't have a case."

"Well, Carson, I wouldn't bet the farm on it if I were you. You got off lucky this time, so take off."

We'd just finished eating when the radio came alive: "Scout 10. Disturbance at 847 W. Central, Apt. 209. Code Two." Metzger O.K.'d the call.

A young woman let us in, holding a wet cloth to her bleeding face. "He did this," she said, pointing to a man sitting in the living room. We could hear children crying in the next room. The man arose from the chair and lo and behold, if it wasn't Barney Carson.

"She had it coming," he shouted. "She didn't have supper ready and gave me a lot of flack."

"Do you want to prosecute"? I asked the woman.

"Yes, I do officers; this is the last straw . . . I'm tired of his abuse and neglect, they're his children too. I'll do whatever it takes."

"You pigs can go screw," Carson spewed; "Like I said, the fuzz can't touch me."

"You got a lot to learn, Sonny," I replied as I took out my handcuffs. "You can go the easy way or the hard way, but you're going. If you choose the hard way I guarantee you a stop at a hospital before going to jail."

"You're crazy Man! I told you I'm protected!"

"Not by me you're not. Now turn around and put your hands behind your back."

"I'll guarantee you something smart guy; you're going to lose your badge over this," Carson sputtered.

I observed a look of disgust on Metzger's face as Carson complied and I knew that the look wasn't for Carson.

Carson was placed in a holding cell until he could be booked for Creating a Disturbance and Assault and Battery. While waiting, Metzger had news for me: "I don't want any trouble . . . maybe we shouldn't have arrested the guy . . . Vise is going to be mad as hell."

"This may come as a surprise to you Metzger, but Vise doesn't sign my pay checks. If you want, you can keep your name off the blotter, but this punk is going to court."

Before I could get back in service, two Vice officers approached me. I knew them.

"Jim, what in hell are you doing? We've spent a lot of time building a case . . .

without Carson it'll all be for nothing."

"Do you know what you've done? You've created a monster. Carson thinks he has a free pass to do anything he pleases. Laws or no laws he thinks he has immunity."

"But look at it from our side . . . "

"You want to look at something, go take a good look at his wife's face. He beat the hell out of her and thinks he can walk away on your say so. And I'll tell you something else . . . If you have to depend on a slime ball like him to make a case, then you better start doing better police work. Regardless of what that punk gets in court, my charges stand."

"You're making a mistake, Moore; a big one."

That was never proven to me. And about two months later I was happy to hear that one, Officer Brian Metzger resigned from the Toledo Police Department.

BUMPER TAG

Working Ten Scout, I was assigned another rookie to break in, named George Lucas. He was short and cocky, but eager to learn, and eventually he became an efficient officer.

It was a foul, rainy, autumn day. The streets were wet and slippery enhanced by a thick accumulation of fallen leaves, especially in the street gutters.

George was behind the wheel cruising the district when we were dispatched to a fire. Making our presence known with our red light and siren, George raced down Ashland Avenue.

"Take it easy, George," I advised. "We're just going to direct traffic at a fire scene."

Cars were stopped in our lane on W. Bancroft, but traffic was moving towards us in the on-coming lane. There was no way to pass the standing traffic and nowhere else to go as we rapidly approached the cars ahead of us. George braked, but our cruiser skidded into the rear of the last car in line, containing four, young women.

We shut down the lights and siren and notified the dispatcher that we were involved in an accident and an accident investigation crew was sent to our location. The noise had been worse than the impact. No one was injured and there was no damage. The girls were more concerned that they were involved with the police, than anything else.

Everyone was relieved when the accident investigation crew determined that a report was not necessary, after all, that's what bumpers are for.

When we got back in service we were dispatched to another fire. George employed the light and siren and once again charged ahead. We were traveling East on W. Central when an oncoming car turned directly into our path, heading for a driveway. George slammed the brakes, locking our cruiser into a skid on wet leaves along the curb. We couldn't stop. It was like a "Keystone" movie: the errant car barely cleared the driveway as we sailed by missing it by inches.

George muted the light and siren as we rolled to a stop at the curb and gasped, "That's it! I've had it! You drive!"

IN THE NAME OF CHIVALRY

After being transferred from the Vice Squad to uniform patrol, Nick Crozier was assigned to work 13 Patrol with me. He had worked in plainclothes for so many years that he had to be fitted for new uniforms.

At 45 years old, Nick was a handsome man. Five foot eleven, 210 pounds, stocky build, wavy dark hair – graying at the temples, with finely carved facial features; sporting dimples and a clef chin.

To say that he was bitter was an understatement. He hardly spoke to me the entire first month we worked together. What made matters worse was that he had been enforcing vice laws for so long that he was virtually ignorant of the current criminal and traffic codes. It was like breaking in a rookie, but an older one, who was set in his ways.

One summer evening, we received a call at 9:15 P.M. to meet a complainant at the corner of Spencer and Gordon Streets. A slim, blond woman about thirty years old was waiting; scantily clad in a slip over bra and panties and wearing house slippers She stated that her husband evicted her from their house and refused to let her back in.

Nick's eyes beamed, "You want back in lady? We'll get you back in. Just leave it to us," he assured her.

"Oh, no," I thought. "Nick thinks he's a knight in shining armor."

We accompanied the complainant to her house on Gordon Street. There was a light on in the front room, but no one responded to our knocking.

We went to the rear door in which a missing windowpane had been replaced with cardboard. To enter, one only had to remove the cardboard, reach in, and unlock the door.

My hand moved towards the cardboard when Nick said, "Stand back." He kicked the door so fiercely that it exploded off the hinges.

The husband was sitting in the living room watching TV from a club chair; drinking a can of beer. The room was tidy except for an ironing board to one side with an iron on it.

"What's going on?" Nick demanded.

The husband calmly replied, "You want to know what's going on? I'll tell you. Last month I gave my wife $400 to pay the bills. This month I get the bills and none of them were paid. I asked her where the money went and she wouldn't tell me. I told her that if she didn't tell me by nine o'clock I was throwing her out At nine o'clock she still refused to talk so I threw her out."

"You can't do that," I informed him. "This is a common-law state. Everything you own is half yours and half hers. By law, you can't evict her from her own home."

"I don't give a damn about any laws," he said defiantly. He finished his beer and set down the can.

"How would you like to go to jail?" I threatened. I was bluffing. I hoped to make him realize the seriousness of the situation and maybe he'd change his attitude. It was a mistake! Nick took me seriously.

"Yeah, let's go!" Nick muttered and he started pulling the man from the chair.

The man resisted and grabbed the iron from the ironing board.

"Watch it, Nick!" I warned, "He's got the iron."

Nick ripped his nightstick from his belt and clubbed the man. He went down. We handcuffed him and hauled him to the wagon.

"Holy, saints," I thought, "we don't have a bloody thing on this guy. We're going to end up in the chief's office over this for sure."

The man suffered a cut from the clubbing so we had to have him treated at a hospital. The bandaged prisoner was booked for Drunk and Disorderly, Resisting Arrest, Assault on a Police Officer and Creating a Disturbance. I was disgusted about the whole mess.

Eventually Nick and I were summoned to a pre-trial hearing. The man's attorney, Jacob Bernstein, requested to talk to us in private.

"I know that Mr. Carter evicted his wife from their home," Bernstein began, "but I'm not sure of all the facts. Perhaps you officers can enlighten me."

"Well," Nick spoke, "he wouldn't let us in so we kicked the door in ---"

"You kicked the door in?" the attorney interrupted, "He didn't tell me that."

"When we arrested him," Nick continued, "he tried to hit me with a flat iron."

"He tried to hit you with an iron?" Bernstein exclaimed, "he didn't tell me that either. Listen, I'm going to plead him guilty to all charges. You won't even have to appear in court and I appreciate your cooperation."

I couldn't believe it, as I emitted a sigh of relief.

That was a sad case and admittedly it wasn't our finest hour. I don't believe an arrest would have been made if I hadn't tried to use psychology and Nick hadn't decided to be chivalrous.

THE GUN DEAL

A recent photo of Libbey High School, where the "gun deal" took place.
The school has been closed for lack of students.

The average workload was seventy cases per officer when I was assigned to work in the Juvenile Bureau as a detective. The summer months were even worse when schools were closed, making it difficult to locate suspects.

One spring morning, the captain assigned me to a special case. The day before, one Lamar Bates, age 17, was involved in a fistfight with another male student at Libbey High School. Losing the scrap, Lamar fled, but a custodian overheard him say: "I'm going to get a gun and do him in." Bates didn't return or follow through, but the captain was concerned.

"I did a little checking on the Bates kid," the captain related, "He was involved in a disturbance last Thanksgiving Day. He crashed a party and before he was ejected, he brandished a gun and fired a shot. Detectives followed it up but no arrest was made and as far as I know, they never got the gun."

"Where's Bates now, captain?" I queried.

"He's back in school. I want you to run out there and see what you can find out."

"I'm on my way. I'll check back with you later, Sir."

To gain more information, I stopped by Tony Gallino's office, a counselor, whom I knew well, at Libbey High School.

"This feud has been brewing between Bates and David Crane for some time," Tony informed me. "It's over a girl, who is presently going with Crane and doesn't want anything to do with Bates. Bates won't take no for an answer. He picked the fight with Crane, backed up by two of his bully-fiends. However, Crane is a big fellow and the two bullies chickened out, leaving Bates to face Crane solo."

"I know the rest, " I interrupted, "Bates took a licking and ducked out threatening to come back with a gun."

"That's right," Tony concurred. "I talked to Bates earlier and he claims he doesn't have a gun."

I decided not to tell Tony about the holiday incident, thanked him for his assistance, and made arrangements to talk to Bates.

Lamar entered the office I was waiting in and sprawled on a chair across from me. He was of average height and weight for his age, dark skinned and fairly muscular.

"Lamar, it seems you're in some hot water," I began.

"Nothin' ah can't handle," he countered.

"You didn't seem to handle it too well yesterday."

"That ol' boy got lucky." He answered sitting up in the chair.

"Like you got lucky last Thanksgiving when that shot you fired didn't hit anyone," I said quickly.

"Ah, didn't intend to hit anyone," he replied, obviously shaken.

"Where'd you get that gun?"

"At a hock-shop on Dorr Street."

"What'd you pay for it?"

"Twenty bucks."

"Where's the gun now?"

"I done threw it away."

"Where."

"Down by Swan Creek, back-a-da school."

"I'll let you in on something Lamar, I'm assigned all the tough cases at Scott, Libbey, and Devilbiss High Schools," I lied, "because the student bodies are predominantly black. I understand and work with youths like you every day. Now, I know that if you paid twenty bucks for something, you're not going to throw it away. I know better than that." This part was true.

"And I'll tell you something else," I continued, "You have a temper and one of these times you're going to really lose it. You're going to get that gun and use it and end up in prison. Then, not I nor anyone else will be able to help you. It will be too late."

Lamar nodded; he was listening.

"Now, I'll tell you what I'm going to do. You give that gun to me and I'll make this fight with David Crane go away. If I don't get that gun, I'll make it look like the biggest rumble that ever happened at Libbey and you'll probably go to court. What's it going to be?"

"Ah, doesn't wanna get nobody else inta trouble."

"You don't have to worry about that, I promise you."

At his direction, I drove Lamar to a house in the 1200 block of Oakwood; I waited in the car. He approached the house and a woman responded to his rapping. He gave her a brief greeting, brushed by her and entered. Obviously bewildered, she hovered in the doorway.

Seconds later, Lamar emerged with a small carton in his hand. He mumbled something to the confused woman and got back into my unmarked car.

The carton contained a 7.65 mm Beretta pistol, a clip, fourteen rounds and a cleaning brush.

I drove Lamar back to Libbey High, then headed for the office.

The captain was sitting at his desk when I entered his office and I dropped the Beretta in the middle of his blotter.

"There's the gun which the dicks never got in that Thanksgiving Day fracas," I declared proudly. I then set the carton with the other items in it next to the gun.

"Nice work!" my supervisor marveled. "You'll get a commendation for this."

But I never did!

THE WARNING SHOT

"Unit 12: Hoag and Hamilton; burglary in progress at a gas station." The Dispatcher's voice was brisk over the police radio.

"Unit 12, O.K.," I answered.

My partner, Officer Bill Marsh, accelerated the aging wagon and within three minutes we were there. The gas station had three bays and the one closest to the main entrance had a hole in the glass large enough for entry. I carefully climbed through the broken glass and found myself high-lighted by a large neon sign which was on the office wall and was the sole light in the building.

Taking cover behind a large mobile tool chest I looked for my partner to enter, but he was no where in sight. A back-up crew arrived, then Bill joined them as they all headed for the rear of the building outside.

There were three cars in the station; one in each bay. Suddenly, I observed an Army fatigue cap travel across the top of the furthest vehicle; I couldn't see who was wearing it.

I also spotted a large carton in the far corner full of shop cloths. In an attempt to scare the burglar and to possibly make him surrender, I decided to fire a shot into the carton. Cocking the hammer on my Colt revolver I carefully took aim and squeezed the trigger. CLICK! The cartridge failed to fire!

A dull, rustling noise at the rear of the car nearest to me drew my attention. My flashlight revealed the burglar crawling on his stomach, attempting to reach the broken window he had entered through.

"Come out before I perforate you," I ordered, aiming my revolver at him. Why I used the word perforate, I'll never know.

A tall, white male stood erect, with his hands raised. He was wearing a complete U.S. Army fatigue uniform. I ordered him to empty his pockets on a counter in the office. He laid out a small amount of change, several used tools and several packs of cigarettes; all looted from the station.

As I was handcuffing the thief, Bill entered through the broken window.

"Where the hell have you been?" I demanded to know.

"We went around to the back," Bill, answered, "We thought he'd run out a rear door, but there is no rear door."

While booking the perpetrator, he stated that he had attended an army reserve meeting before breaking into the gas station. He had no prior police record.

Apparently, he was never aware of my "misfire" and until now neither did anyone else have knowledge about my, "Warning Shot."

CHAPTER 13

TALES NEVER TOLD

EPISODES

1. A DEAF EAR

2. A GRAVESIDE VISIT

3. PAPER FOR WILLY

4. HOT PURSUIT

5. THE AFTERMATH OF ONE CRIME

6. THE WAREHOUSE ARREST

7. WHO NEEDS PRACTICE

8. THE FLASHLIGHT INCIDENT

9. THE FAST DRAW

10. THE CASE OF SHORTS

11. THE JINXED PISTOL

12. THE IMPOSTOR

13. IN THE NAME OF TRUST

A DEAF EAR

Highland Park in South Toledo is frequented by many children during the summer to swim in its large pool. Swan Creek also winds through the park and though some kids will swim in the creek occasionally, it was not advisable because the water was black, filthy and full of debris.

One day as Officer Bill Marsh and I were patrolling in the park along the creek, two young boys approached us. One stated that while they were throwing rocks into the creek another boy fell in and submerged and only bubbles came up where the boy had sunk.

The boys showed us the place where the mishap supposedly occurred. We were skeptical and questioned the boy at length. We ran each fact by the second boy for confirmation and he kept shaking his head in agreement with his friend's statements. Because both boys concurred, we decided to take them at their word.

The dispatcher was informed and a sergeant was sent to the scene. The fire department was alerted and they sent a rescue squad with a small rowboat and equipment to drag the creek in the area where the alleged victim was last seen.

People were stopping in their cars to see what the excitement was about. The spectators became so numerous that another crew was summoned for crowd control. It was like a circus.

The day was hot and humid as the firemen labored steadily in their heavy gear. After dragging the dark waters for a long while they were soaked with sweat and all that surfaced was an old tire, a boot and some soggy logs.

Then two women approached me, identifying themselves as the Mothers of the two youthful complainants. They were concerned because the boys had been away from their homes most of the day.

"I'm especially worried about, Harvey," one Mother exclaimed, "You know, being deaf as he is, I'm always afraid that something will happen to him."

Bill and I looked at each other. We realized that the boy who seemingly collaborated everything his friend said didn't really have a clue about what we were talking about. He was totally deaf! That's why he merely kept nodding his head.

We had played it safe in case the incident was true but now we were certain that the whole thing was a figment of the one boy's imagination. Our problem now was if anyone else found out, especially the firemen, we'd look pretty bad and probably catch hell.

The firemen called it quits. The two Mothers took their sons home. The reporters had already talked to the boys and apparently were duped into believing that they had acted in good faith, not realizing the one boy's handicap either.

The next day the story was in the newspaper with pictures of the kids, the sergeant and myself. To this day no one knows the real facts except Bill and me and a kid who had a big imagination.

A GRAVESIDE VISIT

Reading the "dope" to the patrolmen at roll call was one of my duties as a patrol sergeant. One summer day, on second shift, a report related that several grave markers were vandalized in Calvary Cemetery before dark the prior day.

The cemetery was on my district. As soon as I was free to patrol, I drove to the Parkside Street entrance and cruised throughout the burial grounds. All was serene with no evidence of vandals, so I decided to visit my Mother's grave, but stayed longer than I had intended. When I drove back to the gate, I found it secured with a chain and padlock.

I was in a quandary but I knew of a solution. The caretaker lived on Eastern Ave. across from my sister's house, but I needed to get to a phone.

Leaving my marked cruiser parked out of sight, I climbed over a wall, and walked to the corner of Parkside and Dorr where I used the police call box. I asked the dispatcher to have Sergeant Barnes, who was working the adjoining district, to meet me. He was a trusted friend and I knew he'd be discreet.

The sergeant arrived in short time. I related my situation to him, as we drove to a fire barn from where I called my sister. She agreed to contact the caretaker and have him return to the cemetery to unlock the gate.

Meanwhile, if a call came in for either Sgt. Barnes or myself, we could respond to it together; that was no problem. The hazard was if we both got calls simultaneously; that would be difficult to deal with.

Fortunately, neither one of us received any calls. The caretaker returned in good time and all ended well. In fact, the caretaker was elated that the police were watching the cemetery so closely.

Gates to Calvary Cemetery on Parkwood, which were locked while the author
was on the grounds with his patrol car.

PAPER FOR WILLY

A veteran officer named Clyde Cook and myself were working days and were assigned to fill-in on 11 Scout on a warm, summer day. The district covered the heart of the inner city.

Cook was of medium height and build, about thirty-five with a lot of dark hair. He had a reputation for being stubborn and insisting on doing things his way. He was a no-nonsense officer, with no sense of humor.

After having coffee at one of the drive-ins on district, we decided to attempt to serve several warrants which were issued to us.

One was for Willy Jones on a charge of assault and battery. The plaintiff was his wife, Ruby Jones. According to the warrant, he was known to hang around the "Cold Spot", a bar on Avondale at Division. It was a trouble spot most evenings and weekends and the scene of numerous shootings and mayhem. However, there usually wasn't much action there during the daytime.

According to departmental policy, both officers of a crew were to serve a warrant together. At residences, one officer would go to the rear while the other approached the front entrance with the warrant. When a business was involved, it depended upon the building. There was a locked, chain-link fence around the back of the Cold Spot which would call for both officers to enter the front entrance together.

Cook stopped the cruiser in front of the bar and got out with the warrant in hand. I began to exit when he motioned for me to remain in the car. I started to protest the violation of policy but re-thought it. He was the senior officer, whether right or wrong. In less than three minutes Cook returned to the car. "Not there." He announced. We resumed patrol.

I looked at the photo of Jones on the warrant. He was a black male, 5'9", weighing 140 pounds, no scars or distinguishing marks but he had a pair of ears like open doors on a pick-up truck.

After lunch, Cook relinquished the wheel and I drove. About two in the afternoon we were cruising down Avondale when I observed a man rolling a tire in the street.

"That's him," I exclaimed.

"Who?" Cook asked, bewildered.

"Jones," I retorted as I pulled up beside the man with the tire.

"How do you know?" Cook persisted.

"His ears," I replied.

"Hey, Willy," I called aloud.

The man stopped.; a combined expression of surprise and suspicion was etched upon his face.

"Get in the car," I ordered.

"My ol' lady ain't got paper out on me again has she?" Willy whined as he climbed into the rear seat.

"You guessed it." I handed him the warrant as the cruiser rolled forward.

"Man, this thing is dated yesterday," Willy complained.

"So what?" Cook came to life.

"Well, then why didn't ya pick me up when yo' was in the Cold Spot this mornin'? I'd been out by now. I can't get bonded out now 'til morning and I'll have to spend the night in the lock-up. Damn.

Cook was startled, but he didn't say a word.

In fact, I doubt if Cook ever mentioned the incident to anyone.

HOT PURSUIT

On a summer, July evening in the '60's, the command of the third shift apparently anticipated a busy night. Instead of walking assignments, Officer Albert Jensen and myself were assigned to an extra car; our call number was X-10 and our patrol area was the Old West End.

The only car available was a black 1955 Ford with a white stripe on each side and over 220,000 miles recorded on its' odometer. It was almost midnight when I took the wheel and we headed towards West Toledo.

Jensen was tall and lean, wearing a bushy, brown mustache. It was said that although he had a high I.Q. , he'd unexpectedly do something unusual and seemed to lack common sense

We were traveling West on Delaware when we observed two cars drag-racing South on Collingwood at a high rate of speed. Before we could obtain a clock on their speed, they stopped for a red light at W. Woodruff. In an attempt to avoid detection, I drove into a gas station on the Northeast corner, but when the light turned green, both cars started off slowly, so we knew that they had spotted us.

When the cars reached Monroe Street, side by side, they turned in opposite directions. I was about to pursue the West bound car, which had two occupants, but Al insisted that I follow the East bound car, which had a lone driver.

We attempted to pull him over as we approached Macomber High School at 16th. Street, but he sped away and a chase was on. I told Al to contact the dispatcher and inform him of our activity and he took the "mike" from the dashboard.

Our suspect turned from Monroe, North on to Michigan, which was one-way South, sped through the intersection of Jefferson, then abruptly turned West onto Madison, which was one-way West.

Our red lights and siren were flashing and blaring as the suspect passed 17th. Street and reached the Jefferson Street Extension. I managed to pull along his left side and sharply turned my steering wheel to the right, sideswiping the moving auto. However, he managed to pull ahead and I sensed that he was about to try to ram us back. I slammed on our brakes and the suspect went flying by the front of our vehicle, over a curb and back onto Monroe Street, fleeing in a Westerly direction.

Our aged cruiser had stalled and the motor was steaming. As I worked the starter I saw that Al was still holding the "mike" in his hand and had not said a word into it. "For crying-out-loud," I shouted, "Get hold of the dispatcher!"

Al finally found his voice and called the dispatcher.

Miraculously, the motor cranked over and I revved our speed up until we were just behind our errant driver as he crashed the red light at W. Bancroft and then Detroit Avenue, both large and busy intersections. The only reason he made it through them was the effect of our lights and siren behind him. The suspect continued on Monroe through red lights at Cardinal and Auburn, the latter being a busy street, too.

As the culprit approached N. Cove, he encountered a roadblock set up by 9 Scout; ignoring it, he circumvented the obstructing police car as an officer fired a round from a shotgun at the side of the fleeing auto.

The suspect vehicle veered to the right, jumped a high curb, sideswiped a large tree and bounced back on to the street. The car was motionless as sparks spewed from its under- carriage.

I jumped from the exhausted police cruiser and hurried to the side of the suspect's auto. A young man had a stern grip on the steering wheel and was rocking back and forth in a futile effort to get the car moving again. My adrenaline was flowing and my temples were pounding . The driver's window was open and without hesitation I struck the driver in his face with my right fist; jerked the door open, hauled him out of the car and handcuffed him.

"Is this a stolen car?" I demanded to know.

"Yeah." the suspect admitted, "and so was the other one my buddies were in."

"Where'd you take the car from?" I persisted.

"From the launder mat at Central and Detroit"

I knew where he meant. He was turned over to a wagon crew for transportation to the Safety Building jail for booking.

Al and I drove to the launder mat in the 800 block of W. Central and sitting in front of the building, in question, was another stolen car.

I was never reprimanded for striking the suspect. I don't think the command was ever aware of it and admittedly, I never regretted it. One can't turn the flow of adrenalin off like a tap and it's most difficult to regain your cool and to calm down, when you realize the stupid actions of some jerk could have caused you and your partner serious injury or death. Yet, that is expected of police officers and they do comply in the name of professionalism. However, in this case I failed.

Ironically, the patrolman who fired the shotgun was chewed out at the scene by our shift captain, but nothing more came of it.

I believe that Officer Jensen's "mike fright" was caused by the chaotic pursuit we were involved in. It's no easy task to sit on the passenger side of a police car in a hot pursuit, racing at high speeds through intersections against red lights, most times not knowing who you are chasing or the exact reason why. All you know is that your life is in your partner's hands and that both of your lives are on the line. Believe me, it's scary!

THE AFTERMATH OF ONE CRIME

It was a lazy, Fall afternoon, when four young youths decided to heist a store in a mall on Manhattan Blvd. As they drove away, the driver was careful to obey all traffic laws and maintained a modest rate of speed. However, in spite of their caution, a police car began to tail them.

Officers Frank Boise and Robert Martin were alerted by a police broadcast of a robbery committed by four black males, but there was no description of a car. They observed a car containing four black males and decided to follow it. Ironically, the fact that the suspect's driving was so prudent fueled their suspicions.

Suddenly, two of the occupants rolled the rear windows down, extended firearms and began shooting at the marked police vehicle. Their accuracy being less than desired, the driver greatly increased his speed as the police pursued. Unable to elude the officers, the youths abandoned the car on a side street and fled on foot. Again the two officers pursued.

Officer Boise practiced pistol marksmanship regularly and was considered a good shot, but emptied his six-shot revolver at the fleeing youths in vain.

Officer Martin wasn't fond of firearms and only practiced when it was mandatory. He took aim at the only youth he could see running away and when he recovered from the recoil of the shot the young man was lying on the ground in a heap. Martin ran to the fallen criminal and to his dismay, he was unconscious and not breathing.

The 18 year old felon's death was ruled justifiable and Officer Martin was returned to active duty.

The three survivors were tried in Common Pleas Court. The highlight of the case was when the defense attorney was questioning Officer Boise. " When did you and your partner determine that the youths you were following were suspicious.?"

"When they rolled down their car windows and began shooting at us." Boise, calmly replied.

The three robbers were convicted.

Robert Martin and I lived in the same neighborhood and a few days after the shooting, he approached me as I was cutting my lawn. "Can I talk to you for a minute, Jim?"

"Sure, Bob, what can I do for you?" I shut down the lawn mower to listen.

"I can't get that teenager out of my mind. I keep thinking of his poor family and the hurt his death must have caused."

I thought for a moment, then said: "Bob, you're not to blame. If that boy had his head on right, he wouldn't have been involved in a crime. What's more, he's the one who decided to open fire on the police. Also, instead of running away, he could have given up peacefully. He was the one who made the wrong choices.

As far as you're concerned, you did what you were trained and expected to do. You did nothing wrong."

Bob was listening, but he didn't seem convinced.

"Ask yourself this, Bob: Would you rather it had been you who was killed? It could have been, you know. You have your wife and kids to think about and a lot to live for. Sure, it may take some time, but I'm sure you'll get it behind you."

"I'm sure you're right, Jim;" Bob, took a deep breath, " I know it's going to take time, but I should be able to work it out eventually. Thanks, Jim, you've been a big help."

In due time, Officer Martin was assigned to the detective bureau, where he finished his distinguished career. As far as I know, he is still among the living.

THE WAREHOUSE ARREST

A hole large enough to admit a car was blown in the side of a South End warehouse. While the dust was still settling, two police crews and a sergeant arrived in response to the silent alarm.

A search of the entire interior was conducted. The sergeant even sent an officer to check the top of the box-like structure that was used as an office; to no avail.

"The thugs have to be in here somewhere," the sergeant declared, "we got here too fast for them to have gotten away."

Another search, conducted with a police dog, was also in vain.

Desperate, the sergeant sent another officer to check the top of the office structure again and behold! There, lying on their bellies in plain sight were two black burglars. There was nothing for them to hide behind.. There was no reason for the first officer to miss seeing them. The only difference is that the first officer was black and the second officer was white.

The burglars were arrested and transported to jail.

WHO NEEDS TO PRACTICE

Officer Stan Rafferty was a legend in his own time; it was well known that in his prime, he was involved in shootings with the infamous Purple Gang, out of Detroit, Michigan. According to popular hearsay, Stan eradicated two of their members, in as many shootings.

Now an aging, veteran officer, Stan had great difficulty hitting any of the targets at the Toledo Police Pistol Range. One day, while at practice, he inadvertently fired a shot into the ground very close to his own feet.

The command officer in charge of the range was a strict disciplinarian and not only admonished Stan, but had him barred from using the range. This certainly was overkill, but things were a lot different then.

Stan, looking forward to retirement, responded: "What do I care. Who needs to practice?"

While I was Commandant of the Toledo Police Academy there was a young recruit I'll call Ella Mae Cooper. She was barely 5 feet tall and had to weigh less than 100 pounds. Her issued .38 cal. Smith & Wesson revolver, holstered on her hip, hung almost to her knee. She could barely hold the gun out in front of her even with both hands. Her marksmanship was terrible; needless to say she failed to qualify with the .38 cal. revolver; thus she would not be graduating with her class.

With graduation less than two weeks away, I received an order from the chief of police to re-train her with the revolver. In an attempt to coach her personally, I discovered that her problem was her lack of strength in her arms and hands; she was just too weak to control the weapon well enough to fire it accurately.

Ordinarily a remedy would be for the cadet to perform exercises to increase arm strength, such as holding a dumbbell at arms length for an allotted time; increasing the weight and the time period. However, for results this program would have to be employed for several weeks or months. In Ella's case there was no time for such tactics.

My staff did the best they could and Ella tried valiantly, but there was no measurable improvement in her marksmanship. Again I recommended that she be disqualified. To my amazement I was overruled and she was allowed to graduate with her class.

THE FLASHLIGHT INCIDENT

Working 8 Scout in West Toledo, my partner was driving when we spotted four men in an automobile which had been reported stolen. The dispatcher was informed, but when we attempted to stop the car, the driver sped away and we chased them, as nightfall descended.

Trying to elude us, the driver turned into an alley which dead-ended. We pursued and when the driver realized there was no way to exit the alley he skidded to a stop in an unfenced yard. The four suspects fled the vehicle and raced through the yard and left of the house at the front of the lot and then down the adjacent street, to the right.

My partner followed them directly, but seeing that the culprits headed to the right, I ran to the right of the house in an effort to cut them off. When I reached the front corner of the house one of the felons doubled back and ran squarely into me. I had a three-cell flashlight in my right hand and when we collided I struck him in the face with it, out of reflex.

With my left hand, I then gripped his pant belt in the small of his back which is a method of control and escorted him towards the police cruiser. My lieutenant arrived just as I approached my squad car with my prisoner.

"Your officer hit me in the mouth with a flashlight," the captured man complained to the lieutenant. I flashed my light on his mouth and his lips were bleeding.

The lieutenant was one of those command officers who loved to put patrolmen on report. He looked at me sternly for an explanation.

I knew that if I eluded in any way that I had struck the man deliberately, he'd file charges against me. I looked him in the eye and said: "He ran right into me lieutenant; I had my flashlight in my hand and he ran right into it. It was accidental."

The lieutenant's face told me that he didn't really believe me, but my explanation was feasible. **In all honesty, I did not hit him deliberately.** The collision was like an attack; it was sudden and unexpected and my reaction was simply my reflexes responding in self defense. There were no witnesses and I heard nothing more about it.

THE FAST DRAW

I'm not sure when it was marketed, but there was a revolver holster called the "Clamshell." It was called that because the front of it was spring-loaded and when a release button was pressed it sprung open, not unlike a clam.

139

The advantage of it was that once a revolver was encased in it the weapon couldn't be removed without activating the button, therefore no one could grab an officer's gun by surprise.

However there was a real disadvantage in that the release button was positioned in front of the gun's trigger. To remove the revolver an officer had to press the button with his "trigger finger" which then would be right on the trigger. Under duress an officer could easily discharge the weapon while in the act of drawing it.

Patrolman Paul Williams, wearing a clamshell holster, was dispatched to a home on report of a youth with a gun. Upon arrival Paul was approaching the house when a young lad stepped out from behind a tree holding a gun in his hand.

Paul immediately went for his revolver, but while drawing it the gun discharged, sending a bullet through his right calf.

At the same time Paul's adversary tried to shoot him, but the punk's gun didn't function. Although wounded, the officer managed to subdue his attacker and handcuff him.

What may have saved Officer Williams life is that the gun the youngster possessed was a .32 caliber pistol loaded with .22 caliber cartridges with tape wrapped around them.

THE CASE OF SHORTS

The Buckeye Brewery was on 4 Patrol's district along Bush Street. The employees were very accommodating to the public, in general, as well as to policeman.

Brewery drivers backed their trucks up to a dock and unloaded their empty kegs. The kegs were taken into a large room where they were inspected and if they didn't need to be relined, were washed and conveyed into the "tap" room where they were refilled.

Along one side of the large keg room were two taps built right into the wall and just about anyone who knew about them seemed welcome to imbibe.

Assigned to 4 Patrol with Joe Manning, we were working the second shift and while passing by the brewery about 9 P.M., we observed an employee smoking on the dock. We stopped to chit-chat with him and he asked us if we were interested in a case of shorts.

"Shorts? What are they?" we asked.

"They're bottles that weren't filled to the top; most of them are hardly lacking, but we can't sell them." the fellow explained.

"Hell, yes," Joe responded, "We'll be glad to take one off your hands."

The fellow brought a case out to us and I placed it under one of the bench seats in the rear of the wagon where police gear was kept.

We thanked the guy and left. Joe drove the short distance to Riverside Park (Now the "Jamie Farr Park") We stopped on the road along the river and I got a couple of "shorts" out and Joe and I enjoyed a cold beer.

I can't explain how both, Joe and I, completely forgot about the case of shorts in the wagon when we were relieved of duty. All night long I kept envisioning the crew who relieved us discovering the beer in the wagon. Or if not them, the crew coming on after them. I had no idea how we could explain it to our shift captain.

Reluctantly and full of anxiety I reported for duty the next afternoon. Roll call went smoothly; no one was told to report to the captain. Joe and I hurried to relieve the crew on 4 Patrol and nothing was said.

As soon as the day officers left, Joe and I checked the rear compartment of the wagon and to our amazement the case of shorts was still there; warm, but intact.

"How can that be?" Joe wondered.

"Don't ask me. I'm stunned. I can't believe that both crews missed it."

"Well, let's get the hell out of here while we can," Joe concluded , as he hopped into the driver's seat.

We both lived in Point Place which was North of our district, so we made tracks to Joe's house, where he deposited half of the bottles. Then we went the short distance to my house where I took the case with the remaining bottles.

I'll never know how we got away with it: If both crews saw the case and ignored it or if they failed to check the police gear before going on patrol. It's anyone's guess.

I do know that this incident was never revealed before now.

THE JINXED PISTOL

Patrolman Joe Langdon needed a weapon to carry while off duty. He checked out a hock-shop and found just what he wanted: a Walther 7.65 mm, semi-automatic pistol that had the unique feature of being double-action. That means the weapon's hammer did not have to be cocked, before firing it. With a round in the chamber all one had to do was squeeze the trigger to fire the gun.

Joe's wife, Lois was expecting. The evening of the birth Joe was elated and relieved. Working the third shift, without a day off over a nine day stretch, he was wound-up like a two-bit watch and felt like he was going to burst.

From the hospital Joe went to the Hillcrest Hotel where he knew the bartender, Leo Hamilton. After too long of a time and too many drinks, Joe was feeling no pain.

"Joe, let me put you up here at the hotel," Leo offered. "You can crash in my room."

Joe wanted to but he told Leo: "No. I want to get home."

Driving North on Huron at Lagrange Street, Joe saw the proprietor of the Band Box closing up. Usually a rowdy place, it was quiet that week night and Joe decided to stop for one more drink. The owner obliged him, but Joe wanted another and the owner wanted to leave; an argument ensued and continued outside the bar.

Several men emerged from a building across the street. Joe recognized them as professional gamblers. Knowing they were friends of the bar owner, Joe feared he was in for a beating, so he drew his pistol and ordered the gamblers back into their roost.

From the outside, Joe slammed the door shut and left. He was afraid to chance driving now so he went to Johnnies Coffee Shop several doors down Lagrange Street and ordered a cup of black coffee.

He never finished it. Apparently the gamblers called the police and a sergeant had a crew drive Joe home and placed him on report for "Conduct Unbecoming an Officer" and "Drunk and Disorderly." The sergeant confiscated the Walther pistol.

The Chief gave Joe a 15 day suspension without pay. He also returned his gun.

Nothing was ever said or done about the group of gamblers' illegal activities.

Joe had a strange feeling that the off duty gun had brought him bad luck. He had bad vibes concerning the Walther.

A mechanic who owned a garage in the South end had done some work on Joe's car. About a month later he demanded that the bill be paid immediately. With a large family to support and the poor police salary, Joe was strapped.

"Tell you what," Joe, told the mechanic, "I'll give you something in trade."

After examining the Walther pistol the mechanic agreed. "We're even."

Several weeks later, Joe was passing the garage in his private car and observed an ambulance at the house next door where the mechanic lived.

Joe stopped and made a discreet inquiry. "Yeah, it's a strange case," the ambulance driver related, "the guy committed suicide with a foreign handgun and according to his family his business was doing good and he had everything to live for. They can't think of a single reason why he did it."

THE IMPOSTOR

The Hub Bar where the author arrested a man for impersonating a State Liquor Agent.

The Hub Bar located at N. St. Clair and Jackson was a quiet, place with a serene atmosphere. Once in awhile I'd stop in after work to say hello to the owner and to have a quiet beer. I always paid for my drinks there and didn't expect anything for nothing.

One evening I stopped by and the owner informed me that there was a Liquor Agent present. He pointed out a tall, athletic-looking, white male, about 30 with a receding hairline, standing in front of the juke box.

"Hi," I said, as I approached him. "My name is Jim and I'm a Toledo cop. I understand that you're an AT&F Agent (Alcohol, Tobacco & Firearms Bureau)

He smiled, "Yeah, just call me Steve."

We sat at the bar and ordered beers. I pulled out my wallet and Steve nudged me, "Don't be so quick with the money. These places are always glad to spring for drinks for law men."

"Is that so?" I replied.

Sure enough, the bartender set two beers with two glasses in front of us and waved me off as I tried to pay for them.

"You're not local are you?"

"No, I'm out of Cleveland and I'm here on a special assignment."

"Where are you staying at in town?" I asked matter-of-factly.

"At the Howard Hotel on Madison."

That was a wrong answer. From what I knew agents usually stayed at the Secor Hotel at Superior and Jefferson, a much classier place.

"You know, Steve, I collect badges for a hobby. (I lied.) I'd like to see yours."

Steve hesitated and his face paled. "I may have left it at the hotel," he answered, as he patted his breast pocket in vain.

"Do you know what, Steve? I think you're as phony as a six dollar bill."

The man stood up and glared down at me, "I'm 6'2" and weigh 200 pounds."

Staying seated, I looked up at him and said, "The hardest I've ever been knocked on my ass was by a guy 5'8", when I was in the Marine Corps."(This was true.)

The man sunk back into his seat and crumpled like a deflated balloon.

I grabbed him by one of his arms, placed him under arrest and escorted him to the call box right outside of the bar's front door. A wagon was summoned and he went to jail on a charge of "Impersonating a Law Enforcement Officer."

When I informed the bar owner, he expressed his surprise, but never bothered to thank me for exposing the impostor. I never patronized that bar again.

The crook apparently pleaded guilty, because I was never subpoenaed. Later on I got feed back that the judge let him off with a slap on the wrist because he said he was drunk and didn't know what he was doing.

And there was another fine example of justice in action!

IN THE NAME OF TRUST

In 1965, while working uniform patrol on 18 Scout on the 2nd. Shift, I suffered a staph infection across the small of my back right where my gun belt was worn.

I was in misery, but I discovered that if I sat oblique in the scout car with my back lodged between the back of the seat and the car door, it took the pressure off and was bearable. If I could get rid of the gun belt it would be even more endurable.

I contacted the chief of police: "I really hate to use any sick time, chief, and if I could wear a shoulder holster until the infection clears up I think I can remain on duty."

"I find that commendable officer, but of course you'll have to carry your regular service revolver."

"Absolutely, chief. I'd never work patrol carrying a revolver with less than a 4" barrel. Also, I have a shoulder holster for that size revolver. Thank you very much, Sir."

The following afternoon I reported for work and the shoulder holster made a great difference. About 6: 30 PM my partner and I had reason to go to the Detective Bureau. While there I observed that the chief was on board.

After our business was completed and we started to leave, the chief called to me. As I approached him he said, "Let's see it."

"See what?" I asked.

"Your revolver," he replied.

Then I realized that it was no coincidence that he was at the Detective Bureau. He was there to make sure that I wasn't carrying a snub-nose revolver with a 2" barrel. I was crushed . . . apparently, he didn't trust me.

"I told you that I wouldn't carry less than a 4" barrel on patrol," I reminded him.

"I know, I want to see it."

I decided to play his game: I faltered a bit and acted hesitant, as if he had caught me "red handed".

"Let's see it now." He demanded.

I then pulled out my service revolver, opened the cylinder and handed it to him butt first.

He quickly examined it. Showing no emotion he handed it back to me.

He then left without saying a word.

I was angry. I lied to my partner that my back was killing me.

"Hey, Sarge, you're going to have to get a replacement for me on 18 scout; my back is in agony."

"O.K. Jim. You can leave now if you want; I'll credit you with half-a-day."

I thanked the sergeant and left. I stayed off work until my back was completely healed. So much for TRUST.

CHAPTER 14

HUMOR OUT OF UNIFORM

EPISODES

OFFICER "MOM"

In the '50s when a woman had a baby, it was a week's stay at the hospital. I would always arrange for time off and while my wife was hospitalized, I'd take care of the household chores.

We had a ringer-washer but no dryer. The clothes were washed in the basement and hung on a line outdoors during warm weather.

While my wife was in the hospital for the birth of one of our children, I was doing the wash and had a load to hang out. I was carrying a basket of wet clothes through the kitchen when the phone rang. I set the basket down on the floor and answered the phone When I finished the call I forgot about the basket and fell backwards over it landing smack on my behind. At first I was annoyed then I began to laugh realizing the silliness of the situation.

If that wasn't bad enough, while I was hanging the clothes on a line, a utility man was working high on a telephone pole at the rear of my yard.

"Can you bake a cherry pie, too?" he chortled.

"As a matter of fact I can," I replied. Then shaking out one of my uniform shirts so he could see the police patches, I said, "There are a lot of things I can do." He didn't find anything more to chortle about after that.

TO CANADA IN STYLE

For many years the Toledo Police Revolver Club competed in pistol matches with members of the London, Ontario, Police Department. The matches were the nucleus of grand festivities and camaraderie among the officers which will never be forgotten.

For the record, we were better marksmen, only losing one match in ten years but the "Canucks" could out-drink us any day of the week. At a stag banquet in honor of the first match in London, I drank a beverage called Indian Ale. The alcoholic content was 12% by volume. After I consumed the second bottle I swear my toes tingled.

Each Toledo Officer had to pay all of his own expenses in connection with the matches and attend the weekend affair on his own time. To reduce travel expenses, we car-pooled.

For travel to the second Canadian match, Patrolman Alan Ferry borrowed a new pearl-white Lincoln sedan from a car dealer. Five of us went to London in style.

We decided to reach Canada via the Ambassador Bridge from Detroit to Windsor. Gasoline was more expensive in Canada so we topped-off the tank in Detroit before crossing the bridge.

On the return trip the tank was nearly empty as we approached the United States. We didn't want to gas up until we got back to Detroit. Alas, it appeared that we were not going to make it. The needle was at the bottom of the gas gauge and we dreaded running dry on the extensive Ambassador Bridge.

Just in time, we spotted a gas station within sight of the bridge. Alan was driving and pulled up to a pump. The attendant came to the driver's window and Alan, with a perfectly straight face, ordered: "Fifty cents worth, please."

The rest of us were humiliated and wanted to hide our faces!

However, we reached Detroit and filled the tank there. Who said cops are cheap? The word is frugal !

Jim and his lovely wife MaryAnn at a banquet and pistol match awards ceremony in
Toledo in June 1959

A group of American and Canadian police officers pose at the London Ontario Police indoor range. The author is third from the right, Circa 60's

THE CAPTAIN'S DRIVE

Promoted to lieutenant, I was assigned to Captain Robert Gray's * shift.

Every command officer on the shift played golf except me. One day, the captain invited me to play golf with him and Lt. Cloyce Kirk*, so I borrowed an old set of clubs from a friend and hit some practice balls the day before we were to play.

Arriving at Collins Park in East Toledo, prior to Gray and Kirk, I was wearing jeans, a tee shirt, a ball cap and sneakers. They appeared shortly afterwards. Gray was wearing a colorful golf shirt and a golf cap, both bearing logos, with white golf shoes and trousers with an outrageous checkered pattern. Kirk was dressed similarly with flashy, striped trousers. They reminded me of General Douglas McArthur and his Aide de Camp arriving in pomp and ceremony.

The first fairway paralleled a city street on the right. They insisted that I hit-off first; so in a state of anxiety, I took a 3 iron, teed up and hit a decent drive which rolled just off the right of the fairway. Kirk's ball ended up next to mine.

The captain hit a long drive, but it sliced and landed in the middle of the street, then bounced off the cement and into the side of a car being polished by its' owner in a driveway and then rolled into the man's garage.

Captain Gray looked towards Kirk and me, as if he expected one of us to retrieve his ball. Kirk avoided the captain's stare by looking through his golf bag for some unknown item and I was busy scanning the sky for UFO's. When he realized that neither of us was going to get his ball, he walked over to the man polishing the car and apologized. The man was very good about it and Gray then retrieved his ball from the man's garage.

So, my first experience on the links began with a hectic, although some-what humorous beginning. Then to top it off, when I got home, I discovered that the head of the driver of the set of golf clubs I had borrowed was cracked. It's a wonder that it didn't fly off when I used it.

Eventually, Captain Bob Gray and I became partners in the Toledo Police Golf League and won top honors two different seasons.

THE YELLOW GOLF BALL

Hank Perry was a long-time city employee, whom worked at the police service station servicing police vehicles. He loved to play golf and Captain Gray invited him to play with Lt. Kirk and myself at Ottawa Hills Golf Course to make a foursome.

Hank proudly showed us a sleeve of his new golf balls. They were bright yellow and were new on the market at the time. "I shouldn't have any trouble finding these babies." Hank assured us.

During the course of play, we hit off on a hole with a narrow fairway. Hank hooked his drive, sending his yellow missile to the top of a small, grassy knoll left of the fairway. The rest of us had straight drives and walked to our golf balls lying ahead on the fairway. after the three of us hit our second shot, Hank was still on the hill searching for his ball. Puzzled as to why it was taking him so long to find the brightly colored sphere, we walked over to him. We all broke into laughter when we reached the top of the rise; it was densely covered with dandelions. The whole area was a blanket of yellow! That added up to one lost ball for Hank and a ribbing he endured for the rest of the outing.

A CLOSE CALL

My Father-In-Law was recovering from surgery in St. Vincent's Hospital, so I visited him. I was pleasantly surprised to find that the patient sharing his room was Scott Phillips, a Vice Officer. We had known each other for years. Scott was a heavy cigarette smoker and was in for a series of tests.

While I was sitting at my Father-In-Law's bedside, Scott's doctor came into the room. He was holding an X-Ray, which he spread on a lit wall-panel for Scott to see.

"Mr. Phillips, I have to break some serious news to you." We overheard his Doctor say. "A spot has been discovered on your left lung and I'm not sure exactly what it means. A nurse is on the way up with a machine to take more pictures of it. As soon as they're evaluated, we'll let you know the results." The doctor then left the room.

Immediately, Scott grabbed his pack of cigarettes from his bed stand and threw them in the waste basket by his bed. He then jumped out of his bed and went to his locker and extracted a carton of cigarettes and trashed them, too.

The nurse arrived and took more X-Rays of Scott's chest and left.

As I was getting ready to leave, Scott's doctor returned. "Great news, Mr. Phillips, those last pictures disclosed that the spot is only old scar tissue; nothing to worry about."

The doctor had hardly cleared the door, when Scott bounded from his bed, grabbed the waste basket and retrieved all the cigarettes from it; placing the carton back in his locker and putting the pack back on his night stand.

My Father-in-law and I shook our heads in disbelief.

THE GET-WELL GIFT

Captain Bill Oliver had been a strict sergeant, but as he advanced in rank, he mellowed and the men he commanded liked and respected him.

Being over sixty years of age, Captain Oliver was admitted to St. Vincent's Hospital for an unusual operation, at his age, but one that he had requested. He wanted to be circumcised.

He had tried to keep the reason for his hospitalization as quiet as possible, with no fanfare. When the surgical procedure went as well as could be expected, Bill was pleased; all he had to do now was to recuperate.

The next day he received a package through the mail; there was no sender listed on it. When Bill opened it, he found himself holding the latest issue of Playboy!

THE AUTOGRAPH

Martin Milner, the actor, has always been one of my favorite performers. We are the same age and I've followed his career from his early role in "Route 66" to his last appearances on "Murder She Wrote". His role of Officer Pete Malloy on "Adam 12" was my favorite.

One summer he was in a play with actor Kent McCord at Toledo's Masonic Theater on Heatherdowns. My daughter Charlene, age 16 at the time, asked me to get his autograph. "I'll do my best," I promised her.

After the play, Marty graciously came to the lobby to sign autographs and he was immediately surrounded by a throng of women, of all ages, at least three deep.

"It will take forever to get his autograph with that crowd," I bemoaned to my wife. We did not relish a long wait.

So, I stood at the outer edge of the bevy of women and in a loud voice I called: "Hey, Marty, do you sign autographs for men, too?"

The actor stopped in the middle of a signing and gave me a quizzical look. He finished his signature and approached me, snatched my program from my hand, autographed it and shoved it back to me. He didn't say a word, but I'll never forget the expression on his face; it was one of complete bewilderment. I'll never know what he was thinking at that time; maybe he thought I was queer. I didn't care. I thanked him, joined my wife and left; mission accomplished.

If by some quirk of fate, he should ever read this, I want him to know that my wife and I are still big fans and faithfully watch all the re-runs of , "Adam 12", to this day. To borrow a salutation from another famous actor, Marty: "Thanks for the memory!"

CHAPTER 15

BUCKING THE SYSTEM

EPISODES

1. HOLLOW-HEAD

2. FUTURE CAPTAINS

3. THE HIDDEN AGENDA

4. THE YELLOW CURB

5. PRELUDE TO THE SICK- FAMILY DAY

6. THE MIGHTY PEN

HOLLOW-HEAD

The Jackson Bar was downtown on the corner of Jackson and Superior Streets with a number of small businesses adjacent to it. On the second floor of the business next to the bar was a Dental Laboratory; a quantity of gold was kept there for use in making dentures.

The rear of the Dental Lab contained a row of windows overlooking the alley behind the businesses and a fire escape provided access to the roof and to those windows. Whenever I walked this beat I'd climb that fire escape and check the windows to the lab.

One evening on my first round, about 11:30 P.M., I discovered one of those windows ajar. There was no sign of a forced entry, so I fully opened the window and entered. Everything appeared to be in order. I found a phone number to call and contacted the owner who agreed to meet me there to secure the place.

I had no sooner contacted the Police Box Operator to let him know what I was doing when I heard a car screech to a halt in front of the building; followed by banging on the front door. It was Lt. Hollaman (known as "Hollow-head", to the patrolmen.)

The door was at the bottom of a long staircase, so I called down, "What do you want?"

"Come down here," he demanded.

When I got to the bottom of the stairs, he said, "Come out here."

" I' can't, the door is locked with a key."

"How did you get in?"

"Through a window on the roof."

"Come out here, " he insisted.

So, I climbed up the staircase, went out the window, over the roof, down the fire escape and around to the front of the building.

"Get in the car," he ordered. It had begun to rain.

"I've got the owner coming down to lock the place up," I protested.

"Never mind that. I need you to do traffic. Get into the car."

I had no choice. Once in the car, he informed me: "The theaters on St. Clair Street are about to let out and I expect a traffic jam. I want you to expedite traffic at the intersection of Jackson and St. Clair."

That was ridiculous. It was the last show and there was never a large audience.

Then he jerked as if he had been poked and blurted, "Why didn't you call for back-up?"

"No sign of a forced entry," I calmly replied.

"Some day, Moore, you'll be found dead going into places like that."

"Well, Lieutenant Hollaman, if so, it'll be because I was doing police work, not screwing around with a minor traffic detail." I retorted.

I had expected a sharp rebuke, but the lieutenant quietly stopped at the designated intersection, ordered me to get out and roared away.

Luckily, I had my raincoat stashed in a traffic signal control box at that very intersection. I donned it and waited. After the theaters emptied, it took less than five minutes to direct the few cars of theater patrons through the intersection.

I hit the call box on the corner and let the Box Operator know I was finished with the traffic assignment. I suspected that the lieutenant drummed up that assignment to impress someone, because there was no call for it.

Then a small man, shivering from the dampness, emerged from a doorway.

"Officer," he called, "I think I may be the victim of a ruse. A man saying he was a policeman called me and said my business place was - - "

"That was me, Sir. A window was left open. I was waiting for you when I was ordered to do traffic here." I explained.

I escorted the man to the Dental Lab and the he secured the building.

Afterwards, I thought, "They surely don't call Lieutenant Hollaman "Hollow-head" for nothing!"

The Dental Lab was located at this location, where Lt. Hollaman picked the author up to do traffic.

FUTURE CAPTAINS

Officer Frank Duncan and I were in the same police cadet class and after graduation; we were assigned to the same shift. One evening, we were slated to work together on Scout 14, a South End district.

Just before midnight, we were dispatched to a hit-skip accident in the 700 block of Segur Avenue. A car driven by a youth struck a parked car. The driver then stopped under a streetlight, got out and pulled the right front fender away from the wheel, then drove away.

Several residents on the block witnessed that scenario and noted the license number. We ran a check on the license and after the dispatcher gave us the owner's name and address, he stated that the driver was returning to the scene

Soon a black limousine appeared with a nervous youth, age sixteen, in the rear seat. The driver got out and introduced himself as a former Toledo City Manager.

"I was listening to my police radio and heard the broadcast of the accident. I then saw my neighbor's son drive his car into his garage with a flat tire. I convinced the lad to return to the scene with me, then informed the police. I expect that no charges will be filed against him."

Frank and I disagreed. "Well, Sir, there was damage to the parked car and the youth took time to pull out the fender before fleeing. We intend to cite him into Juvenile Court on two charges: Operating Without Due Regard for Safety and Leaving the Scene of a Non-injury Accident," Frank informed him.

"If he's a first offender the court is sure to be lenient on him anyway." I added.

The former city manager wasn't happy as he drove away with the cited youth.

"Hell, if it hadn't been for the X- Big Shot's intervention that punk would never have come forward on his own." Frank remarked to me.

I agreed and we considered the issue closed and resumed patrol.

About two o'clock in the morning, we had two carloads of young men stopped for racing through two red lights as they zoomed off the Anthony Wayne Bridge. We were issuing multiple citations to the drivers when Lt. Hollaman pulled up. He got out of his car and began to pace up and down as he waited for us to get clear.

The lieutenant approached us as we finished with the two errant drivers. As we suspected, he wanted us to drop the charges against the youth in the Segur Avenue accident.

We refused and gave him our stated reasons. Finally convinced that we wouldn't change our minds, the lieutenant whined, "Oh, I'll never make captain now."

"Look at it this way," I offered, "at least you made lieutenant. We'll probably never get any higher than patrolmen."

(Frank and I stuck to our guns. That was in 1954. Twenty-two years later we were both promoted to the rank of captain.)

THE HIDDEN AGENDA

At. 6 P.M. on a winter day, a man stopped his car in front of an attractive woman standing at Summit and 114ᵗʰ Street in North Toledo. He attempted to persuade her to get into his car, but when she refused he masturbated in front of her, then drove away.

When my rookie-partner and I arrived to interview her, she gave us the most complete and detailed description of the suspect and his car that I had ever experienced in my entire career.

"He was a white male, had a pale complexion, blond hair and blue eyes, about 6' tall, weighting about 150 pounds with a slim build, about 25 years old and had a weak chin with a small scar. He was wearing a blue shirt, dark blue trousers, a camel- hair topcoat, blue socks and brown wing-tipped shoes.

His car was a dark blue, 1964 two-door Ford, bearing Ohio license plates: 5550 E, with white-wall tires," she informed us.

"You understand that if the guy is arrested, you may have to appear in court as the plaintiff," I explained.

"I'll be glad to do it, officers," she assured us. "He was disgusting."

We obtained the man's name and address through a license check. We drove to his house about 6:40 P.M. where we observed a dark Ford in the garage bearing the furnished license number. Snow was melting from the hood, indicating that the car had been recently driven.

As we approached the house, I observed a light in the basement and peered through a window. A man fitting the complainant's description was standing in front of a workbench.

A young blond woman answered our knock. Yes, her husband was home. Yes, he came in a few minutes ago. Yes, she'd call him. What did he do?

The suspect entered the room and we informed him that he had been accused of indecent exposure by a female complainant who gave us his license number. Yes, we were arresting him. Yes, he had a camel hair coat and he would bring it with him.

As we were going out the door, his wife said, "I realize you have to take him in but I know he didn't do anything wrong."

Half way down the driveway, I said to the suspect, "I didn't want to get specific in front of your wife but you are the guy, right?"

"Yeah, Officer. I'm the one. I'm glad you caught me. I knew it would happen sooner or later."

We brought the man to the Detective Bureau and gave them a complete report. We expected to be commended. Instead the Captain of Detectives began to berate us.

"What the hell do you mean busting into a man's house without a warrant and arresting him?"

"We had probable cause, Sir and a complainant willing to prosecute. Her description of him and his car matched perfectly and he admitted to being the perpetrator," I reminded him.

"I don't give a damn what he admitted to, what he looked like or what the complainant wants to do. From now on, you take a report, turn it in and we'll do the investigating. Understand?"

"Yes, Sir." I answered sullenly and left with my partner. The detectives would make a supplemental report and book the suspect.

"I don't think that was fair." My partner said as we headed for our squad car. "We didn't do anything that wasn't by the book."

"There's a hidden agenda, Kid" I replied. "The Dicks won't get credit for this arrest. We do. But they'll have to make a follow-up investigation and do all the paper work for his arraignment in court. In retaliation they want to intimidate us so we won't repeat our so-called "offense." Believe me, we made a good pinch and they know it. The captain can blow all the smoke he wants to, but it's best not to argue with a captain."

THE YELLOW CURB

The woman was a psycho.

A small group started a new church in a tiny building in the middle of the block of an Old West-End neighborhood. When the members began parking in front of her house on meeting nights, she painted the curb yellow in front of her home and demanded that the police issue parking tickets to their cars. Each time she called in, I'd re-inform her that painting her curb yellow did not constitute a "no parking" zone.

This time it was different. A car was parked with its rear bumper barely protruding into her driveway. She complained that the car was blocking her drive. The ironic fact was that she neither owned a car, nor drove. She just wanted to cause trouble for a decent group of people.

I thought I'd resolve the situation by pushing the vehicle forward a foot or two away from the driveway. Not so.

The dispatcher sent us back to her address where we found Lt. Stan (Fibber) McGee waiting. Apparently the woman had called the desk sergeant and he contacted the lieutenant.

I was working with a rookie, so the lieutenant chastised me for moving the car and ordered me to tag it. I refused. I explained that the woman was unstable and made bogus complaints, that she didn't even own a car.

While I was arguing with the lieutenant, the alarmed rookie wrote a ticket and put it on the windshield of the car! Then Lt. McGee said that he was placing me on report. I told him to go ahead.

The following month I was removed from my riding unit and assigned to walking a beat.

PRELUDE TO THE SICK FAMILY DAY

Many police officers worked extra jobs to supplement their inadequate income. When working second shift, I worked from 7:30 A.M. 'til 1:30 P.M. for the North Star Carpet Cleaning Co., driving a delivery truck.

One day I returned home from my extra job to find my Mother-In-Law at my house in tears. Her Mother (my wife's Grandmother) had died that morning. My wife and her Mother were distraught with grief.

The deceased was a grand old lady. She liked me and encouraged her favorite Granddaughter to marry me. I was also saddened by her death.

I thought it best to stay home from work and to comfort them. There were funeral arrangements to be made and many other details to take care of. I could have reported "sick", but I didn't want to lie and I had worked that morning for the carpet company. There was no such thing as a "sick family" day" at that time.

The desk sergeant of the day shift wasn't sympathetic. "Why aren't you coming in?" For the second time I explained the circumstances to him.

"What's that got to do with you?" he inquired.

"Just tell my shift command that I won't be in today." I pleaded in exasperation and hung up.

The next day, immediately after roll call, I had to report to the captain's office. He was a small man for a policeman in those days, with a mousy face, a thin body and a squeaky, high-pitched voice. (My nick-name for him was: Mighty Mouse.)

"The day shift's desk sergeant reported that you refused to come to work yesterday. Is that true?" he demanded.

"No, sir," I replied. "There was a death in the family and under the circumstances I thought it best to stay home with my wife and mother-in-law."

"What did you do?" his voice had a sarcastic edge, "Sit around and hold their hands?"

I felt the blood rush to my temples, my pulse quickened, and I wanted to throttle the little pip-squeak. But I retained my self control and said as calmly as I could, "That's just about what I did, Sir."

"Well," he announced triumphantly, "That's going to cost you a vacation day."

"Yes, Sir," I replied with relief. I had expected a more severe outcome.

It wasn't long after that when, through bargaining between the city and the Fraternal Order of the Police, the "sick family" day was established.

I was just a little ahead of the times.

THE MIGHTY PEN

On Saturdays, the Toledo Art Museum held art classes for children from 8 A.M. until 3:30 P.M. The museum is located on Monroe Street between Collingwood and the extension of Jefferson Ave. There was no parking, standing or stopping allowed in front of the museum and most of the frontage was a signed bus stop.

The format was for the parents to drop their children in the parking lot adjacent to the Jefferson extension, from where they could walk to the near Monroe St. crosswalk.

The Toledo Police Department assigned a patrolman every Saturday from 8 A.M. until 4 P.M. to safely guide the children across Monroe St. to and from the museum.

However, many drivers of the children insisted upon stopping in the bus zone to drop them off and what was worse, would park in the bus zone and wait for them to leave the museum in the afternoon.

The Art Museum post was dreaded by patrolmen for valid reasons: One, It made for a long day on foot. Two, there was no shelter from the elements; not even a place to sit. Three, the assigned officer had to depend upon a squad car for a lunch break and the mobile officers were reluctant to afford relief for fear of the mobile unit being dispatched to a call while the Art Museum officer was being relieved, thus leaving one of the mobile officers at the museum for a prolonged period of time. So, the mobile officer would try to get the museum officer back to his post as soon as possible. It was a trying situation for all involved.

Because of the hardships the museum detail was also used as unofficial "punishment" for patrolmen, whom the command officers weren't too fond of. Admittedly, I caught my share of that assignment.

On one such Saturday, I was frustrated trying to keep the bus zone clear of illegal cars. When told to leave, they would just drive around the block and come right back again. If an officer decided to issue any tickets, by the time it took to tag the first one, the others would hurry away; then the ticketed driver would complain that he or she was the only one to be cited. Meanwhile, bus drivers often had to double park to let passengers on and off the buses.

I decided that enough was enough. I dated and filled out a dozen parking tickets, with the exception of the license number and make of car. I then strolled nonchalantly by the row of illegally parked cars, ignoring them, but surreptitiously I was jotting down their license numbers and car manufacturers.

I walked back to the front of the museum, where I completed the tickets, then strode to the furthest car in the bus zone and placed the appropriate ticket on the car's windshield. By tagging the first car the others could not drive away, as they were blocked in by the car behind them. By the time the drivers realized what was going on, it was too late for them to move.

After receiving a ticket, the driver of the last car remained parked. When I ordered him to drive away he insisted that since he had already been cited that it gave him the right to stay as long as he wished.

"It doesn't work that way, Sir," I advised him. "If you refuse to move I can and will issue more tickets until you do move or I can have your car towed away."

"Let me have your pen," he demanded, "I want to write down your badge number."

"I'm sorry, Sir, but I'm using it. My badge number is only three digits, surely you can remember it: 348." I walked away to attend to some children gathering at the crossing and the belligerent citizen drove away.

About twenty-five minutes passed, when I was informed by a police crew to call the desk. The desk sergeant answered on the second ring. "Moore, here, Sarge. Do you want me?"

"No, but Lieutenant McGee does; stand by."

"Moore, what the hell are you doing out there? A guy just came in complaining that you ticketed a slew of cars while the drivers were waiting for their kids to come out … and something about not letting him use your pen. Haven't you ever heard of Public Relations?"

"Yes I have, Sir, but this was a different situation. First off, I'm tired of bus drivers not being able to get near the curb to let passengers on and off because selfish, lazy or just stupid parents insist upon parking illegally in the bus stop here. Second, that complainant thinks that a parking ticket is a receipt for renting a parking spot in a bus zone and last, I don't know of any regulation that says I have to loan anyone my personal gear; as far as that goes I gave him my badge number loud and clear."

"You haven't heard the last of this," Lieutenant McGee assured me.

But, he was wrong and in fact, that was the last time I ever got that assignment. In my mind I think it was an illustration of the power of the "mighty pen".

The Toledo Museum of Art in the 2500 block of Monroe St.,
where a police officer was assigned as a crossing guard on Saturdays.

CHAPTER 16

WOULD YOU BELIEVE?

EPISODES

LAWSUIT LAURA

The main entrance to the Lion Store was in the 300 block of Summit Street in downtown Toledo. Two almost-life-size statues of lions guarded the entrance. The Lion Store also occupied the building behind the one on Summit, which faced St. Clair Street. The public could enter either store and enter the opposite annex by using rear doors between the buildings.

In the mid-sixties, fellow sleuth Steve Harris and I worked as store detectives at the Lion Store on some of our days off. We were cognizant of a habitual shoplifter we called, "Lawsuit Laura". We conferred the name on her, because whenever she was confronted by a police officer, she would shout: "Touch me and I'll sue you."

She was a black female about age 30, 5'7" tall and thin. She knew all the store detectives, as well as they knew her.

One evening I was sitting in a balcony scanning the interior of the store with binoculars. I spotted Lawsuit looking at some cashmere sweaters on a rack near a door equipped with a two-way mirror. Steve was stationed behind that door.

Lawsuit casually began to cram several sweaters into a large purse. I was sure that Steve would observe her but to my alarm, she sauntered out a door onto St. Clair Street unchallenged.

I rushed downstairs and yanked the mirrored door open. Steve was there but had failed to see Lawsuit's larceny. I updated him quickly and we left the store in pursuit of the familiar thief.

She was walking West on Adams Street. We began to jog to catch up to her when she looked back and saw us. She crossed the street and ran into a parking lot on the corner of Adams and Huron, crouched by the side of a car momentarily, then ran up Huron Street.

Steve chased her while I cut up an alley to intercept her. I exited the alley on Jackson Street and she was headed right for me but she wasn't carrying anything. She stopped a few feet from me and screamed her usual threat as Steve caught up to us.

"Laura, where's the purse?" I demanded.

"What purse? I ain't got no purse, Man."

It was futile. There was no way she could have hidden the bulky merchandise on her person and her hands were free.

Steve and I retreated to the parking lot and checked the wheel-wells of every parked car to no avail. We gave up and returned to the Lion Store.

We entered the store and a sales clerk at a women's accessory counter called to us.

"There's a seventy-dollar purse missing from the display on my counter," she reported.

Lawsuit not only stole the sweaters but also the purse she had put them in.

The only thing Steve and I could figure out was that she must have had an accomplice somewhere whom we overlooked.

THE EDUCATOR

Changing shifts every month, raising a family, working extra jobs and studying for promotions all factored in to taking me over nine years to earn a four-year degree from the University of Toledo.

During that time I was under the tutelage of many fine teachers and I avow that it was worth all my efforts. However, there was one instructor whom I'll call Carl Rankin and it befuddled me as to how he ever obtained a certificate to teach.

The University of Toledo with its impressive tower.

I considered him to be a very poor example for his social science class which included many impressionable teens just out of high school, as well as some seasoned police officers and other adults.

Mr. Rankin always wore a suit and tie, but his appearance was sloppy. His clothes were always wrinkled, his tie dangled loosely from his open collar, and his shoes were never shined.

I don't want to present a lengthy discourse so I'll limit this to one incident which especially distressed me. I don't recall how the subject of suicide came about but Mr. Rankin made the following statements in class:

"If a person is threatening to jump, tell that person to go ahead and jump. What's it to you? Why should you risk your life for someone who doesn't care about his own?"

I saw the faces of the teens in the class. They were taking him seriously. I raised my hand and he gave me the floor.

"A police officer can't do that," I admonished him. "Recently I took a man down from the High-Level Bridge - -"

"All right," he interrupted, "What if half-way down he changed his mind and grabbed you and you both fell to your death? Isn't your life worth more than his?"

"In whose eyes?" I exclaimed. "Are you telling me that his wife and kids don't love him as much as my wife and kids love me?"

Mr. Rankin was stymied. He couldn't give me an answer.

"If a police officer is not prepared to put his life on the line, then he has no right to wear the badge," I added.

He got a break; the bell rang at that time and he dismissed the class.

We got into other heated discussions until I tired of arguing with him. After the mid-term exam, I skipped several of his remaining classes. Although I earned a B grade on both the mid-term and the final exams, he only gave me a final grade of C. When I questioned him about it, he stated that it was because I missed too many classes. How ironic was that?

THE NAKED BURGLAR

"Unit 10. We received a call from the Glenwood Lutheran Church at 2545 Monroe; the caller said he just broke in. Check it out. Use caution."

Bob Skinner executed a U-turn causing the cruiser's tires to screech.

"Wonder what the hell that's all about," he muttered aloud.

"On a summer day at 6 P.M. in broad daylight? Maybe it's a phony." I ventured.

A brief time later we skidded to a stop near the church office. We approached the front door with our revolvers drawn. The door was made of heavy ornate wood with two frosted panes of glass. There was a hole in the pane nearest to the doorknob.

Bob found the door unlocked and we entered into an anteroom. We cautiously approached the open door to the pastor's office and peered in. A teenage male was sitting at a large desk; he had no shirt on. He appeared to be about fifteen with sandy hair; doodling with a pen and paper. He certainly didn't fit the profile of your average burglar.

"Raise your hands and stand up," Bob ordered.

The youth obeyed. Oops! He had nothing on. He was completely nude.

"What the hell are you doing in here?" Bob asked in amazement.

"Please, don't hurt me," the boy pleaded. "I had to get to a phone."

"You're the one who called the dispatcher," Bob realized.

"Yes, Sir. Two men were keeping me locked up in a room. They took my clothes so I wouldn't run away but I broke out a screen and ran to this church. No one was here so I broke in to call for help."

"Well, I'll be damned," Bob shook his head in disbelief. "What's your name?"

"Joel Spencer, Sir."

"Where are the guys you ran away from?" I asked.

"They live in a big house near by on a street that runs into the street this church is on," the youth explained. "I don't know the names of the streets because I'm not from here."

"Where are you from?" I inquired.

"Akron, Ohio, Sir. I ran away from home about a week ago. I met the two men in a park yesterday and they said they'd help me. They took me to their home and gave me some food but then they locked me up."

"Did they do anything to you?" I wanted to know.

"No, Sir. But I don't understand why they wouldn't let me go."

We wrapped the boy in a police blanket and notified a church official that the church office was insecure. We waited until the official arrived.

"Let's take a look at these two clowns," I said to Bob.

Joel pointed the house out on Maplewood Avenue. We left him in the police car and rapped on the door.

The door opened and there stood the "fruity-tooty" twins. Two men in their late fifties, short, with gray hair and similar bland faces. They were even dressed alike in sport shirts and pastel slacks.

Of course they never saw the boy before. Of course they didn't know where his clothes were. Of course we couldn't come in without a warrant. And, oh my, they would never keep someone against their will. They said all this in their lisping, twangy voices complete with effeminate gestures.

We identified them, then booked Joel at the Child Study Institute and made out a report to the Juvenile Detective Bureau. Our job was done, but it was just the beginning for them.

THE FUNNY FARM

The small, white clapboard house at 514 Southard Street was referred to as "The Funny Farm" by police crews working the area. A poor white family with an unknown number of kids lived there.

My only experience involving the family was in answer to a disturbance call when I was assigned to 10 Scout with Bob Skinner on a day tour.

The front door was standing open so we walked in. First I was startled by a life-size statue just inside the door. It appeared to be the likeness of a saint and probably came from a church.

Then something took my hand. When I looked I was even more shocked. It was an adult chimpanzee. He was eating an orange which he held in his other hand.

By the time we settled the dispute, I saw a goat, chickens, ducks, three dogs and two cats, then, as we were leaving, a parrot flew by us.

"You think that's something," Bob laughed, " you should have been with me the first time I set foot in that crazy house.

My partner and I walked into the kitchen and the ol' lady was stirring a large pot of stew on a wood burning stove. A small tot was standing on top of a stool near the stove. He pulled out his penis and began to urinate into the pot. I swear, without batting an eye, the ol' lady stirred the pee right in with the concoction she was cooking."

THE FATAL SHOT

Jeremy Jones, barely out of his teens, thought he was a big man. He had a woman and they were living it up in a motel. There were multiple felony warrants on file for his arrest but that didn't worry him. He was having a ball.

Someone else knew Jeremy was at that motel and tipped the police. Lawmen surreptitiously surrounded the building and assembled a team of officers outside the room in which Jeremy and the woman were bedded.

When the door came crashing in the girl flung herself to the floor between the bed and the wall. Jeremy snatched a gun from under a pillow, but before he could use it he took several hits and tumbled to the carpet from the open side of the bed.

Jeremy left the motel in a body bag. His gun was tagged as evidence. The black community was upset. There was talk of excessive force. When the coroner's autopsy report was released they were really outraged. Jeremy's death was ruled a suicide. The police shot that boy multiple times. How could it be suicide?

The explanation in the newspaper was simple: Jeremy had been shot several times but none of the wounds were life-threatening. The shot that ended his life was a bullet in his head, fired from his own gun.

Probably, during the spate of shots fired in rapid succession no one distinguished Jeremy's shot from the shots fired by the police.

Perhaps, Jeremy did not want to submit to arrest and did not want to be jailed. Those could be the reasons he fired the fatal shot. Or another theory is that he could have fired his gun as he was falling from the bed and the bullet accidentally struck him in his head. Apparently, either way it was Jeremy who fired the fatal shot!

(TO2) TOLEDO, Ohio, April 21 - PROTEST MARCH - Civil rights leader Rev. Floyd Rose, left of woman with sign, and others march through rainy streets Tuesday to protest the police shooting of a young man in a hotel. The protesters said they disagree with recent findings that two police officers were justified in shooting

THE GREAT DIVIDE

Professor Maynard Tipton's slight, thirty-four year old frame was erect but very thin. His dark brown hair, pulled back into a ponytail dangled to the middle of his back. A haggard beard couldn't conceal his weak chin. He wore what appeared to me to be the same clothes to every class. I observed stains on the fingers of both of his hands, presumed from nicotine, but who knows? The stains could have been from Marijuana.

He taught the subject at the University of Toledo, which I disliked the most: Mathematics. I took Math. only because it was a requisite for graduation. When I attended his class for the first time, I knew instantly that Tipton and I were from two different worlds and that sooner or later out worlds would collide.

His evening class was from 8:30 P.M. until 10:00 P.M. on Monday, Wednesday and Friday. Assigned as a Patrol Lieutenant on the third shift, I didn't have to report for duty until 11:00 P.M.

About once a week Tipton liked to spring a quickie exam. Twenty minutes before dismissal, he'd pass out a questionnaire containing five or six problems. When students finished, they could leave. The grades on these tests constituted a percentage of each student's total grade for the semester.

Because I had almost an hour between the end of class and when I had to attend roll call, I took my time; sometimes being the last to leave. One such evening, as I placed my paper on Tipton's desk, he asked me: "What do you do as a Police Lieutenant?"

His gambit was unexpected. "I supervise from three to four Patrol Sergeants, whenever a serious crime or incident occurs on one of their districts, such as multiple alarm fires, shootings, rapes or major disturbances."

"You mentioned rape, lieutenant. You know I think the majority of those reported are charades. I really think that rape should be classified as a simple assault and battery."

"Is that so?" I was astonished but remained noncommittal. "Is there anything else you'd like to see changed?" I was curious.

"Well, of course, certain segments of our society have been striving for over a decade to decriminalize the possession or use of marijuana. Personally, I think it should have been legalized a long time ago."

That I expected but making rape a misdemeanor? I couldn't fathom his reasoning, especially because I knew he was married.

I decided to give him something to digest.

"Would you care to know what I think, Professor?"

"By all means, lieutenant, speak your piece."

"Our country is so lenient that anyone can travel from Canada to Mexico or from California to New York without so much as a visa. Because we have a Bill of Rights anyone can practice any religion without fear of persecution; can assemble or hold peaceful demonstrations; can own firearms and are protected from illegal search and seizure; are assured due process and as long as you obey the law and don't harm anyone except in self-defense you can do about whatever you want."

"So what's your point, lieutenant?" Tipton suddenly waxed impatient.

"My point is this, Professor: if a person can't live within the confines of the laws of our country and without maliciously harming someone, then upon conviction of murder, kidnapping or rape, such persons should be executed immediately.

Upon the third conviction of a lesser felony, such as robbery or burglary, perpetrators also should be executed. The method is irrelevant: hanging, electrocution, injection, whatever. Our society would get rid of a lot of scum and those with two convictions hanging over them would have to walk a fine line."

"Lieutenant," Professor Tipton seemed aghast, "you're a cruel man."

This, from an educator who wants to reduce the crime of rape to simple assault and battery. Who's the cruel one?

AN UNACCEPTABLE TERM

During the summer of 1970, I attended a Social Studies class at the University of Toledo, taught by a tall, black female. I'll call her Miss Terry and in my opinion, she was a very intelligent and capable instructor.

However, during one session she stated that one should not criticize blacks for using the "M.F." word; that it didn't have the same connotation that non-blacks may attribute to it.

My Mother had passed away about a month before this and I was still grieving over her death. The instructor's words hit a nerve and I became incensed. I raised my hand and she bid me to speak.

"Recently I lost my Mother. To me she was a saint; always sacrificing for my siblings and me. She worked so very hard. I remember her washing clothes in a large tub and scrubbing them on a wash board, which was jammed up against her stomach. She wrung the clothes out by hand and spent hours ironing them."

One day I asked her, "Mom, why do you work so hard?"

She looked me in the eye and replied in a soft voice: "I have to earn my keep."

"Ma'am, with all due respect, telling me that I must accept the word Mother coupled with an obscene word is an insult to my intelligence."

I sat down and the instructor abruptly changed the subject. I figured that I had just got myself a failing grade.

At the end of the semester, I was amazed. The instructor graded me an "A" for the course.

CHAPTER 17

CHALLENGES

EPISODES

CHALLENGES

Police officers may be challenged in situations where circumstances are confusing or deceptive. They may have little time to render a crucial decision . . . one that could either save a life or cause a death.

How well they are trained and equipped are important factors.

When police lack proper equipment, they may have to improvise.

They must outwit and outdo their adversaries, yet stay calm and use good judgment.

Is an armed man a culprit? He may be a victim defending himself.

Is a person intoxicated? Someone in a diabetic stupor has the same symptoms.

Following are some situations in which I faced such challenges.

THE TOURNIQUET

"The man was crazy, officers. He came in here, looked around, then smashed the glass case with his bare hand. He ran out bleeding bad."

The complainant was the owner of a smoke shop in a brick, two story building at the 901 Washington.

"Did he take anything?" my partner Bill Marsh asked.

"Not that I can tell. It would have to be smokes, that's all that's in the case. Now there's blood and glass all over everything."

We got a brief description of the man and then traced his bloody trail along the sidewalk to a door leading to the second floor. We found the injured man in the darkened hallway at the top of the stairs trying to conceal himself behind a folded day-bed.

"Come out with your hands up," my partner, Bill, commanded.

A tall, thin, black male stood up holding his right hand over a bloody gash in his left forearm. When he removed his hand from the wound, blood spurted out like a fountain; an artery had been severed. We had to stop the bleeding or the man would go into shock and die.

We had a first aid kit but it did not contain a tourniquet. Desperate, I took my nightstick from my belt, slipped the man's arm through the rawhide thong to a point above the wound and spun the baton like a propeller. The twisted thong became a tourniquet and shut off the flow of blood like a tap.

We transported the man to Mercy Hospital for treatment. His wound was cleansed, sutured and bandaged and he was given a tetanus shot.

We then booked him as a "safe keeper" for psychiatric evaluation. It would be up to the court to commit him, depending upon the results of the evaluation. At least he didn't bleed to death.

THE COMMAND

Officer Ed Burton was a military veteran and also a veteran police officer with fifteen years on the job. Ed was only 5'10" tall, with a medium build, but his demeanor was gruff and aggressive. He also had a reputation for being overly officious.

Ed always worked a wagon and he drove the entire eight hours, because he didn't like writing reports or riding in the back of the wagon. This was his prerogative as the senior officer.

Ed and I were working an extra day so we were assigned to 5 Scout. Five's district was the far Northeast end of Toledo, called Point Place and was seldom manned. Many streets in Point Place dead-ended at the watery edge of Lake Erie. It was considered a quiet area.

At mid-morning, we received a, "man with a gun," call on 321st Street. As we arrived, a woman hailed us.

"Officers, my husband has been drinking and running around the neighborhood shooting at street lights and traffic signs. We live across the street and I ran to my friend's house here and called you because I'm afraid of him."

"Where's he now, lady?" Burton asked.

"I think he's in our garage. Be careful. He has a lot of guns."

We walked across the street. The garage was detached from the house and had two large doors; one was closed and the other open. The suspect was crouched in the open doorway reloading a nine-shot .22 caliber revolver.

A car was parked in front of the closed door, so I positioned myself on the far side of it holding my revolver at the ready.

Burton, leaving his gun holstered, walked up the driveway and openly confronted the armed man and gave him a command: " Drop the gun!"

The crazed gunman ceased loading and looked up.

I could read his mind, "Can I close the cylinder and shoot both cops before they can shoot me?"

He knew he could take Ed, who was standing in the open, with his revolver still holstered, but I posed a problem. He wouldn't be able to get me with the car in the way while I had a clear shot at him and he knew that I was waiting to take him out.

"I said, drop the gun!" Burton, commanded a second time.

The shooter swept us with his eyes once more still calculating. Then conceding the odds were against him, reluctantly let his revolver drop to the ground.

Burton rushed in and handcuffed the defeated outlaw.

I didn't re-holster my firearm until the culprit was placed securely into the back of our squad car. He was extremely dangerous.

Besides the .22 caliber revolver, we confiscated a .38 caliber revolver, a .45 caliber pistol, a 7.65 mm pistol, two .30 caliber rifles and a 12-gauge shotgun.

I never mentioned it to Ed, but to this day I truly believe that my training and cautious tactics prevented him from being shot and possibly killed.

SHOTS FIRED

The Summit and Cherry area was a small community of its own, housing many of the local inhabitants in the numerous apartments above the stores and bars in the immediate vicinity. Many of the dwellers were retired and thriving on pensions.

There were sixteen bars in a two block radius. The patrons were a mix of the retirees, lake sailors, hookers, young punks and the curious; the latter coming from the greater Toledo area as well as from Michigan, which bordered Toledo's northern border.

During evenings, especially on weekends, there were multitudes of people from so many levels of society carousing in the locale that it was inevitable for altercations to occur; some ending in mayhem. Because of the potential for trouble, a foot patrolman was assigned to the corner of Summit and Cherry on a twenty-four hour, seven-day schedule.

I was assigned to Beats 41 to 44 regularly, which encompassed the area between Jackson Ave. and Cherry St. from Summit to Erie St.

On a lazy Sunday afternoon, about 2:00 P.M., I was anticipating getting off duty when I observed and unmarked police car parked in front of the Evergreen Bar on St. Clair Street, a couple doors South of where it connected to the Cherry and Summit intersection. A certain detective was having his usual "pick-me-up" inside the bar, before going off duty.

Strains of a Pat Boone recording floated on the warm, stagnate air as I ambled to the car to listen to its police radio.

Bam! Bam! Two shots exploded in the bar across the street. I grabbed the police radio's "mike" in the detective's car and informed the dispatcher: " This is Moore on 41 to 44; shots fired in the Delmonty Bar. I'm going in."

Running to the St. Clair Street entrance of the café, with my revolver in hand, I cautiously peered through the open doorway.

The day bartender, Jimmy Coleman, was lying on his back in the middle of the bar's floor. A large man was hovering over him with a snub-nosed revolver gripped in one hand.

"Drop the gun," I ordered the man.

The armed man looked up and said, "It's not what you think, officer."

"Drop the gun or I'll drop you," I warned, as I aligned my sights on him. He was agitated but straightened up and tossed the gun to the floor, behind him.

Picking up the snub-nosed weapon I asked, "What's this all about?"

"My name is Barry Johnson," the large man responded, "and it's like this ... I've been in here most of the day with a woman friend while Jimmy was tending bar. When he got off duty, he sat with us and then tried to get fresh with the woman. I told him to back off and we had words. He left in a huff and then came back with a gun and fired two shots at the ceiling and yelled: 'Now what you got to say?'

Hell, Johnson continued, that didn't scare me. I was in the army. I took the gun away from him and knocked him on his ass. That's when you got here."

"That about it, Jimmy?" I queried.

"Yeah, I guess so," Jimmy replied sullenly as he got up from the floor rubbing his right arm. He was still wearing his work apron.

"Where'd you get the gun, Jimmy?" I inquired.

"I had it upstairs in my apartment; it belongs to my boss. Will I get it back?"

"It will stay impounded for thirty days, then your boss can see the chief about getting it back."

A back-up crew arrived. I asked them to put a 10-4 on the air and to tell the dispatcher that I confiscated a gun and to send me a wagon.

"Who are you arresting?" Johnson asked anxiously. "I don't have to go to jail do I?"

"No. But if a cop ever tells you to drop a weapon again you'd better do it quicker. Another officer may have shot first and asked questions afterward, I replied. "I'm charging Jimmy with endangerment. He foolishly put lives in danger when he fired the gun inside the bar."

The wagon crew arrived but that didn't end a surprisingly challenging day. I had to go to the Safety Building to write an Incident Report and to file an Affidavit at the Clerk of Courts Office. It never fails: On a quiet Sunday, when I was looking forward to getting home, I end up working overtime.

THE PHOTO IS LOOKING WEST ON CHERRY FROM THE CHERRY STREET BRIDGE TO SUMMIT STREET, KNOWN AS THE "CORNERS".
THE SUMMIT AND CHERRY STREET AREA WAS "HONKY-TONK", WITH NUMEROUS CHEAP BARS AND A SMATTERING OF OTHER SMALL BUSINESSES.
THE EVERGREEN BAR IS PICTURED DIRECTLY ACROSS FROM THE WHITE TRUCK, ON THE LEFT EDGE OF THE PHOTO. THE DELMONTE BAR CAN NOT BE SEEN.
FURTHER DOWN CHERRY STREET, ST. FRANCIS DE SALES CATHOLIC CHURCH RISES ABOVE THE SKYLINE, ALTHOUGH ITS STEEPLE WAS DESTROYED BY FIRE MANY YEARS AGO AND NEVER WAS REPLACED.
IN THE EARLY '80'S THE "CORNERS" WAS RENOVATED; THE BARS GAVE WAY TO MODERN BUILDINGS AND A LARGE PARKING GARAGE. HOWEVER, ST. FRANCIS CHURCH REMAINS THE SAME.   CIRCA 1950'S

ST. CLAIR STREET AS IT INTERSECTED SUMMIT AND CHERRY STREETS WITH ITS
INFLUX OF TAVERNS. THERE WERE AT LEAST SEVEN ON THIS BLOCK ALONE,
INCLUDING THE DELMONTE, WHERE THE "SHOTS FIRED" INCIDENT OCCURRED.   CIRCA 1950'S

THE DRUNK

One Patrol was considered the "protectors" of the Safety Building which housed the Toledo Police Station, jails and courts. The unit worked out of a small office in the police barn (garage) and received their calls via phone. The concept was if some type of emergency occurred in the building, One Patrol would be close by and ready to respond.

Officer Bill Phalen and I were assigned to the unit as replacements for the regular crew while they were on a day off.

On a mild, October day we received a dispatch to a small factory on Water Street just North of the Summit and Cherry area, near the railroad tracks. Reportedly, a drunk had entered the premises and refused to leave.

When we arrived at the building, we were directed to a short bulky man sitting on a stool in front of a machine. "He's been sitting there for almost and hour," the foreman complained. "He won't say anything and we can't get him to leave."

The man was wearing two pairs of pants, two shirts and a suit coat over a jacket. All of his outer clothing was damp. He seemed to be in a stupor and unable to communicate.

"My guess is that he came off a boxcar. I think he's a hobo," I said.

"Probably so," Bill agreed, "Let's throw him in for drunk."

"I can't smell any intoxicants on him." I reported.

179

"That's because he smells so bad." Bill suggested.

"That wouldn't matter. I got as close as I could to his mouth and there's no odor of an alcoholic beverage."

"What do you want to do? We can't leave him here." Bill argued.

"We'll run him out to the Maumee Valley Hospital and let them check him over."

We brought the man to the hospital and got him to recline on a table in an examining room.

A nurse came in and took his temperature; it was 104 degrees. The man was burning up. The nurse called for help and another nurse and an intern began to undress him. When they took his shoes off, Bill and I had to leave the room; the stench was nauseous. The man was admitted for observation and we returned to duty.

The next day, I returned to One Patrol but Bill was assigned to a different unit. My new partner and I had an ambulance run from downtown to the Maumee Valley Hospital. Before we left the hospital, I saw the nurse who had worked the day before.

"How is that guy we brought in yesterday with the high temperature and the extra clothing?" I asked.

"He died last night." She calmly informed me, "He had meningitis."

When I got back to the Barn, I got hold of Bill via phone.

"He died of meningitis!" Bill exclaimed. "If we'd booked him for drunk and he'd croaked in jail, all hell would've broken loose."

"That's for sure, Bill. Listen, you'd better get the uniform you wore yesterday, cleaned as soon as possible and tell your wife about this; you can't be too cautious."

"How about you? You had your face on top of his."

"Not much I can do about that now."

(Author's note: Police officers face perils every day, which the majority of the public seldom realize. They have to make decisions that may determine life or death for someone, based on skimpy information or evidence at the location of a serious incident; many times within a brief time span. It's all part of the job.)

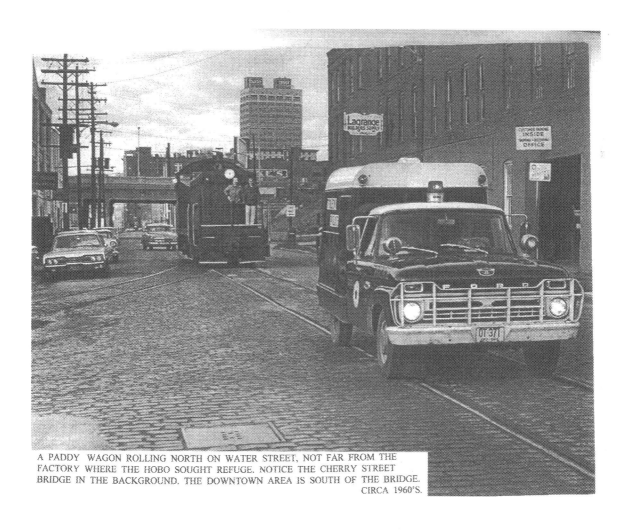

A PADDY WAGON ROLLING NORTH ON WATER STREET, NOT FAR FROM THE FACTORY WHERE THE HOBO SOUGHT REFUGE. NOTICE THE CHERRY STREET BRIDGE IN THE BACKGROUND. THE DOWNTOWN AREA IS SOUTH OF THE BRIDGE.
CIRCA 1960'S.

CHAPTER 18

WORST POSSIBLE SCENARIOS

EPISODES

A BRIDGE TOO DARK

On a summer night, a bulletin was read at the third shift's roll call: "One Dennis Olsen, white, male, age 17, 6'1" tall, 140 pounds, blond hair, blue eyes, last seen wearing a blue shirt and jeans is missing from 505 South Avenue. He threatened suicide after a break-up with his girlfriend. Attention 14 Scout."

Dave Freeman and I were working 14 Scout. Radio traffic was light throughout the warm, humid night. There was no action, even the bars were quiet. We checked the business places, gas stations and usual trouble spots until we were thoroughly bored. Everything was serene.

Dawn began to break just after 5:00 A.M. Out of dull desperation for something to do, Dave drove slowly along a dirt road between railroad tracks and the Maumee River. The desolate trail wound its way behind a row of warehouses and under the Anthony Wayne Bridge.

We were approaching one of the huge cement supports for the bridge when I observed something which looked amiss in the pale morning light. At the base of the massive structure there was a strange item resembling a bag or bundle.

Dave stopped the car and we both walked toward the object. Suddenly, to our horror we could discern the body of a young man crumpled against the bridge support. He had suffered compound fractures of both legs. It was evident that he had jumped from the bridge, hitting the ground feet-first, shattering his ankles. Apparently still alive and presumably in excruciating pain, he dragged himself to the base of the bridge support, propped himself in a sitting position and died. Death was probably caused by a combination of loss of blood and shock.

"I'll bet you anything," Dave surmised, "that he thought he was over the water when he jumped. It's impossible to distinguish between the water and the land at night because everything under the bridge is pitch black. What a shocker."

"No telling how long he had sat there alone and suffered." I added.

"Well it's over for him now," Dave lamented. "Let's get hold of the dispatcher and get someone out here to pick up the poor soul."

Distant view of The High Level Bridge from which a youth jumped.

Close-up of area of the High Level Bridge where a youth jumped.

Base of bridge tower where youth's body was discovered.

A FLAWED DESIGN

A group of children crowded around the ice cream wagon. The van was unique because it was round and decorated like a carousel. Recorded organ music played as the attendant filled the young, waiting hands with cold treats.

Unobserved, a nineteen-month-old child sat down in the street directly in front of the cheerful vehicle, to eat his ice cream.

The driver's seat was in the exact middle of the machine, making it impossible for the vendor to see anyone in the street. He started the motor and drove over the child.

Paul Thomas and I, working 13 Patrol, were dispatched to the scene. The child was unconscious. We ordered an ambulance. I observed what appeared to be a tire mark on one of the baby's cheeks. He was breathing, but dark blood oozed from his lips, which was a bad sign. The ambulance was taking too long.

"Paul, get the kid inside the wagon. We're taking him." I averred.

A shudder rippled through the tiny body as Paul lifted the toddler from the pavement.

On the way to Maumee Valley Hospital, the tardy ambulance was speeding towards us. The scream of the two sirens drowned one another out. The ambulance and our wagon were approaching the same intersection unaware of each other. When I suddenly saw it I refused to give way and the ambulance jumped a curb to avoid colliding with us..

At the emergency room, Paul placed the limp child on a table in an examining room. He was the exact image of my youngest son; blond, blue-eyed, with dimpled cheeks.

A doctor came in and held a stethoscope to the child's chest, looked up and said, "This kid's deader than hell. What'd you bring him in here for?"

Tears welled in my eyes and I clenched my fist. He had no idea what we went through to get the child there; racing against time. And for his arrogance, I wanted to slug him! But, I knew if I did, I'd be in big trouble . . . and that was the one thing that I couldn't afford.

We were informed that the child's Mother was in the waiting room. I had to tell her that her baby was gone, but before I could utter a word she saw it in my eyes. I embraced her and she sobbed in my arms. I wanted to cry too, but a six-foot, two-inch, uniformed cop can't allow that to happen. Again, I had to suppress my feelings. What made matters worse, is that I recognized her. She was employed as a clerk for the police department at the Safety Building.

A TRAGIC EXIT

Police officers see a lot of tragic incidents during their careers but the most devastating case I ever investigated was the suicide of a young, attractive, Mexican woman.

It happened in a little house near St. Peter and Paul's Catholic Church in the South End. She lived with her Mother and her five-year-old son. She wasn't married but kept company with the boy's Father.

On the day before, according to her Mother, that man abandoned the Mother of his child. He told her that he never wanted to see her again and she believed that she could not live without him. She was only about twenty years old.

Mid-morning of the fateful day, she laid on her single bed with her son beside her. She placed the muzzle of a 12-gauge shotgun to her forehead, just above her eyes ... and pulled the trigger!

The top of her skull and her brains were splattered all over the ceiling and walls of the tiny room. How the shotgun blast and her grisly death impacted her son, I can't even imagine.

God, rest her soul.

THE PERSONAL ELEMENT

Mark Sullivan owned and operated a carry-out on Airport Highway on 13 Patrol's district. Over the years I worked that unit, we became friends. I'd stop in for a bottle of pop and we would hash over the latest news events.

Eventually I was promoted to sergeant. I was working the second shift one evening when a serious accident occurred on the Old Dixie Highway, located in North Toledo. The road was poorly lit.

There was a small factory operating on Dixie and a bar was located across the street. Apparently some of the factory workers would spend their dinner break at the bar.

On this particular evening, a worker was returning to the factory when he was struck by a speeding car. After hitting the pedestrian, the careening vehicle sideswiped a telephone pole and tipped over, but no one in the car was injured.

When I arrived, the worker's body was lying in the roadway. His left leg had been ripped off at the hip and was about fifty feet from the body. When the coroner's men arrived, they had a difficult time getting the mutilated man into a bodybag.

When police handle a case like this, they can be objective because the victim and other parties involved are strangers. Officers may sympathize and may feel empathy for a victim but that really doesn't affect them personally, so they can remain objective.

When the patrol crew got the situation under control, it was near the end of my tour so I drove to the Safety Building. When I arrived a man was waiting to see me; it was Mark Sullivan.

"Hey, Mark, what can I do for you?" I greeted him.

"I understand you were at the scene of a bad accident on the Dixie," Mark asked in a quiet voice.

"Yeah, Mark, I just came form there."

"The man who was killed was my Father." Mark's face was grim, "and I just wanted to ask you how it happened."

Now, the personal element was injected. The identity of the man whose leg was ripped off; the man whose guts were coming out where that leg had been; the man whose lifeless form was difficult to put into a body bag was established as Mark's Father. And Mark, a friend, is present wanting to know how his Father died.

There was a lump in my throat. I pondered for what seemed a very long time before I replied, choosing my words carefully.

"Mark, I can only tell you this: I believe that it happened so fast that your Dad never knew what hit him. I don't think he suffered for a moment." Mark thanked me and left.

From work I went directly to the Cabin Club, a neighborhood tavern on Alexis at Ganymede and had a drink. I've stopped for a drink on the way home on other occasions, but this time, I needed it.

MY NUMBER COMES UP

The night of December 5, 1971 was bitterly cold. I was the West End sergeant of the third shift. As soon as I could get on the street, I headed for the Elbow Room on Sylvania Avenue at Bellevue Road. I parked behind the building and entered through the rear kitchen door.

"Hi, Betsy," I greeted the cook. "How about one of your great pizzas with pepperoni and mushrooms?" They had the best pizza anywhere in town.

I entered the main room and stood at the end of the bar. The place was crowded as usual. The bartender set a cup of "Irish" coffee in front of me. I knew all the employees as well as the owner because I worked there off and on. Sometimes I tended bar when they were short-handed.

When my order was ready, I had regular coffee with the pizza. I had a hunch that it was going to be a long night and I'd need the nutrition. Little did I know then how right I was.

About 2:00 A.M. a complaint of a rape came in. One of my crews was dispatched to an address off Reynolds Road near Dorr Street. When I arrived the officers were putting a description of the rapist on the air. I authorized them to transport the woman to St. Luke's Hospital.

The victim stated that her attacker was wearing a shirt with "Stan" embroidered on it. I left the scene and decided to scan the area for the suspect.

I was near the Squirrel Cage, a bar on Dorr at Reynolds, when a white Cadillac sped out of the parking lot, stopped at the corner for the green light, waited until the light turned red, then made a left turn onto Reynolds Road through the red light. There were two men in the car.

The rape victim's house was a short walk from the bar. It was possible that the perpetrator could have left the bar on foot, committed the crime and then returned to the bar. The other man could have waited at the bar during the commission of the crime.

I decided to stop the Cadillac and check out the occupants. Perhaps one of them was named Stan. I relayed my intentions to the dispatcher.

The driver readily responded to my flashing lights and pulled over. I positioned my cruiser behind and to the left of the stopped car as a measure of protection for myself.

"Good evening, may I see you driver license, please?" I asked the operator. I scrutinized the men as I was talking. They were well dressed and both obviously had been drinking.

"Certainly, sergeant," the man replied politely. He took his billfold from a pocket but could not locate his license, "I know it's in here," he said nervously.

The air was frigid. I pulled the collar of my reefer up but I was beginning to shiver as the man searched his wallet.

I heard the motor of an approaching vehicle accelerating with a whining noise. Looking up, I realized that the auto was heading directly towards the rear of my squad car. I estimated its speed at seventy miles per hour. If the driver didn't change direction immediately, there was going to be a collision.

Watching the vehicle rapidly decimating the space between it and my cruiser, I realized that I was in danger. My first impulse was to run across the highway but I checked myself, thinking that if the driver swerved at the last moment, I'd be run over. At that point I didn't know what to do. I stood motionless, holding my portable radio in my left hand, my eyes fixed upon the approaching missile.

The zooming motorist smashed into the back of my cruiser, forcing it into the Cadillac. The violent impact propelled the erratic sedan into a broadside-skid directly at me. I extended my arms in a futile effort to defend myself. My only thought was: "This is it. I'm going!"

The car swept into me throwing me to the pavement on my back. Everything was moving too rapidly to register. At one point, the dark form of the car loomed over me and my mind pleaded, "God, don't let it roll on me." When all motion ceased, I was lying on my back, with my right shoulder pinned to the roadway by the car's left, rear wheel.

The two men I had stopped came to my side. I gave an order to one, "Get the keys from this car before that S.O.B. runs over my head." And to the other I directed, "See if the police radio in my car is working and tell the dispatcher that I need help."

The first man immediately reported that the driver who hit me was unconscious. "Get the keys anyway," I insisted.

By that time a police crew arrived. They pushed the car away and helped me to my feet.

The fingers of my left hand were cut and bleeding, the index finger was broken. I was wearing leather dress boots with eight-inch tops; the right one had a deep gash above the heel and was partially off my foot. My ankle pained me but I realized how fortunate I was to be alive.

The errant driver regained consciousness. He suffered a laceration on his forehead. We were both taken to St. Luke's Hospital where he refused to give a blood sample for alcoholic content.

He was reminded of the "Implied Consent Law", whereby Ohioans, when obtaining a driver license, accept the condition that they must submit to either a breath-test or give a blood sample if charged with drunk-driving. A refusal results in an automatic one year suspension of their driving privilege and a three day jail sentence.

"So I get three days," he shouted. "What the hell do I care!"

I was undressed and placed on a table with a sheet covering me.

"My right hip is really paining me," I complained.

"I'll be right with you," a nurse sweetly replied.

She came to me with a hypodermic needle, flung back the sheet, and injected it into the middle of a large purple abrasion on my hip. I must have landed on my holstered revolver.

To relieve pressure, the doctor had to remove the nails from the middle and index fingers of my left hand before suturing the lacerations.

"Your right ankle is severely sprained," the doctor informed me. "There isn't much we can do for it. It probably would have been better if it had been broken."

I didn't follow his logic then, but later, I realized what he meant for it gave me trouble for many years.

"You say your right wrist is hurting?" the doctor responded.

An X-ray revealed that it was broken in two places so it was set and a cast was applied.

There were no beds available so at 4:00 A.M. that morning, a fellow sergeant drove me home. When my wife opened the door, I greeted her limping heavily, with my left hand bandaged like a white boxing glove and my right hand and wrist encased in a cast.

My number had come up, but by the grace of God, I survived.

CHAPTER 19

WHAT WERE THE ODDS?

EPISODES

1. A REMEMBRANCE

2. SPARED

3. INSTANT CLEARANCE

4. ECHO OF FATE

5. AN AMERICAN TRAGEDY

6. THE DEAL

7. THE HERO

8. JUST SHOOT ME

9. SHADES OF MAYBERRY

A REMEMBRANCE

On a June summer evening of 1964 while working 13 Patrol in South Toledo, I entered a diner called the "Kitchen Nook" at Airline and Fearing Boulevard. I had just sat down when an attractive young lady in her mid-twenties with long red hair approached me. She was with a young man.

"Do you remember me?" she inquired with a smile.

I had to admit that I honestly did not recognize her.

She laughed and introduced me to her fiancée.

"When I was sixteen," she related, "I was struck by a car and you took me to St. Charles Hospital in a police ambulance."

Instantly, I recalled the entire incident: It was my first emergency run when police wagons were still used as ambulances.

"I remember now. You had stepped from between parked cars trying to cross Oak Street when you were hit. It was a bizarre accident because you were actually struck by the outside rear-vision mirror on the car and not by the auto per se."

I recalled the scene. She was sitting in the street with a deep gash on the left side of her face. It was a hot day and there was congealed blood on her clothes and on the pavement.

"I remember picking up the broken mirror by the curb," I continued.

"I felt sorry for your poor partner," she said. "When he got the stretcher from your police car, he struck his head on something sharp and had to have stitches. Remember?"

"Yes, someone had left one of the folding legs sticking out and he caught it just above his right eye." I couldn't help but chuckle at the thought. "When they got through with him at the hospital, he was as bandaged up as you were." We all were laughing now.

"Well, we have to be on our way but I knew it was you the second you walked in," the lovely redhead said.

"After ten years I'm flattered and I'm glad that I was of service to you. I wish you both the best of luck and a happy marriage."

I never met her again but I pray that she fared well and that her marriage was blessed.

SPARED

On a muggy July evening working an inner-city district, my partner and I were dispatched to a shooting. Upon arrival, a large woman was being placed into an ambulance. She had been shot five times.

The ambulance crew informed us that her husband was the shooter and after they got the woman out of the house they heard a single gun shot from within the dwelling. They proceeded to take the victim to Mercy Hospital.

With a back-up crew, we searched for the husband to no avail. Then we heard moaning from a bedroom. We located the man sprawled between a bed and a wall. He had tumbled there after shooting himself in the head. He also was rushed to Mercy Hospital.

Our report indicated that both victims appeared to be in critical condition. It didn't seem that either would survive.

Later that evening, word was received from the hospital that although the woman suffered five wounds, none of them were life-threatening and she was expected to recover.

The husband lost a lot of blood but his prognosis was positive.

They both lived. Whatever the odds were, they beat 'em.

INSTANT CLEARANCE

A detective's goal is to solve or clear as many cases as possible; the sooner the better as new cases keep coming in.

While I was assigned to the Juvenile Detective Bureau, I had a case involving a fourteen-year-old boy, who admitted to committing numerous burglaries in the South End of Toledo but he didn't know all the addresses.

He also admitted to taking money from a house in which an elderly woman lived alone. She repeatedly left her front door open with the screen door unlocked while she watered her backyard garden.

One day the youth entered the woman's house while she was in the rear yard. He discovered that she kept four, twenty-dollar bills in her bedroom dresser and he took one. On three more occasions he entered her house and each time, he stole another twenty dollar bill.

That very day, the woman went to pay a bill and realized that the money was missing. She called the police and a detective was sent from the burglary squad to investigate. It happened that the detective and I worked as partners in uniform patrol prior to our assignments in plain clothes.

Driving the youth in an unmarked car, I had him direct me to the homes which he had invaded. Eventually, after the youth had pointed out several houses which he had victimized, he directed me to the elderly lady's house.

The detective was about to leave as I drove up. I called him to my car and told him that the youth with me was the perpetrator of the crime he was investigating.

"Wow!" he exclaimed, "That's the fastest I've ever had a case solved."

THE ECHO OF FATE

For several years Officer Dave Freeman and I were partners. One evening in the sixties we were working 13 Patrol in the South End and were dispatched to a modest home in a quiet neighborhood. It was simply a: " Call for police".

A nineteen-year-old white woman, who was obese and had a bad case of acne, phoned her aging parents and told them that she was bringing her boyfriend home to meet them. Upon arrival, she introduced them to a dark Negro male with "processed" hair. Her parents panicked and called the police.

They thought that their daughter was under their jurisdiction until she was twenty-one and forbade her to associate with the man. We had to explain to the shocked parents that in Ohio a child is considered an adult by law at the age of eighteen and that their daughter was free to go with whom she pleased.

We said as much to the daughter but convinced her for the sake of keeping the peace, to have the man leave and for her to stay the night with her parents. The man agreed and left and that is how we resolved the matter at that time.

Five years later Dave and I were no longer partners but were randomly assigned to 13 Patrol for a tour on the second shift. During our shift we answered a call for police at the same address that we were dispatched to five years previously. We were met by the same woman and her Mother. (The Father had passed away.) Only now the younger woman had four small children clinging to her and the complaint was that her husband was harassing them.

While we were there the husband drove by and we recognized him as the same fellow she had brought home five years ago as her boyfriend. Now, according to the daughter, he was threatening to kill her.

Because we, the police, did not actually witness the man do anything that we could arrest him for, all we could do was to advise her to obtain a "Restraining Order" and if and when he should bother her, to call the police and show them her copy of the said court order.

A restraining order would give police the authority to make an arrest, in the event her husband was harassing her, without actually witnessing any unlawful acts.

Five years between calls for police by the same family, answered by the same officers, in regards to the same individual. What were the odds?

AN AMERICAN TRAGEDY

When I was about twelve, I lived next door to a family named Kent. The Father was a slight, mild man with a quiet wife. They had two daughters; the eldest one was named Rita. She and I were the same age and in the same class at Westfield School.

The Kent household was usually serene until the Father imbibed a few beers, then he would become abusive and argue loudly with his wife.

Rita grew into a lovely teenager with snow-white skin and raven-black hair. She also happened to have a strawberry birthmark on the back of her left hand.

Her parent's were very strict. She was not allowed to date or to attend school events or any activity away from her home. Once, when I telephoned her to ask her to a dance, she quickly stated in a whisper that she didn't dare. Later I learned that she was chastised because I had called her.

One of my earliest assignments, working with a veteran officer on 14 Scout, was in response to a disturbance call at the Kent residence. Nothing had changed; the ol' man was inebriated and had been arguing with his wife and someone called the police.

While my partner counseled them in the kitchen, I looked at family photos displayed in the living room. Rita was not in a single picture.

The Kents never recognized me. Before we left, I inquired of Mr. Kent, "You have two daughters don't you?"

"No!" he answered gruffly, "We only have one daughter."

I knew better but said no more.

Twelve years later, as a detective in the Juvenile Bureau, I was looking for a fifteen-year-old delinquent named Josh Culbert. He had dropped out of school and was a suspect in numerous cases of vandalism all over the South End. No one knew where he was staying. From school records, I learned the address of his Mother, in a low-income housing project: the McClinton Nunn Homes on Dorr Street.

Mrs. Culbert answered the door. She was wearing a faded, pink, soiled robe. Her hair was disheveled. She wore no make-up. She appeared haggard and was obviously ill.

Yes, Josh was her son. No, she had no knowledge of his where-a-bouts. He was incorrigible. She explained that after she had bore him out of wedlock, the father abandoned her and Josh. She took the name Culbert and raised the child by herself. She further volunteered that she was thirty-five, on welfare and dying of M.S. She appeared older.

Then I observed the birthmark on the back of her left hand. The woman was Rita Kent. She confirmed it when I asked what her maiden name was. She didn't recognize me and I didn't have the heart to enlighten her.

Josh was taken into custody two days later.

I never saw Rita again but over the years I've thought of her often. Her life was a tragedy. An attractive, healthy, spirited girl, raised by Victorian standards. She apparently rebelled and was impregnated, probably by the first boy she got close to. She and the baby were abandoned by the baby's Father and when she needed them most, her parents had forsaken her too.

What were the odds of being dispatched to her parent's house when I was a rookie and then being assigned to a case involving her twelve years later?

THE DEAL

The wintry night air nipped our faces as my partner, Tony Monetti, and I left our warm squad car and trudged towards the bungalow in the snow. We had no idea of what the trouble was. The dispatch was simply, "A call for police."

We followed a path of footprints to a side porch. There was a door at the far end containing a window with two vertical panes of glass. The window was plastered with steam from the heat inside and rivulets of moisture trickled in erratic patterns down the smooth surfaces.

I knocked on the door, peering intently through the wet trails of condensed water on the inside of the glass. I could discern the image of a man standing in the center of the kitchen under the ceiling light. His left arm was extended and bent at the elbow. A dark substance appeared to be running down the man's forearm. Could it be blood?

"Come in," the man called.

The knob turned in my hand, but as the door gave I suddenly realized what I was staring at. The substance wasn't blood, it was leather. A rifle sling! The man was waiting for us to come through the door with a rifle in his hands.

Leaving the door ajar, I jammed my back against the side of the house and warned my partner, "He's got a rifle!"

Tony went to the rear of the house in a crouch. He quickly returned. "There's no back door," he reported.

We drew our revolvers as I called to the armed stranger. "Look, Mister, we don't know what's been going on. We got a call for police and we just want to talk to you."

"We can talk," replied the man. "Just throw your guns inside."

"We can't do that," I retorted. " Tell you what; you put your rifle down and we'll holster our guns."

"I've got a better idea," the man offered. "You guys holster your guns and I'll hold mine over my head; then you can come in."

"That's a deal." I agreed but Tony was emphatically shaking his head, "No".

"Don't worry, Tony," I whispered, "I can take him."

Opening the door wide I entered a darkened dining room and carefully stepped over a shattered vase lying on the floor. I held my right hand over the butt of my revolver, ready to draw instantly while keeping my eyes riveted on the man's rifle.

Due to years of target practice and competing in combat pistol matches there was no doubt in my mind that before the man could lower his rifle to any degree, I could draw my service revolver and fire two or three rounds into his chest. No brag, just fact.

Holding his rifle over his head, the man remained statuesque.

However, when I reached the kitchen doorway, I was taken aback.

"I know you," I exclaimed. "I don't remember your name but we went to high school together."

"I recognize you too," the man admitted. "My name is Joe Lansing."

"Well," Tony announced, "since we're among friends, you won't be needing this," and he grabbed the rifle from Joe Lansing's hands.

"Hell," Joe said, "That ol' thing's so rusty it probably wouldn't even fire."

"Probably not," I agreed. Now that the situation had been neutralized, it was important for Joe to save face.

Tony proceeded to eject five .30 caliber, full- jacketed, armor-piercing rounds from the bolt-action rifle.

"I'm Officer Jim Moore and this is my partner Tony Monetti; now what brought all this about anyhow?"

"Well, I've been working a lot of overtime lately," Joe related, "and I think my wife is seeing someone else. Several times I've come home early and she wasn't home. My wife, Yvonne, always says she was at her sister Angela's place.

Tonight, I accused her of two-timing me. She threw a vase at me and locked herself in the bedroom; then she must have called the police."

As if on cue, a young woman wearing a black satin negligee, opened down the front over a black satin nightgown, entered the kitchen. The ensemble clung to her curvaceous body as close as nature would allow, exhibiting the sleek outline of her hips; then draped to her shapely calves. Her raven-black hair cascaded down her back almost to her waist. Standing about five-foot-two, her ample bosom was straining against the bodice of her nightgown. Her complexion was flawless and her face was adorned with a delicate nose and pert lips, accentuating her dark, alluring eyes. She was stunning!

"I told you before and I'll tell you again," she addressed her husband, "I am not cheating on you. I have no interest in any other man." Her voice was smooth and calm but her eyes were ablaze. "I'm sorry that I got so upset, but I'm tired of being alone so much of the time and then you dare to accuse me of being unfaithful; that is more than I can stand for."

"It looks like you two have settled down so we'll get back in service," I said wanting to escape the torrid house. "Before we do, though, allow me to make a couple of suggestions:

Joe, perhaps you can cut down on the overtime and spend more time with Yvonne; I'm sure she would appreciate that.

And Yvonne, when Joe must work extra, how would it be if you had your sister Angela come here to your house? In that way, you'd be here when Joe got home," I concluded.

"Officers," Yvonne, replied, " I, and I'm sure I speak for Joe, too; we really appreciate the way you handled this situation, with the gun and all. It could have turned out very differently. We want to thank you very much."

"Yeah," Joe, sheepishly agreed, staring at the floor.

"And," Yvonne, added, "we'll certainly take your advise under consideration."

"What about my gun?" Joe inquired.

"We'll have to confiscate it. After thirty days, contact the chief's office and you'll be directed on how to get it back," Tony explained.

Back on patrol, Tony mimicked Joe Lansing: "Hell, that ol' rifle won't shoot. It's all rusty."

"Yeah, right." I chimed in. "The first shot will just blast the rust right out of the barrel and if the bullet doesn't kill you, peritonitis will set in and finish you off." We both broke up with laughter.

What remarks we may have exchanged concerning Mrs. Lansing are better left unrepeated.

THE HERO

There was an officer, I'll call Tom Dwyer, who spent a lot of his off-duty time in a South-end bar called Sam's. One afternoon while he was sitting in the bar drinking, a man entered and strode directly to the kitchen. Shortly afterwards, a woman screamed and there was popping noises, like firecrackers. Dwyer realized that the explosive sounds were gunfire. Apparently, there was a shooting in the kitchen.

The Toledo Police Department had a strict rule that all sworn officers be armed at all times, as they were expected to handle any crime occurring in their presence, whether on-duty or off-duty.

From what I heard and in my opinion, Dwyer, apparently was unarmed. He left the bar but he knew that he couldn't leave the area because most everyone in the bar knew he was a cop. If he fled he would be disgraced. He went to his car and checked the trunk, to no avail.

Desperate, Dwyer went to the front door of the bar and as the armed suspect emerged the officer displayed his badge and placed the man under arrest. The felon shoved his firearm into Dwyer's chest and pulled the trigger. Click! The gun was empty.

What were the odds?

The suspect surrendered to Dwyer without further resistance.

Dwyer was touted in the news as a hero; a title he deserved, considering the nerve it took to apprehend the shooter, especially if Dwyer was unarmed.

JUST SHOOT ME

A patrol unit was dispatched to a residence in South Toledo to investigate a disturbance. When they arrived, they saw a man at the front door holding an infant. When the officers approached the door, the subject threatened to kill the baby with a twelve-inch serrated knife.

The suspect shut the door and retreated to the kitchen. One officer kept him under surveillance from outside of the kitchen window, while the other officer summoned the district sergeant via radio. Being the district sergeant, I responded.

Upon arrival the officers briefed me and I started toward the house. My intentions were to try to reason with the man, but suddenly, he charged from the front door wielding the knife above his head screaming, "Shoot me! Shoot me!"

I stood motionless, drew my service revolver and commanded: " Drop the knife!"

The attacker was a pale thin person in his thirties with stringy, sandy hair. He stopped in his tracks several feet in front of me, still brandishing the knife and yelling for me to shoot him.

Pointing my revolver at him from my hip, I repeated my order: " Drop the knife!"

During this stand-off, the two patrolmen simultaneously used their nightsticks; one striking the man's wrist and dislodging the knife and the other felling him. He was placed under arrest, handcuffed and placed in the crew's wagon.

The prisoner was taken to the Maumee Valley Hospital for treatment and I followed the crew there. He was identified as Donald Lowell.

While waiting to be examined, Lowell complained: "My wrist hurts."

"If you hadn't acted like a damn fool, you wouldn't have been hurt," I replied.

"Why didn't you shoot me?" He asked earnestly.

"You've been watching too many TV shows," I retorted. "Police officers only use lethal force as a last resort."

A wry expression crossed his face as he spoke again, "You don't recognize me, do you sergeant?"

"No. I don't recall knowing any Donald Lowell," I mused.

"I changed my name," the man said with a smirk. "When we attended Jones Junior High together, my name was Donna Lowell"

SHADES OF MAYBERRY

When we were kids, Tony Monetti and I both lived in the 700 block of Jervis Street. We both were appointed to the Toledo Police Department during the same year and for awhile we were assigned to the same patrol shift.

The Unger family, with four boys, lived in the 500 block of Western Avenue, a couple of streets over from Jervis. They were a tough and somewhat rowdy family but we all knew each other. After the kids were grown Mr. and Mrs. Unger separated but never divorced. Mr. Unger stayed in the homestead on Western Avenue while Mrs. Unger lived and worked in a different part of Toledo.

One summer afternoon, in 1970, Tony was sent to the ol' man's house to check for the safety of the occupant. Although no one answered the door, everything seemed all right except for one strange factor: the door of the kitchen refrigerator was wide open.

Tony called for a sergeant to authorize a forced entry. I was dispatched. We discovered an unlocked window in the front room of the house. Upon entering, we found Mr. Unger lying face-up on the floor in his underwear; he was dead. The room was used as a bedroom and a double bed in front of the window had concealed his body from view from the outside.

We surmised that he was at the refrigerator when he suffered some kind of attack and went to the bedroom where he collapsed and died. The appliance door was left open.

There was an address book by the telephone listing Mrs. Unger's work number.

"Hello, Sarah? This is Jim Moore. Tony Monetti and I are at the ol' man's house. He passed away. Yeah, someone called in to check the house and we found him. Apparently natural causes. Do you want us to call Gordon? Okay, we'll contact him and the coroner. Gordon can make the necessary arrangements for the body. Sorry to be the bearer of bad news. Yeah, you're right; everybody's got to go sometime. Well, take care and I'll probably see you at the funeral."

Gordon, the eldest son, was notified. He arrived the same time as the coroner. The body was removed and we chatted with Gordon for a brief time and then Tony and I went back in service.

No, this was not Sheriff Taylor and Barney Fife in Mayberry. It just seems like it.

At the time, Toledo covered 86 square miles with a population of nearly 400,000 citizens and the Toledo Police Department had an authorized strength of nearly 700 sworn officers.

What were the odds of Officer Monetti and I, both responding to a call involving a family we both knew from childhood, with virtually no contact with that family for twenty-five years? I doubt if even a bookmaker could answer that one.

CHAPTER 20

COMMAND INCIDENTS

EPISODES

AN ERROR IN JUDGMENT

Working the third shift as the East Side Sergeant, I was approaching Main and Front Streets when I saw 3 Scout traveling through the intersection. I also observed a man standing in the doorway of Murphy's Department Store, located at that corner; when he saw the police car he ducked back against the door.

I should have contacted 3 Scout on the air and had them check the suspicious man, but I had recently been transferred from the Juvenile Detective Bureau to Uniform Patrol and was use to doing things on my own; so I decided to check the man myself.

Pulling my marked car to the curb, I motioned the man to the passenger side of my car.

" Get in," I told him. He complied and seated himself next to me.

"Do you have any identification?" He nodded and took a Social Security card from a pocket and handed it to me. He was about 5' 9" tall and weighed about 140 pounds. He was a white male, with dark brown hair and eyes, wearing blue jeans, a plaid shirt and a soiled, dark green jacket. The name on his S.S. Card was Harold Palm and from the first three digits of the S.S. number I knew he was from a western state, if the card was truly his.

I contacted the dispatcher and relayed all the afore mentioned info, with a request for warrants, on the man in my car. While I was waiting for the dispatcher to get back to me, I realized that if the man was wanted for anything and decided to resist arrest, my holstered revolver was between us. I also was beginning to regret that I hadn't alerted 3 Scout and had them check this subject out. The bottom line was that I had made a serious error in judgment.

"Sergeant," the dispatcher's voice was stoic, "that subject is an escapee from a mental institution in Wyoming."

"O.K. Dispatcher," I acknowledged the information. "I'll need transportation."

"Two Patrol, the sergeant needs transportation at Front and Main for a fugitive."

"Two Patrol, on the way."

I deliberately called for transportation instead of a wagon, in a feeble effort not to alarm the mental patient at my side, but in the long run it didn't matter. The fugitive was no fool and in all probability knew that I was summoning additional police officers to take him into custody.

My mind was racing for ways to protect myself if the deranged fellow should go off the deep end before the wagon crew arrived.

I spoke in a jovial voice as I guarded my revolver with my right elbow: "Well, you certainly have come a long distance from Wyoming. Did you hitch-hike all this way?"

"No, not all the way," the stranger replied, easily, "I took a bus as far as my money could take me; then I had to hit the road."

Keeping a sharp eye for any furtive movements on the fugitive's part, I kept him talking the best I could. The wagon arrived in good time and the man was transferred from my car to the wagon, without any problems.

I was lucky and I knew it! And I made a silent vow never to be that careless again.

A SILENT WITNESS

Heading East, a car pulled along side of me as I was waiting for a red light at Alexis and Jackman Roads.

"Sergeant," the driver called out, "do you see that maroon car up ahead?"

I acknowledged that I did.

"She's been speeding and darting from one lane to the other. She's an accident looking for a place to happen."

The light turned green and the car in question took off with screeching tires. She passed two cars, then changed lanes without signaling, passed two more cars and then changed lanes again without using her directional signals.

I maneuvered behind her and employed my red light and sounded the siren briefly. She pulled into the mall at the corner of Alexis Road and Lewis Avenue and stopped by the Bargain City store.

As I approached her car, she greeted me with a large smile, "Did I do something wrong, officer?" she crooned.

She was in her twenties, brunette, with a lovely face; her skirt was raised as high as possible, revealing shapely thighs.

"A motorist complained about your driving, Miss," I informed her, ignoring the display. "Then I also observed you operating in a reckless manner. I'm going to have to issue you a citation."

Immediately she burst into tears, "Oh no, officer, please don't do that. I'm awfully sorry. I didn't mean to do anything wrong." She whipped out a hanky and began to dab her eyes.

I walked back to my marked car and wrote out a citation, charging her with, "Operating Without Due Regard for the Safety of Others".

When I handed the ticket to her, she evolved into a wild woman. She snatched the ticket from my hand and snarled, "Give me that, you son-of-a-bitch. I'll see you in court and I'll have your badge for this."

I turned my back in the middle of her tantrum and returned to my command car. She then drove away.

Before I could start my engine, the complainant got out of his car and walked over to me. He had been parked nearby and witnessed the entire episode with the errant driver.

"If you need a witness, sergeant, I'll be glad to appear in court with you," he said. "That woman certainly deserved the ticket."

"That's most kind of you, Sir," I replied, "but it shouldn't be necessary."

He returned to his car and left.

I remained parked for a few moments absorbing the realization that if I had given in to that woman's charade, I probably would have had a strong complaint lodged against me by a formidable and not so silent witness.

A CHANGE OF ATTITUDE

The Southern Michigan Sportsman Club is still located on Temperance Road in Temperance, Michigan. In 1963, I was elected Vice President of the club and proudly held the office of President through 1964 and 1965.

An eighteen-member Executive Board ran the club, consisting of five officers, three trustees, six directors and four reps of the activity factions within the club: rifle, pistol, archery, and shotgun.

One of the directors, Dick Weston, had a negative attitude towards police officers. He never missed an opportunity to make a derogatory remark whenever a police matter was discussed. Other than that, he wasn't a bad guy and we got along.

Dick was a top salesman for a supply company and one day I wanted his advice on what product to use on a newly tiled floor in my home. He lived in a district I supervised as a sergeant, so I stopped by one evening while I was working.

He greeted me at his door like a long-lost brother. "Come in, come in. Boy! Am I glad to see you. How about a beer?"

"No thanks, Dick." Yeah, I thought to myself, "I'll be in the kitchen drinking a beer and he'll be calling the chief from another room."

"Guess what?" he beamed. My wife got me one of those police scanner radios for Christmas and I can't believe what goes on. Holy cow! A call came in for a crew --- a guy had a gun and his wife had a knife --- damned if I'd even answer such a call," he exclaimed.

I laughed aloud, "We have to, Dick. That's what the job's all about,"

The change in Dick's attitude was inconceivable to me. Apparently, the police radio gave him an insight into police work which he was never aware of before. I was elated. Law enforcement officers can use all the friends they can get and Dick became a good friend.

A HAUNTING EXPERIENCE

The people living at 1240 Hamilton took pity on a stray dog. They began to feed the under-nourished canine, which appeared to be part Collie and part Shepherd. Soon it took shelter underneath a shed at the rear of the yard.

Eventually the dog became pregnant and dropped a litter under the shed. The problem now was that the dog became over protective of it's brood and threatened anyone who even walked by the front of the house.

The people, who befriended the dog, finally had to call for help. Their next door neighbor began to hang some clothes in her backyard and the dog jumped the fence and chased the frightened woman back into her house.

An employee of the Humane Society was sent out, but couldn't get the dog to leave her litter under the shed, so the police were called to aid him. The district crew and I, the district sergeant, arrived at the same time.

"What I'm going to do," the H. S. officer explained, " Is to throw a firecracker under the shed to scare the dog out. When she appears I'll try to capture her with my snare. If I miss her, I want you officers to be standing by with firearms to destroy her if she tries to escape. But do not shoot her in the head; it has to remain intact so she can be tested for rabies."

The younger officer of the crew took the shotgun from their car and "jacked" a shell into the chamber. He was a rookie, whom I didn't know. The H.S. officer flipped a lit firecracker under the shed and upon its explosion the frightened dog emerged on the run. The H.S officer tried in vain to snare the mongrel, but she was too fast for him and the dog headed for the street. Before I could head her off the rookie fired and struck the stray in her back legs. She dropped on her right side and was writhing in pain; she obviously was crippled. I had no choice but to end her misery. I shot her with my .38 cal. service revolver once, twice, three times and finally used all six bullets, before she died. One bullet struck a tit and milk ran out instead of blood. I felt terrible about killing her and I'll never forget it. It may have been necessary; it may have been official, but it was a haunting experience indeed.

The litter? A young boy volunteered to get the pups from under the shed, which the H.S. officer took into custody; eight little balls of tawny fluff.

A MATTER OF TACTICS

Patrolman Lyle Owens was working a project at Fems, a fashionable women's' store in a West end mall . It was a quiet Friday, summer evening, about 8 P.M. when no less than eight men, dressed in three-piece suits, ties and wearing derbies, marched into the store. They were members of a black Islamic group and very militant.

They immediately began to harass the female patrons, badgering them to buy a newspaper which their group published; their methods were very crude. They had a reputation for being violent, so Owens called the dispatcher for help.

Unit 9 was sent along with myself, the district sergeant. We arrived together. However, when the three of us entered the store, the eight men were standing at attention in a single file by the cashier's counter.

Owens filled us in, but the group's leader denied that they did anything wrong and insisted that they were only interested in selling their newspaper. There was no customers left in the store and therefore no complainants.

The store owner supported the officer's statement, but indicated that he mainly wanted the men out of his store and wasn't enthusiastic about signing a complaint against them. The back-up crew and myself did not witness any action that an arrest could be based on.

"Do you have a city permit to sell your paper?" I queried the group leader.

"No." he replied, "I didn't know that we needed one."

"Yes, and such a permit can only be obtained through the city's Service Director during regular business hours," I added.

(I wasn't sure if there was such a permit, but it served the purpose.)

"All right, sergeant, we'll take our leave." With that the leader gave a command and the entire line of men marched from the store.

The store owner looked relieved. Owens didn't have anything to say, so the crew and I left. It was near hit-off time and I was riding home with Captain Pat McNulty,* so I headed for the Safety Building.

Pat and I were about to leave for home, when Acting Captain, Lt. Al (Curly) Bronson said that he wanted to see me. Pat and I both sat down in his office.

"Officer Owens called me and said that he was upset because no arrest was made at Fems," Lt. Bronson began. "I called the chief and he - - "

"You called the chief?" I interrupted. "What the hell for?"

"Well," Curly looked defensive, " I wanted to be sure that an arrest could have been made and he told me that an arrest can be executed for any ordinance that has a penalty clause. For disturbing the peace there's a minimum fine of ten dollars."

"Look, lieutenant, in the first place Owen's badge is as big as mine and he had plenty of probable cause, according to him, to make an arrest before me and 9 Scout arrived. He didn't do it! When Unit 9 and I arrived there was nothing going on . . . there was no complainants and the shop owner didn't want to sign a complaint.

Further, there were eight of them and four if us; what if we had tried to arrest them and they resisted and that shop got torn apart? Who'd you think would be calling the chief then?"

"Yeah, and all for a ten dollar fine." Captain McNulty added.

"No, I think under the circumstances the situation was handled the right way. You know, Lieutenant Bronson, if Owens can't handle these projects, he shouldn't be working them."

Captain McNulty and I left the office with Lt. Bronson scratching his head.

When the next captain's exam came up, Curly didn't take it. I wasn't surprised.

WHOSE TOUGH

Officer Gary Daniels was working a one-man traffic car on the afternoon shift, when he informed the dispatcher that he had stopped a car for traffic violations. He gave his location as the Anthony Wayne Trail and Woodsdale.

A few minutes later he came on the air again: "Dispatcher, I need backup at my location; I have a hostile driver."

"Thirteen Patrol assist Unit 510 at the Anthony Wayne trail and Woodsdale with a hostile driver."

"Thirteen Patrol O.K."

"Sergeant Two to dispatcher. I'm near by, put me out, too." I radioed.

"Sergeant Two O.K.. Unit 510, Sergeant Two is en route, also."

The A.W. Trail is a divided highway, which begins at the South edge of Toledo's downtown area and continues through the South End to the city of Maumee and beyond.

When I arrived, the officer and a young man were struggling on the grassy median strip, which separates the South and North bound lanes. I slammed my cruiser to a skidding stop and alit with my nightstick in hand. The belligerent driver had managed to throw the officer to the ground and then came at me. I jabbed him in the solar plexus with my club and he folded over with a grunt. A whack across the back of his neck sent him to his knees; I grabbed him by his collar and the back of his pants belt and draped him against the hood of the traffic car. Officer Daniels helped me handcuff him.

Thirteen Patrol arrived and as Daniels and I escorted the arrested male to the wagon he paused and said to us: "You guys aren't so tough."

"You're right" I replied, "But then, who's wearing the handcuffs?"

REQUEST DENIED

Crews had to summon their district sergeant whenever they wanted to force an entry into any building, whether it be to check for the safety of the occupant or to serve a felony warrant.

For forty dollars more a month a sergeant had to shoulder a lot of responsibility, which it seemed that many patrolmen took for granted. The sergeant had to appraise a situation and decide whether to allow a forced entry. Concerning felony warrants, if the sergeant wasn't convinced that the felon was actually in the building, a crew may have to be told to back off and try another time. In that case crews were usually disappointed, but disregarded the fact that if the felon wasn't in the dwelling, the city had to pay for any damages caused by the forced entry and that would definitely reflect upon the sergeant's judgment.

On one occasion, a white crew spotted a black man whom they knew had numerous misdemeanor warrants on file for his arrest. The suspect fled and the officers pursued him to a residence, which he entered and locked the door . A backup crew was summoned to cover the rear of the property to prevent the fugitive from escaping.

In answer to the original crew's knocking, a small, elderly woman answered the door. The crew requested entry to arrest the suspect, to which the woman answered, "He ain't here!" She then slammed the door shut.

The crew requested a sergeant and I was dispatched.

"What do you have?" I inquired

"We chased a man into this house and he has a dozen warrants out for him. We know they're all traffic warrants, but we also know he's in the house."

"Have you seen him since he ran inside?" I inquired.

"No." the officers replied, "but we know he's in there."

"Has someone been covering the back?"

"Yeah, 11 Scout was sent for backup and is staked out behind the house."

I knew that 11 Scout's crew consisted of two black officers and that one of them was very militant. When he finished low on a Sergeant Exam, he was very vocal because he wasn't promoted immediately. When asked about the dozens of officers ahead of him; he had no answer.

In my mind there was a strong possibility that the militant officer on Scout 11 would allow the suspect to flee. With only misdemeanor warrants involved, I couldn't take the chance.

"Fellows, we're going to pass on this one," I told the crew.

"What! Why?" they protested.

"In the first place, the warrants are only for misdemeanor offenses and secondly, there is a good chance that your man is not in the house; you'll have to take my word for it. You'll see him around another time, I'm sure."

I put both crews and myself back in service and as far as I was concerned, that ended the matter. To this day I'm certain that I made the right decision.

THE OAK OPENINGS ARREST

Boy Scout Troop # 434, of Meadowvale School of Toledo, Ohio, was a struggling troop of seven boys and two leaders. In February of 1969, I re-organized it, using methods prescribed by the Boy Scouts of America, into a solid troop of 30 Boy Scouts supported by a strong committee of adults, including Assistant Scoutmasters and myself, as Scoutmaster.

From a tent manufacturer located on Hawley and Hamilton Streets, I obtained tents at wholesale prices: Two-man tents @ $22.00 each and a large, one-of-a-kind, Leaders' Tent for only $36.00.

In July of 1970, our troop obtained a permit to camp a weekend in Oak Openings, a multi-acreage spread of natural wilderness South of Toledo. We set up our camp late Friday afternoon in a remote area; 14 two-man tents, the leader's tent and two dining flys.

Two active Committeemen: *Ron Lett and *Dick Keith and Assistant Scoutmaster Harvey Dunn shared the Leader's tent with me.

It had been a long day, so after a campfire session, the whole troop hit the sack early, about 9:30 P.M. About mid-night, the Senior Boy Scout Leader woke me up.

"There's someone out here with us, Mr. Moore," he reported.

"There can't be, Fritz, we're about as far back as you can get."

"Well, someone is running around and knocking our tents over."

I was in pajamas and I donned sandals, then awoke the other leaders. I went outside the tent and saw a strange youth, about 15 years old, near one of the scout's tents. The tent had been tampered with and he was holding one of the aluminum tent poles in one hand. I started for him and he shook the tent pole menacingly towards me.

"When I get you, I'm going to take that pole and wrap it around your neck," I warned.

He took off running and I chased after him. Ron Lett caught up with me and we could see a total of three male figures running ahead of us; they were heading for the parking lot.

One of my sandals fell off and then I lost the other one. The ground was cool and was getting moist under my bare feet; we were nearing a swamp. Suddenly, the tallest of the punks we were pursuing darted off into the swampy area.

"I can't go any further, Jim", Ron Lett gasped, as he fell behind. I knew he had a respiratory problem, yet he was the only one to assist me. Dunn was in perfect health, but had stayed in the campsite.

My breath was getting short too, but I plugged away on the trail until I reached the parking lot. There was only one car parked in the entire lot, a red, Ford Mustang. As I approached it I observed a six-pack of beer on the rear seat. The car was locked; then I couldn't help but see the two youths trying, in vain, to hide under the car.

"Come on out-a there", I ordered. Then I stooped down and grabbed each by a leg and began to pull them from under the car. When they got to their feet, I was surprised that one of them was nearly as tall as I was.

"How old are you?" I asked the tallest one.

"Seventeen." he replied.

"And you?" I referred to the punk who had thrown away the tent pole.

"Fifteen," he said.

Grabbing them each by the back of their pants belt I informed them that I was taking them to the Ranger's Quarters, which was a short distance from the parking lot and that the Sheriff's Department would be called. I didn't tell them that I was a police sergeant.

En route I was concerned that they may resist, but apparently they figured that they were in enough trouble and remained subdued; for which I was glad.

The Ranger answered his door, half asleep, as I pushed the punks into the small cabin. I explained the situation to him and he agreed to contact the Sheriff and to watch the vandals until the Sheriff arrived.

I ran back to the campsite and got dressed. The other leaders did a good job keeping the troop calm and assessing the damage. Two tents were severely damaged, so four of the tents had to accommodate a third scout. It worked out.

When I returned to the parking lot, a Sheriff Deputy had already arrived and had the two delinquents in the rear of his cruiser. Just then, the third member of the raiding party came ambling out of the woods.

"Those lousy mosquitoes are biting the hell out of me," he complained.

"How old are you?" I demanded.

"Nineteen," he replied. He then admitted that he and the other youths had saw us setting up camp in the afternoon and planned to return at night , "to scare us." They had been shooting pool and drinking in bars, prior to raiding our camp.

My first impulse was to escort him back into the woods where he, without doubt, would have a slight accident. However, I decided to use this incident to illustrate to the scouts how our justice system works. The intruders were all charged with Malicious Destruction of Property and the adult was also charged with being Drunk and Disorderly.

A trial was held in the Maumee, Ohio, Municipal Court. I appeared with several of my scouts, so they could see "justice in action". What a joke! When I presented a damaged tent pole to the judge, he exclaimed: "Show that to the defense attorney, not me."

I did as he requested, but thought: "Who's judging this case anyway?"

I also realized that there was no mention of the youths drinking in bars prior to the raid. The adult should have been charged by the court with "Contributing to the Delinquency of Minors."

Then it dawned on me; a bargain had already been made between the judge and the defense attorney. I figured that the juveniles would be found guilty of damaging the tents and ordered to make restitution; the adult would be found guilty of D.& D. and pay court costs, with all other charges dropped, because he obtained an attorney. I was right on all counts!

The only thing I was glad of was that our troop was reimbursed for the cost of two new tents. So much for justice.

The author in his Scoutmaster uniform at Camp Pioneer, OH. July '70.

Troop 434 of Meadowvale School camping at Oak Openings

The Author standing by a two-man tent, like the ones damaged.

GOOD INTENTIONS TURNED SOUR

Working the afternoon shift on a cool, autumn day as the South Toledo patrol sergeant, I viewed a car speeding East on Western Avenue. I clocked the car 10 miles over the limit in the 700 block of the residential street and decided to give the male driver a verbal warning.

When he stopped for a red light at Broadway, I pulled along side of his car and motioned for him to pull to the curb. He looked astonished; pointed to himself and his lips said, "Me?"

When I nodded affirmatively, he gave me a scowl. When the signal turned green, he audibly jammed his car into gear and quickly drove left onto Broadway, making a dead stop at the curb to his right..

Approaching the car, I judged the driver to be in his late twenties with a heavy, dark beard. I observed a pile of text books on the seat next to him, indicating that he was attending college, so I surmised that he was a rebellious, anti-establishment student with a hostile attitude.

Requesting to see his driver license, he began to look into a billfold, when I noticed that his right hand was bleeding. There was a deep laceration in the underside of his palm, stemming from the base of his little finger to his wrist. My first thought was that he had been involved in a knife fight.

Then, I observed that the gearshift was missing from the steering column of the car and where it had been was a protruding shaft of razor-sharp metal. Apparently, when I ordered the angry man to pull over, he moved the gearshift with such force that he broke it off and the momentum of his arm caused his hand to contact the projecting metal shank, inflicting a deep gash in his hand.

When I brought the condition of his hand to his attention, he sullenly reached over the back of his seat with his left hand and grabbed a dirty, cloth glove from the rear floor and calmly put it on his right hand over the bloody wound.

He repeatedly refused any kind of medical attention, including summoning an ambulance to take him to a hospital. Citizens can not be forced to accept medical attention against their will, unless they are incapacitated or unconscious. This man was neither and I couldn't convince him to change his mind.

Now I had to issue him a citation for speeding. If I didn't and he decided to sue me, I would have no way to support my "probable cause" for stopping him in the first place and I'd be defenseless against a lawsuit. It was ironic, because I never intended to cite him, but I had no choice.

A COP WHEN NEEDED

The patrol sergeants usually came off the streets and gathered around the Desk Sergeant's area in the Safety Building, about a half hour before the next shift's sergeants came on duty. On third shift, that would be about 6:3 0 A.M.

On the morning of July 13, 1969, for reasons I can't explain, I decided to stay on the street and hit off my district via call box. I parked my marked car on E. Woodruff at Canton to use the call box there, when I saw a man staggering towards me from Cherry Street.

I figured him for a drunk trying to get home, but as he approached the intersection he appeared to be injured and there was blood all over his shirt. I immediately drove my cruiser across the intersection to the curb nearest to him, got out and intercepted him.

"What happened," I asked.

It was difficult for him to speak; his lips were cut and swollen, his nose was bloody and he had bruises on his face.

"I was waiting for a red light at Woodruff and Cherry, when six Mexicans jumped out of a car and dragged me from my car. They beat me and robbed me of my billfold and watch, then stole my car."

I immediately informed the dispatcher of my discovery and ordered an ambulance, then proceeded to obtain pertinent information from the victim:

"What kind of car did you have?"

"A '68 Cadillac, light yellow with white upholstery. I don't know the license number, but it is an Ohio plate."

"That's all right," I assured him. "How about your billfold and watch?"

The billfold is brown leather with about $200 in it and my watch is a gold Rolex.

I relayed the information to the dispatcher and it was broadcast immediately to all police units. The ambulance arrived and had just driven away with the victim, when 7 Patrol radioed that they were in pursuit of the stolen Cadillac, West on Lagrange Street, from East Bancroft and that it was occupied by several Mexican youths.

The police unit chased the Cadillac up an alley, where the thieves abandoned it and fled on foot. They arrested one of the robbers, who was trying to hide in a garage. The others escaped, but were later identified and arrested through information obtained from the one arrested youth.

The officers of 7 Patrol and myself were issued a commendation, which read in part: ". . . these officers are hereby commended for their alertness, good observation and quick action, which led to the arrest of a suspect less than one-half hour after the crime was committed."

After a bit of pondering the only explanation I could entertain for staying on the street that morning, instead of going into the station, was that the victim's Guardian Angel brainwashed me!

An Unidentified Patrolman using a call box.

FEAR DEFINED

On a day shift, working with Officer Bill Phalen on 1 Scout, the downtown scout car, we were dispatched to a disturbance call at the Library Bar at Jefferson and 11th. Street. When we arrived, we found Lt. Paul "Whitey" Whitman sitting in his marked car on Jefferson just past the bar.

The first thing that came to my mind was: "Why didn't the lieutenant check the call out?" Personally, I figured that Lt. Whitman was afraid to go it alone. Mind you, he wasn't required to, but when Bill and I entered the bar we discovered that there was a side door on 11th. Street and all the persons involved had left the scene by that door.

There was nothing going on and the bartender wasn't very cooperative, so we went back in service. Bill and I didn't say anything to the lieutenant, but some things stay with you indefinitely.

While attending the University of Toledo, I was privileged to have Mr. Don Gray*, as a tutor. He taught physiology and he was an outstanding instructor.

During one of his classes, he presented a lecture on fear and the physical reaction people may experience during a fearful situation: one's hands may become moist with perspiration; hair on the back of the neck may feel like it's "standing up" and one may become nervous, with shallow breathing and the sensation of not getting enough air.

At the time I was a lieutenant in patrol working the 3 P.M. to 11 P.M. shift. About 4 P.M. on a sultry afternoon, 11 Scout was dispatched to the Cold Spot on a "Man With A Gun" call. The notorious bar at Avondale and Division Streets had bullet holes all over it's interior from past disturbances and shootings.

When the call was transmitted, I was driving a marked car on Avondale and was almost directly in front of the place. My first instinct was to drive around the block and let the district crew take the initiative. Then the incident at the Library Bar bolted into my mind rousing one of my pet peeves: command officers not responding directly to dangerous calls and letting the patrolmen take all the risk.

After parking my cruiser in front of the house next to the bar, I entered the hell- hole alone. A barmaid rushed to me and reported: "There are some men drinking in the backroom and one of them has a gun."

While approaching the room I felt nervous and the hair on my neck felt like it was raised; my breathing was shallow and my hands felt sweaty. The door to the room was ajar and I could see six men sitting at a table playing cards. One player, just right of the door, had his chair tilted back; a large revolver was stuck in his belt.

Stepping into the room, I kicked the chair out from under him and as he plummeted to the floor I grabbed the gun from his person . . . it was a toy cap pistol! But, the fear was real.

Scout 11's crew arrived, so I let them resolve the matter and went back in service.

A COWBOY TACTIC

The district sergeant was out of service, so I, the district lieutenant responded for him. A crew had pursued a man wanted on felony warrants, into a large Victorian house on Robinwood. A woman inside had answered the door, but refused them entry.

The crew now wanted permission to forcibly enter and search the house for the felon. Just as I arrived two men and two women strutted out the front door "dressed to the nines" and sauntered away on foot. We figured it was a ruse to get us to leave.

While waiting for an additional crew to arrive I checked the front door. It was made of solid oak and was locked. The rear door was a thin pine door, which was also locked. The second crew arrived

"Are you sure you saw the man in the house?" I inquired of the first crew.

"Yes, Sir," they said in unison. "While we were waiting for you, we saw him looking out an upstairs window."

"O.K. men, we'll go in," I had decided.

An officer kicked the rear door open and the five of us entered the kitchen of the house. There was a basement door just inside to the right and it had a screen-door hook securing it. No one could have went through the door without unhooking it, so we didn't search the basement, but I stationed one officer at the rear door, so no one could sneak out behind us.

The first floor was cleared, but we made an astonishing discovery in the living room. Sitting in the middle of the room, like an object de art, was almost the entire front of an automobile: Fenders, hood, radiator and front bumper, all standing upright. I don't know how it was erected or what was holding it together and we didn't have time to be concerned about it at that time.

Three officers and myself took the stairs to the second floor hallway which had three, small bedrooms off of it. A loaded revolver was found under one mattress, but no trace of the fugitive.

A fourth bedroom on the second floor was situated across the front of the house and was searched to no avail. However, there was a small doorway off that bedroom, which revealed a very narrow staircase to a dark attic. The wanted criminal had to be up there and the staircase was the only way to him. Of course none of us relished climbing those steps, presenting an obvious target, if the man was armed.

Something had to be done. Taking a shotgun from one of my officers I placed my uniform hat on the muzzle; then holding the gun above me, started up the stairs, bobbing the hat as if it were on my head.

When I was about halfway up the steps the fugitive called out: "Don't shoot."

"Come on down," I ordered.

The man complied without further incident; was placed under arrest, handcuffed and taken to jail. Shades of Tom Mix!

A LASTING IMPRESSION

According to departmental policy, the use of tear gas had to be authorized by a patrol lieutenant, which I was at the time. Only patrol lieutenants were equipped with a tear gas kit.

A domestic violence case evolved into a "barricaded man" situation on the East Side. A man had struck his wife so she fled the house and called the police. Her husband refused to let anyone in or to talk to anyone. Armed with a shotgun, he locked himself in an upstairs bedroom.

Upon my arrival, the man fired a shot at my cruiser from his bedroom window. I bailed out of my marked vehicle and took cover.

The sergeant at the scene reported that the house was surrounded. The man would not communicate with police or his wife, but wanted to see his Mother who was supposedly en route.

Time was on our side, so we waited. However, after an hour, the Mother had not arrived and the man's wife was demanding action; it was getting dusk and nightfall was near.

I decided to use tear gas in an effort to either drive the man from the house or to persuade him to surrender. There was one hitch . . . I had no training with a tear gas gun, nor did my sergeant. I knew how the gun operated, but I had never fired one.

Episodes from many TV shows came to mind where-in the TV cops aimed and fired tear gas into various buildings, never missing the targeted window or door and always with successful results.

Believing it was time to take action, I reached into the dark trunk of my marked cruiser and took a shell from the gas kit at random. After loading the gun, I aimed it at the middle of the open window of the bedroom the man was in. I figured if the shell went high or low, there was a chance it would go through the window.

The gun was hefty and the rigid trigger required a tremendous amount of pull. Suddenly, with a belch of orange flame, the gun fired. The powerful recoil slammed the butt of the gun into my upper arm with such force that I had to struggle to keep my balance as pain seared through my right shoulder.

The shell sailed high, struck the house just above the window, then arced away whistling like an aerial bomb and landed in the street. A prevailing breeze caused its' fumes to gas my sergeant and myself.

Apparently, the sound of the blast and the impact of the shell on the house alarmed the man so fearfully that he tossed his shotgun out the window and surrendered.

The next day I looked at the house in the daylight. The projectile had left a perfect imprint of the entire shell in the aluminum siding above the window. Then I learned that the round I fired was designed for a distance of 150 feet. The window was only about a third of that distance from where I fired.

Believe me, it made a lasting impression.

SERGEANTS TOM KENNELLY AND GERALD WHITTY INSPECTING THE TEAR GAS GUN AND EQUIPMENT IN A POLICE COMMAND CAR. CIRCA 1960'S

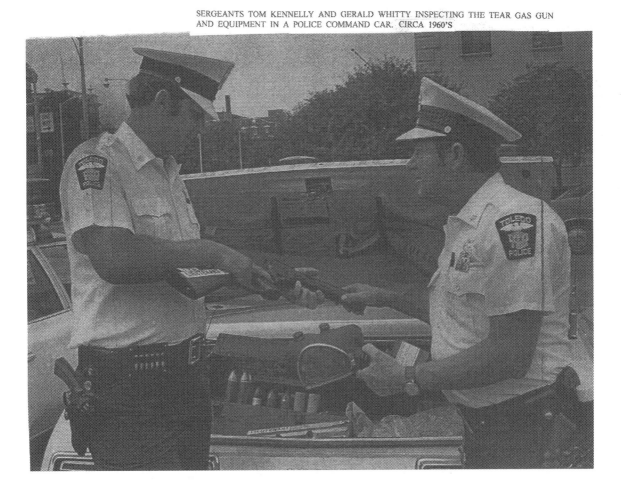

A RECOMMENDATION IGNORED

Not long after I had returned to full time duty, as a patrol lieutenant, I was assigned to Captain Donald Hickey's* shift, working afternoons. Capt. Hickey was a great guy to work for. (After his retirement he was appointed Sheriff of Lucas County, Ohio)

Because of my investigative experience he assigned all complaints against any personnel on our shift, to me, for investigation.

One afternoon upon my arrival for work I found two large butcher knives and three smaller knives on my desk with a note from the captain. Apparently, one of our crews had arrested a deranged man the evening before and left him at the Toledo Mental Health Center. They neglected to search the man and when the crew left he attempted to castrate an attendant with one of five knives he had on his person.

The crew also failed to make an Incident Report on the case. The first thing I had to do was to have the dispatcher's office trace the original call and find out what crew was dispatched.

The dispatcher's office immediately reported back that Officers Rodney Carr and Omar Henry, working 11 Scout, were sent to 1520 Fernwood on report of a 918 (a deranged person). There was no other information, because they didn't come back into service until after our communication personnel had been relieved of duty.

After roll call I had the officers report to me. Carr had three years of service and Henry was a six-month rookie; both officers were black males.

"Yes, they went to the Fernwood address, which was a duplex, and the demented man lived upstairs. Yes, they investigated and found that the man was trying to cook moldy potato peelings over an open fire in the middle of the living room. Yes, they put out the fire and took the man into custody.

No, they couldn't explain why they failed to search the man or why they left him alone with a sole attendant. No, they couldn't give a good reason for not making the required Incident Report, except that when they were through with the call it was past time to go off duty.

"You're very fortunate that the attendant wasn't seriously injured or killed," I informed them. "There is absolutely no excuse for not searching that man and for not making out the required reports.

I'm placing both of you on report to the chief with a strong recommendation for a suspension without pay. You're dismissed."

Upon receipt of my report, Captain Hickey submitted the case to the chief with his added recommendation for the officers to be suspended without pay.

We were both flabbergasted when we learned that the officers merely received a verbal reprimand. Why was the chief so easy on them? You figure it out.

THE ROLE OF ARBITRATOR

On a summer day in 1975, as a lieutenant assigned to the Traffic Bureau, I was sent to see a complainant in South Toledo. All I knew was the matter concerned the conduct of a traffic officer's son and the complainant's name was Wilkins.

I was met at the door by Mrs. Wilkins and invited inside.

"Thank you for coming right out," she said, with a concerned tone of voice.

"I'm Lt. Moore and I'm not entirely aware of what this is all about, Mrs. Wilkins; maybe you can enlighten me."

"Well, lieutenant, Officer Ray Ostrowski lives a few doors down the street; we don't know him too well, but his son Paul cuts our grass. The boy is about 16 years old and we've never had any trouble with him, but today he apparently had been drinking and was carelessly running the lawnmower into our flower beds and damaging them. When my husband admonished him, Paul became belligerent and used profanity towards my husband. He then told us what we could do with our flowers and stalked off. He even left his lawnmower here.

We called his Father, but he refused to discuss the matter with us and said as far as he was concerned, his son had done nothing wrong. So we called the police department and talked to Officer Ostrowski's boss, Captain McNulty; he apparently sent you to handle the situation."

"Just what do you expect me to do, Mrs. Wilkins? It's pretty much a civil matter."

"Well, we don't want to make any real trouble for Paul, but I think he at least owes us an apology. If he does that we'll consider the matter closed, but of course we'll have someone else cut our lawn in the future."

"Well that's your prerogative, Ma'am, but let me ask you this: If Paul's Father worked for Toledo Edison or for the gas company or at a factory, would you have still called his boss?"

Mrs. Wilkins hesitated, "Well, I suppose not - - "

"I'm sure you wouldn't have," I interrupted, " but, I'll have a talk with Officer Ostrowski and I'm sure that everything will come out all right."

From the Wilkins residence I walked to the officer's house and as I reached the front walk Patrolman Ostrowski emerged. "What's going on," he demanded. His voice was stern and he appeared hostile. "You're not talking to my kid, he's sleeping."

"Simmer down, Ray. I don't want to talk to Paul. I talked with Mrs. Wilkins and she feels that Paul owes her and her husband an apology for his conduct."

" Well she can go - - "

"Let me finish . . . Ray we go back a long ways and I'm not about to hurt you or anyone else. Personally, I don't think she's asking for too much. On the other hand I told her that if you were employed by Edison or some other company she wouldn't have called your boss. She agreed.

I look at it this way: it's really a civil matter. I'm not making any kind of report on this incident, but you have to live in this neighborhood and it's only common sense that it's better to be on good terms with your neighbors, than not. You do what you want, I have to get back to work."

"Yeah, you're right. Later we'll both go see the Wilkins . . . and thanks."

"No problem, Ray." And with a wave I added: "Don't forget to get your lawnmower."

A GIFT FOR THE CAPTAIN

My right wrist had been fractured in two places and was the more serious injury of my encounter with a drunken driver. (Covered in "My Number Comes Up" episode). While on light duty I was promoted to the rank of lieutenant in January of 1972.

Captain Don Gruppi and I had known each other for 17 years. Now, he was a pudgy, balding man, who always took the easy way out and was hard pressed to make a decision on his own. At the time he was a Patrol Shift Commander.

After I was off light duty I was temporarily assigned to Capt. Gruppi's command, working the second shift. Lt. Ron Owens was also on the shift and seemed to have a close relationship with Captain Gruppi.

Ron, at 5' 9", was grossly obese, with a huge gut overhanging his gun belt.

On a quiet day our shift began as any other. Roll call was held and the troops were dispersing to their districts. Lt. Owens and I were conversing at the long counter which ran across the entire width of the desk sergeant's cubicle.

An unassuming man entered the main door and approached the desk sergeant, whom was at his station behind the broad counter. The visitor was of medium height, on the heavy side, fifty-plus, with mixed gray and sandy hair, dressed in nondescript pants and shirt.

"Can I help you, Sir?" The desk sergeant inquired.

"Yes," the man replied in a soft voice, "I want to see the captain."

"May I ask the nature of your business, Sir?"

"Well," the man hesitated. "I have something to give him and it's sort of personal."

"I see," the sergeant said. He picked up the phone and dialed three digits.

Captain, there's a man here to see you; he says his reason is personal. Right, Sir."

"The captain will be right out," the sergeant informed the man.

As Captain Gruppi emerged from his office, the man intercepted him at the office door and insisted that he had to see him in private.

"All right, if you must," Captain Gruppi agreed.

The two men had hardly entered the office, when Captain Gruppi called out in a loud voice: "Owens. Help!"

Lt. Owens ran into the office, leaving the door open. I also hurried to the office and when I entered, I observed the captain standing behind his desk; his hair mussed; his face reddened and he was gasping for breath. Lt. Owens was sitting on the floor between me and the visitor, who was standing by the far wall flexing his fists.

Skirting around Lt. Owens's bulk and without thinking of my fragile wrist, I landed my right fist solidly into the man's face. I then pulled him from the wall and threw him across the captain's desk, face up. A patrolman appeared and began to strike the man repeatedly on his head with a slapper. "Hold off!" I cautioned the aggressive officer.

As the man was handcuffed, he shouted: "Why didn't you kill me? My back pain is more than I can stand. I thought if I hit a high ranking officer, I'd be shot."

The man was led from the office by a uniformed crew to be booked for assault and battery on a police officer.

"That guy's nuts," Capt. Gruppi exclaimed. "He said he had a gift for me and began to empty his pockets onto my desk. He said this is my billfold and this is my last will and testament and this is for you … and at that he hit me with his fist. Some gift!"

THE NAME OF THE GAME

When I was promoted to captain and placed in charge of the training academy, I wasted no time in having the lieutenants and sergeants trained in the use of all types of tear gas weapons.

I also arranged for mock-up buildings to be erected and equipped with pop-up targets at the windows and doorways to present realistic situations which have occurred in city neighborhoods.

All of these programs were funded by a government grant which I had successfully applied for as Training Commander of the Toledo Police Department.

Many police departments, at that time, supplied their officers with re-loaded .38 caliber ammo for target practice for economical reasons. The cartridges could be re-loaded by police personnel at a great savings.

Re-loads contained only 2.7 grams of gunpowder while factory ammo contained 3.5 grams of gunpowder, a significant difference in force. The variance in the powder charge made a great difference in recoil. The recoil of the re-loaded shells was mild while factory ammo caused a severe recoil due to the greater concussion when fired. Thus, it was more difficult for a shooter to recover composure for a consecutive shot when using factory ammo.

During practice police officers employ ear-guards to protect their eardrums from the noise caused by the explosion of the bullets. For obvious reasons, officers are not equipped with ear-guards while on patrol.

To personally verify the difference in the two grades of ammo I went to the police pistol range at dawn one morning before reporting for duty. When I fired a factory bullet from my revolver a streak of orange flame belched forth from the barrel which would not have been visible in broad daylight. My shooting arm was propelled straight up from the recoil which was several times greater than that of the practice ammo. The explosion was so pronounced that it caused a ringing in my ears.

I was convinced that all officers who worked the streets, including detectives, had to be made aware of what to expect when they fired their weapons in the course of their duties with factory ammo.

A program was created, executed and proved to be successful. Most of the officers were astounded at the difference in recoil, as well as the noise factor without ear-guards.

However, there was one negative note: I was informed that a certain officer was going to sue me because the exercise caused him to suffer an earache.

Although I suspected the officer of frivolity I took the matter seriously enough to do some checking. I gained information that the officer in question was an experienced deer hunter and hunted with a .30 caliber high-powered rifle.

I sought him out and mentioned to him that I heard that he was a deer hunter. He boasted that he always got a deer on every hunt. I told him that I also heard that he hunted with a high-powered rifle. "That's right," he assured me. Then I inquired of him if he wore ear-guards when he hunted and shot deer. His face reddened as he admitted that he didn't. That was the last I heard about any lawsuit.

Author, Captain James B, Moore, prior to his retirement. Circa 1980.

THE JIMMY CARTER ESCORT

Jimmy Carter, a nominee, at the time, for the office of the President of the United States was coming to Toledo. My rank at the time was lieutenant and I was second in command of the Traffic Bureau. I'm not sure how it happened, but I was chosen to be in charge of the escort detail.

Working with the Secret Service I was responsible for escorting the candidate and his entourage from the Toledo Express Airport to Southwyck, a shopping mall in South Toledo, where Mr. Carter would address a rally in his honor.

It was scheduled on an afternoon in the last week of October 1976. A small detail of uniformed officers was assigned for crowd control at the mall, but a large turnout was not expected because it was on a week day.

When Jimmy Carter arrived on schedule, he was directed to a black limousine in which he would ride with several Secret Service Agents. The lead car, another black limousine, contained the Secret Service Agent in charge, myself and another agent-driver.

All of the law enforcement personnel could communicate via police radio.

Following Mr. Carter's limo was two Greyhound Busses; the first carrying the candidate's entourage and the second one filled with news reporters, photographers and their equipment.

The procession was preceded by a Toledo police officer driving a marked police car. His function was to stop traffic at main intersections to allow our vehicles to travel as a unit without stopping. When the motorcade cleared an intersection, a second marked cruiser at the rear of the procession would speed ahead and stop traffic at the next important intersection. Thus the two marked cars would "leap-frog" each other to control traffic along the whole designated route.

A crowd of only 3000 to 4000 thousand people was expected. When our caravan reached the mall we were stunned. There were people shoulder to shoulder covering the entire surface of the parking lots and as near to the front doors as the thin line of patrolmen would allow. It was impossible to drive our string of vehicles through the throng and get anywhere near the front entrance. (A later official crowd estimate was 12,000 persons.)

Orders were then issued via radio for our motorcade to drive to the rear of the mall's edifice which, to our relief, was clear. All members of our group dismounted and entered the building through a rear door. I was the last person to go in and was walking backwards to assure that no one else entered behind me. Satisfied, I turned around and almost walked into Mr. Carter. He was very gracious and shook my hand.

The rally seemed to be a success; after it ended our group exited via the rear door to the vehicles. Secret Service Agents ushered the candidate into the rear of his limousine and to their dismay Jimmy Carter went right out the opposite car door. He hurried to a tall, chain-link fence across the rear of the mall and began to greet the throngs of spectators jammed along the other side of the metal barrier, grasping the multitude of fingers extended through the fence. The Secret Service was fit to be tied. Several minutes passed before they finally persuaded Mr. Carter to return to the limousine.

Then as our procession was carefully exiting through the mulling crowds, towards Byrne Road, we received a message that a man with a rifle was observed in the vicinity of Byrne Road and Airport Highway. The head agent turned to me and asked:

"Is there an alternate way to by-pass that intersection?"

"Yes," I replied, "We can take Byrne Rd. to Heatherdowns Blvd. then to Reynolds Rd. which will take us back to Airport Highway."

The only draw-back was that Heatherdowns, a two-lane street, was a little narrow for the busses to navigate. However, cars traveling in both directions voluntarily hugged the roadside and some even stopped along Heatherdowns and their occupants alit to cheer and wave at the candidate's passing motorcade.

However, a certain reporter, who was with the entourage panned the operation in the newspaper. She criticized the following.

1) The motorcade's original plans were changed and they arrived behind the mall rather than in front of it.

2) A member of the National Press Corps. was injured when a car he was waiting for ran over his foot. He refused treatment and left with the rest of the entourage.

3) Departure was delayed and the motorcade stopped, jolted and forced traffic off of Heatherdowns Blvd. on the return trip to the airport.

Although I was quoted in her article, the reporter had never interviewed me.

When the entourage arrived, as previously stated the crowd was immense and we unloaded at the rear of the mall and entered through the rear door, which proved to be advantageous.

I don't know how we could possibly be blamed for a reporter getting his foot run over when It appeared to be from his own carelessness.

We got a late start from the mall because of Mr. Carter's enthusiasm to please the crowds along a rear fence, as stated, and we took an alternate route on Heatherdowns Blvd. to avoid a possible sniper at Airport Hwy. and Byrne Rd. True the roadway was narrow for the busses, but it really wasn't that bad.

If the reporter had done her homework, she would have been aware of these facts.

Mr. Carter's entourage was escorted to the airport on time and as far as I was concerned: "All's well that ends well."

CHAPTER 21

ABOVE AND BEYOND

EPISODES

1. THE FREIGHT ELEVATOR

2. IN DEFIANCE OF ORDERS

3. YOU CAN'T WIN THEM ALL

4. HIGH STAKES

5. LOVE THY NEIGHBOR

THE FREIGHT ELEVATOR

It was less than two years since my graduation from the Toledo Police Academy. I had worked with Patrolman Larry Peters, my first partner, for about four months.

On a sunny October afternoon working 4 Patrol, we answered a call for an ambulance at the Security and Exchange Building on the corner of Huron and Madison; an office building in downtown Toledo.

We were directed to take our stretcher to the top floor; someone had suffered a heart attack. The victim was lying on a leather couch in his office and was having trouble breathing. In those days we carried no oxygen.

Larry and I lifted the ailing man onto the stretcher but when we attempted to enter a passenger elevator, we discovered that the stretcher was too long to fit inside.

Someone suggested the freight elevator, so we lugged the stretcher with the distraught gentleman strapped to it, to that elevator.

An associate of the victim had the presence of mind to run ahead and get the elevator and was raising the wooden gate for us when we got there. Although the elevator accommodated the stretcher the lift moved down the shaft with the speed of a snail. When we stopped on the main floor the stricken man's face was ashen.

We placed our burden in the wagon. I hopped into the rear and barely got seated next to the stretcher when Larry had the truck racing West on Madison with the red emergency light spinning and the siren blaring.

Peering out the rear windows, I saw buildings, cars, intersections and pedestrians swishing away, rapidly becoming distant images. I was swaying from side to side as the wagon swerved while being maneuvered and bullied through the stubborn, slower-moving traffic.

The victim's appearance remained the same. His breathing was shallow and I prayed we would reach the hospital in time. There were closer hospitals but the patient's physician would be waiting at the Toledo Hospital.

When we turned on to North Cove, I detected the odor of burning rubber and saw a trail of white smoke in our wake, but the hospital was in sight.

The paddy wagon slid to a halt in the emergency driveway emitting singed vapors from the rear wheels. The motor was thumping and steaming in distress.

Larry and I practically jogged with the stretcher into the Emergency Room. The hue of the heart patient's face had changed to an eerie gray. He was quickly transferred onto a gurney as waiting medical personnel hovered around him like a swarm of bees.

I folded up the stretcher and carried it to the overheated wagon.

"Well, I hope he makes it," Larry sighed.

"I wouldn't take any bets on it Partner."

"Speaking of bets, I'm not sure if we should chance driving to the service station or not," Larry pondered.

"Will the wagon start?" I asked.

"Yeah, but I burned the brakes out getting here."

On the following Christmas Eve the Desk Sergeant presented us with identical packages wrapped in plain, brown paper. They each contained a bottle of ten-year-old scotch with identical notes:

"I'll never forget our ride in the freight elevator. If it hadn't been for you and your partner, I would never have made it. Merry Christmas to you and yours."

It was signed, "George Taylor,* Attorney at Law."

Larry and I voiced the same thought: "I'll be damned, he made it!"

231

The Security & Exchange Building as it appears today.

IN DEFIANCE OF ORDERS

Patrolman Ed Burton was doing what he liked best . . . driving a paddy wagon. He had seniority and the favor of many command officers to assure that he would always be assigned to a patrol-wagon district.

He liked a wagon because in his own words: "When I make an arrest, I don't have to battle some jerk while waiting for a rookie to find me. By that time, I can toss the bastard in the back of the wagon and haul him to jail myself."

Officer Burton was doing just that one day, transporting a drunk to jail, while Officers Brock and Wondergem on 11 Scout, were responding to a disturbance call on Officer Burton's district.

Officer Rollie Brock was the senior officer and had worked the inner city for many years. He was renowned for his great respect for the people of the black community and had a solid reputation for going out of his way to help them whenever he could.

Also a veteran street cop, Officer Dean Wondergem was no stranger to the inner city but had only recently been partnered with Rollie.

Both officers towered over the woman, who opened the door for them. A man standing towards the rear of the room, wearing a bathrobe, was also short.

Rollie entered first with Dean behind him. "What seems to be the trouble?" Rollie asked the woman."

"I'm the landlady here," she informed them, "and this man, wearing a robe, is boarding here. Officers, ah wants somethin' done about him. He's two months behind in his rent and when I asks him for it, he done gave me a lotta lip. My daughter tried to talk to him and he done slapped her face and she ran out-a- here crying, so I called for you."

"What do you have to say?" Rollie addressed the man.

The boarder fired three shots through the pocket of his robe. The first shot struck Rollie's neck, the second bullet hit him in his chest and the third one drilled through his left arm and lodged in Dean's right hip.

Later, investigation disclosed that Rollie actually managed to draw his revolver and fire one shot but the bullet was never located.

Dean hobbled to the squad car and radioed for help.

With Burton's unit out of service, the dispatcher sent other crews.

"Twelve Patrol to dispatcher," Burton blurted into the mike, "we're not far from Eleven's location. We're going there."

"Continue with your present assignment, Twelve," the dispatcher answered with a stoic voice. "Bring your prisoner in."

"But we're close by," Burton protested.

"I repeat, Twelve, bring your prisoner in. Two crews are on the way."

"Dispatcher, you're breaking up, I can't read you," Burton shouted into the mike; then turned the radio dial to "off ".

Officer Ed Burton stomped the accelerator to the floor and the patrol wagon lurched forward. His partner and the drunk in the rear compartment clenched the metal armrests with white-knuckled fists to keep from bouncing off the sides of the truck.

Twelve Patrol was the first unit to arrive at the scene and when Ed came to a screeching halt, what he saw anguished him.

Officer Rollie Brock was staggering along the sidewalk, bare-headed, with his revolver dangling from the trigger-finger of his gun hand. He was covered with blood and was in a state of shock.

Ed's partner threw the rear wagon doors open as Ed ran to Rollie, picked him up and carried him to the wagon. Ed's partner, along with the prisoner, lifted Rollie into the rear of the truck as Ed jumped back into the driver's seat and sped away.

Officer Dean Wondergem was in good shape and would receive help from the other crews, which were arriving.

"Twelve to dispatcher," Burton radioed, "we're on our way to Mercy Hospital with Officer Brock. He's hurt bad. Call ahead and have them meet us outside the Emergency Room with a gurney. He's going to need blood."

When Twelve Patrol arrived at Mercy Hospital, the staff began working on him even as he was being rolled from the parking lot into the emergency room. Rollie had lost so much blood that he only had a fifty-fifty chance of survival.

Meanwhile, the boarder had retreated to his upstairs room where he took his own life with the same gun he used to shoot the officers.

Officer Burton, by disregarding orders, saved Rollie Brock's life!

For aiding in the transport of Officer Brock to the hospital, Officer Burton had the drunken prisoner exonerated. That's the kind of officer Ed Burton was.

YOU CAN'T WIN THEM ALL

On a sweltering evening in July of 1970, I was a volunteer bartender at a dance held in the Knights of Columbus Hall on Secor Road. The place was packed.

While a lively set of square dances were in session, I decided to take a break. I had just sat down in the kitchen when a man staggered in from the outside and collapsed to the floor. I recognized him as one of the guests who had been dancing.

His mouth and chin were covered with vomit. He apparently went outside for air, became ill and entered the kitchen seeking help. It appeared to me that he had suffered some kind of attack. He was unconscious and not breathing; nor could I detect a heartbeat

Several persons responded to my call for help. I directed one specific person to call 911 and proceeded to administer CPR to the prone man.

The kitchen became crowded and I had to ask people to move back, to allow me room to aid the victim. I also received a lot of good-intentioned advice and even some criticism which I didn't have time to consider.

It wasn't long before paramedics relieved me and an ambulance transported the victim to St. Vincent Hospital.

Before the dance ended, it was learned that the stricken man was D.O.A. (dead on arrival). I felt extremely sad. Had I done something incorrectly? Had I done enough? Was it my fault? These questions plagued me for weeks until I had to seek the answers.

I went to the Emergency Room of St. Vincent Hospital where an empathetic doctor took pity on me. He checked the filed case and informed me that the man had suffered a blood clot in his heart.

"Nothing could have saved him." He assured me.

I certainly was sorry that the man expired, but I confess that I was relieved to know that I hadn't caused his demise in any way.

Over the years I have participated in many First Aid Programs, including C.P.R. I have always stressed one factor which I repeat here, "If you have done your best as a first-aider or first responder and a victim should not survive, *do not blame yourself!* We are only human and our capabilities can not exceed God's will."

HIGH STAKES

On a cold evening of February 1975, I was anticipating the end of a tour on second shift. Then about 10:00 P.M., there was a report of a "jumper" on the Anthony Wayne Trail Bridge. Being the District Patrol Lieutenant, I rushed to the scene.

All the other bridges spanning the Maumee River are drawbridges, but the A.W.T Bridge is a suspension bridge. It's designed in the form of an arc, high in the middle to allow lake freighters to go beneath it. Toledoans commonly refer to it as the "High Level Bridge."

Two enormous towers, on either side of the apex support huge suspension cables which, in essence, suspend the bridge. It is the towers from which people, bent on committing suicide, usually leap.

The top of either tower can be reached by walking on the large cylinders encasing the suspension cables. Small steel cables, strung above the cylinders, serve as "railings" and aid the climbers in their ascent. Each tower stands 225 feet above the river and the distance from the traffic lanes to the water is 115 feet.

When I arrived, a sergeant had already directed patrol units to block off traffic at either end of the bridge. The fire department had rigs on the bridge standing by. Four patrolmen had ascended a cylinder and were near the summit of the West tower several feet from a man, who was threatening to end his life.

Apparently it was a stand-off. The man didn't jump, but wasn't descending. It was folly to try to over-power him; it would be extremely dangerous. The officers appeared stymied.

I decided to confront the confused being in an attempt to resolve the impasse. There was a raw gusty wind, so I handed my cap to someone for safekeeping. The cylinder was slippery from moisture in the night air. The wind whipped about my bare head, stiffening my face and scalp and blurring my eyes as I resolutely gripped the small cables with gloved hands and worked my way to the patrolmen.

"He's scared, lieutenant," one of the officers said in reference to the wavering civilian.

"Aren't we all?" I replied.

Sidling past the patrolmen, I addressed the frantic man. "What's your name?"

"Robert," he replied.

" I'm Lt. Moore, Robert. What do you want to do?"

"I just want to get down from here," Robert pleaded.

I stretched my left, gloved hand towards him, "I'll tell you what, your take my hand and look into my eyes. Don't look down or anywhere else. We'll just take small steps and I'll get you down. It doesn't matter how long it takes, we've got all night."

The man did as I directed and I began stepping backwards, leading him down the cylinder. I couldn't help but think, "This distraught person could change his mind in a heartbeat, jump and take me with him." I kept inching backwards but kept a death-grip on the cable with my right hand.

The firemen had ladders set at the lowest level of the large cylinder and when Robert and I reached that area, ready hands helped us both to the pavement of the bridge. I then retrieved my hat.

The rescued man's wife was waiting nearby. They were allowed to embrace but then Robert was escorted to a police car and taken to the Ohio Medical College for a mental evaluation.

The problem was resolved. The firemen cleared out and the bridge was re-opened. Subordinate officers were responsible for the reports so I returned to my office. The succeeding shift was already on duty and the personnel of my shift had all left.

I trudged the cold walk to my car but I didn't mind because I had a strange inner warmth surging within me.

I never met Robert again and I never did learn his full name but I've thought of him over the years and have always willed him well.

235

THE ANTHONY WAYNE BRIDGE; A FORMIDABLE SIGHT OF THE MASSIVE STRUCTURE.

A CLOSER VIEW OF ONE OF THE HUGE TOWERS AND THE CYLANDERS ON EITHER SIDE, WHICH PEOPLE HAVE CLIMBED WITH THE INTENT OF JUMPING INTO THE MAUMEE RIVER BELOW.

LOVE THY NEIGHBOR

Winter months in Toledo could be treacherous. At times it would be mild and rain, but then the temperature would drop, freezing everything in a sheath of frozen water. Trees would topple over from the icy weight while walkways and streets would become massive sheets of ice. If there was snow, it would compound the hazardous conditions. This was the scenario one February evening when I was working the third shift. I was a lieutenant and North Toledo was my district.

Calls for help exceeded the normal demand. Auto accidents were rampant, taxing our resources to the limit. Several eighteen-wheelers had jacked-knifed on I-280. Police crews were throwing salt on the highway by hand to help the truckers.

The demanding, exhausting tour of duty finally ended in the early morning. When I arrived home I couldn't believe my aching eyes. One of the large trees in my front yard was down, completely blocking my driveway.

Too numb to care, I parked on the street. I mumbled to my wife that I'd do something about it after I had some sleep and crashed into bed.

When I awoke in late afternoon I looked out my bedroom window and to my utter amazement the tree was gone. My wife excitedly explained to me that the neighbors, knowing I had worked all night, got together and cut the tree up and hauled it away.

"They were afraid that all the sawing would disturb you but you slept right through it." she gushed. "Isn't it wonderful?"

It was one of the rare times in my life when I was absolutely speechless.